D1927898

EMPLOYMENT LAW FOR CHARITIES

EMPLOYMENT LAW FOR CHARITIES

By the Trowers & Hamlins Employment Department

Edited by Emma Burrows

JORDANS

2003

Published by
Jordan Publishing Limited
21 St Thomas Street
Bristol BS1 6JS

British Library Cataloguing-in-Publication Data
A catalogue record for this book is available from the British Library.

ISBN 0 85308 858 6

Typeset by Jordan Publishing Limited
Printed by MPG Books Ltd, Bodmin, Cornwall

AUTHORS

Emma Burrows, General Editor

Simon Armstrong

Alex Bush

Cara de la Mare

William Downing

Joanne Easterbrook

Brett Elgar

David Holden

Penny Markham

Simon Whysall

PREFACE

INTRODUCTION: WHAT MAKES CHARITIES SPECIAL EMPLOYERS?

At 31 December 2002 there were 186,582 registered charities in England and Wales. Last year the charitable sector is recorded as employing 563,000 paid workers, which represents 2.2% of the total UK workforce, and an unknown number of volunteers; an estimate of unpaid charitable work in relation to direct service activities is valued at over £8.1 billion (the Charity Commission's *Annual Report 2001–2002*).

As a substantial employer in the UK, the charity sector is obliged, in the same way as other employers, to ensure that it complies with employment law. In addition, charities have other considerations.

Charities are complex employers. Board members (to whom all charity staff will report, directly and indirectly) are voluntary and unpaid. They often do not have the same expectations as an executive team in a more corporate structure. They may not come from the same professional or economic background as the staff who report to them; this cultural difference is something that charities have to make allowances for.

Charities also often have a complex cultural mix. It is fairly common, especially with large charities, for a charity to operate charity shops, which necessitates the setting up of a separate subsidiary to deal with the retail business. Other charities operate group structures, so that a group of companies exists, some of which are charitable and some not. This means that a charity might employ different sorts of people within the same group which will give rise to different employment considerations.

Many charities come from local beginnings and want to retain a workplace and a culture of volunteers that can sometimes be at odds with a more corporate feel perhaps now required by law and regulators.

In addition, charity staff can sometimes have different needs and aspirations to other employers. The Audit Commission's report in 2002, *Recruitment and Retention: A public service workforce for the 21st century*, deals with employees in the private sector providing public services. The Audit Commission found that, due to privatisation, the proportion of private sector workers in education, health and social care has increased dramatically. The report found that people providing public services from the charitable sector have different priorities and identify their employment with public service. They value 'making a difference', flexibility and working with people over other reasons for work such as pay and benefits. This means that charities do not and should not have the same preoccupations as corporate bodies when settling reward and remuneration of their staff.

The Charity Commission is the government agency which is responsible for the regulation and direction of charities in England and Wales. Some organisations are not regulated in the same way as 'exempt charities' and are subject to the regulation of other agencies, such as the Housing Corporation and the National Care Standards Commission. This book does not seek to cover the requirements of these regulations, although some reference is made to such requirements in passing.

It is not an exaggeration to say that, as employers, charities sometimes find themselves struggling to cope with many different expectations.

These expectations come at a time when all employers face major changes to working practices and law in the workplace. The growth of employment law since the Labour Party came to power in 1997 is extraordinary. In 2002, new employment law came into force on so many different days that it is now proposed that there should only be two days a year when new law is introduced, to reduce confusion. All employers, large and small, must now cope with an enormous increase in the rules they must comply with. Whether we like it or not, we are moving to rigid employment practices that provide for prescribed systems of work, and in the case of instances such as increasing diversity, encourage major social change. No employer can afford to ignore these.

This book is a guide to up to date employment law and good practice as at 1 September 2003. It is designed to bring some light to the new regulatory environment and is meant to be a practical guide. Where possible, we have provided you with practical examples and case studies.

We hope that you will find it interesting and practical, and we value any feedback.

Emma Burrows, Head of the Employment Department
Trowers & Hamlins

1 September 2003

ACKNOWLEDGEMENTS

Among our many charity clients, I would like to thank Clare Smith, Director of HR at Leonard Cheshire, for her invaluable guidance on what charities identify as relevant issues.

I would also like to thank all those who contributed to the book and its organisation; most especially my PA, Lindsey Syddell, and our encouraging Commissioning Editor, Martin West at Jordan Publishing.

CONTENTS

CHAPTER 5 – REFERENCES

CHAPTER 6 – CONTRACTS OF EMPLOYMENT

CHAPTER 7 – DIVERSITY WITHIN THE WORKPLACE

CHAPTER 8 – PAY

CHAPTER 9 – PENSIONS

CHAPTER 10 – WORKING HOURS

CHAPTER 11 – HOLIDAYS

CHAPTER 12 – DEALING WITH SICKNESS ABSENCE

CHAPTER 13 – CONFIDENTIALITY, VICARIOUS LIABILITY AND INTELLECTUAL PROPERTY

CHAPTER 14 – PRIVACY

CHAPTER 15 – CONSULTATION OBLIGATIONS AND THE RELATIONSHIP WITH TRADE UNIONS

CHAPTER 16 – THE WORK–LIFE BALANCE AND FAMILY FRIENDLY RIGHTS

CHAPTER 17 – TIME OFF FOR PUBLIC DUTIES

CHAPTER 18 – HEALTH AND SAFETY

CHAPTER 19 – MANAGING ADVERSE INCIDENTS

CHAPTER 20 – DEALING WITH EMPLOYEES' COMPLAINTS, GRIEVANCE PROCEDURES AND THE PUBLIC INTEREST DISCLOSURE ACT 1998

CHAPTER 21 – DEALING WITH ALLEGATIONS

CHAPTER 22 – DEALING WITH MISCONDUCT AND POOR PERFORMANCE

CHAPTER 23 – RESIGNATION, DISMISSAL AND SETTLEMENTS

CHAPTER 24 – EMPLOYMENT TRIBUNALS

CHAPTER 25 – REDUNDANCY AND RESTRUCTURING

TABLE OF ABBREVIATIONS

ACAS	Advisory Conciliation and Arbitration Service
ACOP	Approved Code of Practice
AML	Additional Maternity Leave
CAC	Central Arbitration Committee
CHAI	Commission for Healthcare Audit and Inspection
CPS	Crown Prosecution Service
CRB	Criminal Records Bureau
CSA 2000	Care Standards Act 2000
CSCI	Commission for Social Care Inspection
DDA 1995	Disability Discrimination Act 1995
DPA 1998	Data Protection Act 1998
EA 2002	Employment Act 2002
EAT	Employment Appeal Tribunal
EEA	European Economic Area
EOC	Equal Opportunities Commission
EPA 1970	Equal Pay Act 1970
ERA 1996	Employment Rights Act 1996
an ETO reason	an economic, technical or organisational reason entailing a change in the workforce
European Convention on Human Rights	European Convention for the Protection of Human Rights and Fundamental Freedoms
GOQ	genuine occupational qualification
GSCC	General Social Care Council
HRA 1998	Human Rights Act 1998
HSC	Health and Safety Committee
HSE	Health and Safety Executive
HSWA 1974	Health and Safety at Work Act 1974
ICD	Information and Consultation Directive
the Lawful Business Practice Regulations	Telecommunications (Lawful Business Practice)(Interception of Communications) Regulations 2000
LGPS	Local Government Pension Scheme
NCSC	National Care Standards Commission

NMW	national minimum wage
NMWA 1998	National Minimum Wage Act 1998
NMWR 1999	National Minimum Wage Regulations 1999
OML	Ordinary Maternity Leave
PHI	Permanent Health Insurance
PIDA 1998	Public Interest Disclosure Act 1998
PTWR 2000	Part-time Workers (Prevention of Less Favourable Treatment) Regulations 2000
RF(SE)A 1985	Reserve Forces (Safeguard of Employment) Act 1985
RIDDOR 1995	Reporting of Injuries, Diseases and Dangerous Occurrences Regulations 1995
RIPA 2000	Regulation of Investigatory Powers Act 2000
RRA 1976	Race Relations Act 1976
S2P	State Second Pension
SDA 1975	Sex Discrimination Act 1975
SERPS	State Earnings Related Pension
SMP	Statutory Maternity Pay
SNB	special negotiating body
SSP	Statutory Sick Pay
TUPE	Transfer of Undertakings (Protection of Employment) Regulations 1981
ULR	Union Learning Representative
WTR 1998	Working Time Regulations 1998

Chapter 1

CATEGORIES OF STAFF AND OF EMPLOYMENT RIGHTS

1.1 INTRODUCTION

The past two decades have seen enormous changes in labour markets which have given rise to changes in work patterns and types of workers. The notion that most members of staff in the UK are engaged as employees working '9 to 5' is now far from accurate. Any analysis of this area is hampered by a lack of consistency in the terms used to describe the wide variety of working relationships that exist. Individuals providing services in the workplace are traditionally classified as 'employees', 'workers' and 'self-employed'. Charities are more likely to engage employees, workers and volunteers. The position regarding volunteers is dealt with in more detail in Chapter 2. This chapter looks at charities' relationships with employees and workers.

Over recent years, the number of categories of staff has increased further to include fixed-term workers, part-time workers, temporary workers (whether supplied through an agency or direct to the charity), and casual workers who are contracted to work on an 'as and when required' basis, or on a zero hours basis.

The European Union is now considering the different types of employment with a view to rationalisation across the member states.

1.2 THE SPREAD OF EMPLOYMENT RIGHTS

It still remains the case that the majority of employment rights are available only to employees and not to workers. Under the Employment Relations Act 1999, the Government has within its power the ability to extend identical rights to workers, although it has not, as yet, done this. A chart setting out the rights of employees and workers is set out at the end of this chapter.

1.3 WHAT IS AN EMPLOYEE?

As a result of the better rights that employees enjoy, it is important for a charity to be able to identify whether or not the individuals who provide services to it are its employees. Depending upon the degree to which certain criteria are satisfied the individual may be viewed as self-employed, a worker or an employee. The individual could also be a volunteer. The most effective method of identification is a careful analysis of the contract between the charity and the individual.

1.3.1 Three-part legal test

Courts generally adopt a three-part test to determine whether a contract of employment exists. A contract cannot be a contract of employment unless the following elements are present:

(i) **Mutuality of obligation**
Generally speaking, there must be an expectation that the employer will give the individual an opportunity to provide his or her services, and must oblige the individual to provide those services when the employer gives that opportunity.

(ii) **Control**
This means that the employer must have ultimate control over the individual to the extent that the employer can order and direct that individual. It does not mean that the employer has to supervise the way in which the individual performs his or her role.

(iii) **Personal service**
There have been a number of conflicting cases on this point, but the general thinking appears to be that where a contract contains a power to substitute the individual's services for those of another there cannot be a contract of employment. The individual must provide personal service to be an employee. However, it would also appear that a limited power to delegate would not prevent the contract from being a contract of employment.

1.3.2 Other relevant factors to consider

If all three parts of the legal test are met, the contract may be an employment contract. The next stage is to analyse a number of additional factors.

Does the individual in question:

- have responsibility for investment and management?
- take a degree of financial risk?
- have an opportunity to make a profit?
- provides his or her own equipment?
- engage his or her own assistants?
- constitute an integral part of the business?
- provide services under the control of another, who determines what services must be provided, and when and how those services must be provided?

Other factors to be considered in the contract are whether:

- there is an entitlement to receive payment during sickness;
- he or she is permitted to participate in benefits such as pensions or private health insurance which are normally reserved for employees;
- he or she is subject to the disciplinary procedure or permitted to raise formal grievances against the charity;
- he or she is prevented from providing services to another service provider;
- the employer pays tax and national insurance on sums paid to the individual in consideration for the services provided.

It does depend on individual circumstances but, if all these points are present, it is likely that the contract will be an employment contract.

1.4 RIGHTS OF WORKERS

Even if the individual is not an employee, if a member of staff carries out work on a continuing basis for a charity, he or she may nevertheless be a 'worker' and enjoy rights which do not depend upon the existence of a contract of employment (see the chart at **1.6**).

1.4.1 Part-time workers

Part-time workers are people who are paid wholly or in part by reference to the hours which they work, and are not full-time workers, having regard to the employer's custom and practice. Under the Part-time Workers (Prevention of Less Favourable Treatment) Regulations 2000, a part-time worker has the right not to be treated by his or her employer less favourably than a comparable full-time worker, unless it can show an objective justification. In seeking to compare the treatment of its part-time and full-time workers, a charity cannot restrict the examination to the workplace within which the part-timer is based, but must look at all its workplaces to see if any comparable full-time staff work in the organisation. If no comparator exists then the worker will find it difficult to bring a claim under the Regulations.

Less favourable terms could include provisions relating to salary and benefits under the contract. Part-time workers are also protected from the right not to be unfairly dismissed on the grounds of their status, or to be subjected to any other form of detriment. Some women who work part time are also protected under the laws of indirect sex discrimination. For further guidance on the meaning of indirect sex discrimination, see Chapter 7. Men who work part time may also rely on their right not to be discriminated against on grounds of sex if they are able to point to a comparable female part-time employee who has been treated more favourably than they have been.

1.4.2 Fixed-term employees

Workers and employees who are employed for a specific task, or for a set period of time, are fixed-term workers. Fixed-term employees are protected by specific law; fixed-term workers are effectively temporary or casual staff (see **1.4.3** and **1.4.4** below).

Under the Fixed-term Employees (Prevention of Less Favourable Treatment) Regulations 2002, employees are protected from less favourable treatment on the grounds of their status as fixed-term employees. Employers cannot treat fixed-term employees less favourably on the grounds that they are employed on a fixed-term contract unless less favourable treatment is objectively justified. Employers can, however, justify individual terms which are less favourable if the overall contract offered to the fixed-term employee is as favourable as that afforded to a permanent employee. Under the Regulations, when terminating an existing fixed-term contract, the employer must inform the fixed-term employee of available vacancies in the establishment, In addition, fixed-term employees are no longer able to waive their right to redundancy payment. The Regulations also provide that a fixed-term contract will be converted into a contract of indefinite duration, to which the minimum notice provisions will apply, where an employee is employed under a contract purporting to be a fixed-term contract, and that contract had been previously renewed by the same employer over a period of more than four years.

Despite lobbying, the Regulations apply only to employees, not workers.

1.4.3 Agency workers

Agency workers are normally contracted to an agency, which in turn supplies their services to the client. For a summary of employment law on agency workers, see Chapter 3. Charities are likely to engage temporary workers, for example to work on a campaign, or where a member of staff is absent on long-term leave.

1.4.4 Temporary workers

'Temps' are either agency workers (see Chapter 3) or casual workers (see **1.4.5**) or fixed-term workers (see **1.4.2**).

1.4.5 Casual workers/zero hours workers

Casual work is work that is temporary or occasional. Casual workers have no fixed hours and may be called upon as and when work is available. Casual work is frequently unskilled or seasonal work and is undertaken to meet fluctuating demands for work. It may include work carried out on an 'on call' basis so that work may or may not be accepted according to choice. There may be periods when a casual worker is not working. Indeed, the nature of the relationship will be on an 'as and when required' basis so the worker cannot be obliged to accept the work, but neither is the charity committed to offering work.

Zero hours contracts are arrangements by which individuals agree to be available for work as and when required, but no particular number of hours or times of work are specified. Although zero hours contracts may suit some individuals who require earnings occasionally, there has been concern that such contracts may be subject to abuse, for example, where the individual is asked to remain on the premises while not receiving work. Arguably, this would be a breach of the National Minimum Wage Regulations 1999 and the Working Time Regulations 1998 (see Chapters 8 and 10).

1.4.6 Other staff

Directors and trustees

Directors or trustees of a charity are not employees as such, but by virtue of their appointment may become office holders. A director or trustee may still be an employee or a worker depending on the degree to which some or all of the other remaining factors of the tests set out above at **1.3.2** are satisfied. This is particularly the case in small charities where trustees carry out the day-to-day operational work of the charity.

Workers' co-operative

The status of workers in a co-operative depends on the circumstances surrounding their arrangements. So, for example, professional musicians who associate to form an orchestra might be regarded as a co-operative of self-employed persons, but in an ordinary industrial co-operative, the workers should be regarded as employees of the co-operative. Where the co-operative has been registered as a company, or is registered under the Industrial and Provident Societies Act 2002, it will have become incorporated. In either of those cases, the court would have little difficulty inferring that the individuals who worked for it were either workers or employees.

Consultants

In most cases where a consultant is truly independent from the charity, his or her status will be neither that of worker nor of employee. However, there are certain categories of self-employed individuals whose position cannot be viewed as wholly independent from the charity and what it does. Where a consultant has provided expert advice or services to the charity under a short-term contract or under several contracts in a series which is not continuous, it is likely that the consultant will be viewed as self-employed. On the other hand, where the engagement is on an open-ended basis and where some of the characteristics set out at **1.3.2** are present, the consultant could be either an employee or a worker.

1.5 HOW DOES A CHARITY PROTECT ITSELF?

Most employment claims arise when staff are not treated in accordance with their rights.

The safest advice for charities is to ensure that they are clear about the status of those individuals who work for them. In most cases, the position will be clear, in that the charity will wish to establish an employment relationship between itself and the individuals who work for it. The looser the arrangements are, the more difficult it is for the charity to control and direct what the individual actually does on a day-to-day basis. The downside is that, as employees, individuals will have greater rights.

There are other cases where a charity may engage workers or volunteers, or contract with consultants, where the factual relationship is such that those individuals could be deemed to be employees. It is sensible for the charity to take a view on this before any dispute arises.

Once the charity has established the nature of the relationship between itself and its staff, it must ensure that contracts are properly drafted. Section 1 of the Employment Rights Act 1996 sets out the statutory obligation on a charity to provide its employees with a written statement of terms and conditions within 13 weeks of the date of commencement of employment. Further details concerning these requirements are given at **6.3**.

In other cases where a charity wishes to rely upon temporary, casual workers or volunteers, it must ensure that the nature of the relationship is not one where employment status can be inferred. The best advice for a charity in these circumstances is to ensure that none of the factors listed at **1.3.2** are present in the relationship between the charity and its staff.

It is always advisable to have a contract drawn up setting out the position. The absence of a written contract will not necessarily lead to the conclusion that individuals are not employees.

CASE STUDY

Arthur and Sam work for Sun Sign, a charity concerned with environmental protection. They have worked for the charity for 3 years. Employees with the charity receive both holiday pay and sick pay, but Arthur does not. The charity states in his contract that he is engaged on an 'as and when required' basis and is not to be regarded as an employee. Sam is regarded by the charity as an employee.

Arthur is engaged to deliver leaflets. He is paid according to the number of leaflets he delivers, although he is guaranteed a minimum payment of £100 per week. He travels around the local area delivering the leaflets using his own car. The charity is responsible for paying all expenses on the car, except for the petrol which Arthur pays for himself. He receives no holiday or sick pay, although 6 months ago he was asked to attend a disciplinary hearing following an altercation with one of the charity's employees. He pays his own tax and national insurance on his earnings, and may substitute another worker to deliver the leaflets, if he wishes, although this is normally only done with the permission of Sun Sign.

Sam, who currently works full time as a marketing administrator, has asked her manager whether she may change her hours to part time. Her request has been refused on the basis that no other employee has been permitted to work part time, but even if her request is granted, Sun Sign says she has no right to participate in the organisation's bonus scheme.

Answer

Arthur

Although engaged on an 'as and when required' basis there are several factors which could indicate that Arthur is engaged either as an employee or as a worker. The guarantee of a minimum payment (although not described as a salary or wage) could indicate that he has the status of an employee. However, all other factors generally point to him being either a worker or self-employed. He provides his own transport for delivering leaflets, and pays for the petrol himself, although Sun Sign are responsible for covering all other expenses. On balance, it would be fair to say that he is responsible for providing his own equipment.

Arthur does not have the benefit of a contractual entitlement to holiday pay or sick pay, but was asked to attend a disciplinary hearing. Treating Arthur in this manner could be construed as being inconsistent with his status as self-employed, particularly if he attended a formal hearing and a warning was issued to him.

If he is able to substitute other workers to fill his role when on holiday or at any other time, then this factor is one which is likely to indicate self-employment, but if the charity is required to approve who may take over his role then this factor itself indicates that there is an element of control over him by the charity, which points towards him being an employee or worker.

The fact that he pays his own tax and national insurance contributions on what he earns could be a factor indicating self-employment, but this will not always be conclusive, particularly when there are other factors present which indicate employee/worker status.

Overall, the position regarding Arthur's status is unclear since there are factors pointing in different directions.

Sun Sign is best advised to clarify the position by making him an employee, or to treat him as self-employed.

Sam

Sam has made a request to work part time which has been rejected. In the absence of a justifiable reason for refusing her request, Sun Sign could be exposed to a claim for indirect sex discrimination unless the charity is able to show that it would not be possible for her to carry out her job properly on a part-time basis. The fact that the charity has not previously permitted anybody to work part time will not be justifiable. Sam may also have a claim under the Part-time Workers (Prevention of Less Favourable Treatment) Regulations 2002 if Sun Sign denies her the right to participate in the bonus scheme which is made available to full-time employees.

1.6 STATUTORY RIGHTS AVAILABLE TO ALL WORKERS OR EMPLOYEES ONLY

The following table shows which statutory rights are available to all workers and which are available to employees only.

Statutory right	*All workers*	*Employees only*
Written statement of terms and conditions of employment		✓
Written statement of reasons for dismissal		✓
Protection against unlawful deductions from wages	✓	
Itemised pay statement		✓
Guarantee payment		✓
Insolvency payment		✓
Remuneration on suspension on medical grounds		✓
National minimum wage	✓	
Statutory sick pay		✓
Time off for public duties		✓
Time off to look for work or arrange training in the event of redundancy		✓
Time off for antenatal care		✓
Time off for dependants		✓
Time off for pension scheme trustees		✓
Time off for employee representatives		✓
Time off for study or training (young persons)		✓
Time off for members of a European Works Council		✓
Refusal to work on a Sunday (shop and betting workers)		✓
Not to be unfairly dismissed		✓
Notice of dismissal		✓
To be accompanied at a disciplinary or grievance hearing	✓	
To be informed and consulted about collective redundancies		✓
Paid annual leave, rest breaks and maximum working week	✓	

Statutory right	*All workers*	*Employees only*
As a part-time worker, not to be treated less favourably than a comparable full-time worker	✓	
As a fixed-term employee not to be treated less favourably than a comparable permanent employee		✓
Protection of acquired rights on the transfer of an undertaking		✓
Protection against detriment for exercising right in respect of the National Minimum Wage Act 1998, Part-time Workers Regulations 2000, Working Time Regulations 1998 or Public Interest Disclosure Act 1998, and the right to be accompanied at a disciplinary or grievance hearing	✓	
Protection against detriment for exercising rights in respect of health and safety cases, Sunday worker, pension scheme trustees, employee representatives, time off for study and training (young persons), trade union membership, family and domestic leave, members of European Works Councils, under the Fixed-term Employees (Prevention of Less Favourable Treatment) Regulations 2002		✓
Protection for making a protected disclosure	✓	
Time off for trade union officials		✓
Time off for trade union activities		✓
Parental leave		✓
Maternity leave		✓
Adoption leave		✓
Paternity leave		✓

Chapter 2

VOLUNTEERS

2.1 INTRODUCTION

The position regarding the status of those not automatically regarded as employees has caused immense difficulties for all employers. However, the position of volunteers has proven to be even more complex, which is a matter of concern especially for charities, who often make great use of volunteers.

Volunteers are not expressly excluded from legislation which would otherwise give them rights to bring employment claims except under the National Minimum Wage Regulations 1999. There are quite obvious policy considerations involved in not permitting volunteers of charities to claim a minimum wage, given that many charities have limited resources. The same considerations have not been applied to any other potential claims a volunteer may have, with direct financial consequences for charities.

It is still important to consider the position where a volunteer develops employment rights. If a volunteer is deemed to be either an employee or a worker he or she would be able to assert a variety of statutory rights against the charity (see the main rights as listed in the table at **1.6**).

2.2 CONSIDERATION NOT THE DETERMINING FACTOR

As set out in Chapter 1, one of the most important issues to be considered when ascertaining employment status is whether there is mutuality of obligation between the parties. This, in itself, normally implies that there is a legally binding contract in place between the individual and the charity. In most cases, in order for there to be such a contract some form of meaningful 'consideration' (ie salary or wages) must be paid to the individual.

It remains quite difficult to determine whether a volunteer may be able to assert rights as an employee or worker. So far, the courts have been unable to set out the minimum criteria necessary for a volunteer to achieve status as a worker or employee. It is far easier to determine whether someone is *not* an employee or worker.

2.3 HOW TO DETERMINE THE STATUS OF A VOLUNTEER

There are many factors which a tribunal will consider when attempting to ascertain the status of a volunteer. All or some of these factors could convert an individual's status from that of a volunteer to an employee or worker:

(a) **Mutuality of obligation.** Is there an expectation that the charity will offer work and that the individual will be expected to accept all work offered?
(b) **Personal service.** Where the individual is unable to attend work, is he or she permitted to appoint a substitute, in which case an employment relationship is more likely to be inferred?
(c) **Written documentation.** Are there any contractual documents in place between the parties which contain any provisions which one would normally find in an employment contract? In particular, is there any kind of contractual provision which would entitle the charity to terminate the relationship with the volunteer?
(d) **Set hours and/or performance criteria.** Is there an expectation that the volunteer will work a set number of hours every day or week or that the quality or quantity of his or her work will be assessed?
(e) **Control.** Is the volunteer required to report to any other individual in the charity? The more control the charity has over the volunteer, the greater the likelihood that he or she will be viewed as employed.
(f) **Similarity of work.** How does the work undertaken by the volunteer compare to that undertaken by other individuals who are employed by the charity? Where there is a high degree of overlap between the tasks and responsibilities of volunteers and employees, a tribunal is more likely to infer the existence of an employment relationship.
(g) **Remuneration.** Does the volunteer receive any kind of remuneration for the work he or she does? If the volunteer receives payment which is or might be construed as consideration for any work done, then it is likely that he or she will be viewed as a worker, or possibly an employee, depending on the other factors present.

Example

In the case of *Migrant Advisory Service v Choudray* (unreported) 28 July 1998 (EAT), it was found by the EAT that the £25 per week 'expenses' paid to the applicant were in fact a sham, since in reality she did not actually incur any expenses. There were no travelling expenses as she walked to work, and no subsistence because she went home for lunch. The payment made to the volunteer was therefore regarded as salary. In particular, if payments are made whilst the volunteer is off sick or on holiday, this is highly supportive to the volunteer's case that he or she is either an employee or a worker.

(h) **Appraisals or performance reviews.** Where undertaken, these indicate that there is an element of control over what the volunteer does, and could support an argument of mutuality of obligation between the parties.

2.4 CONCLUSION

It is important for charities to look very carefully at the arrangements they have in place for volunteers. There may not be any formal written documentation entered into between the parties, but any oral representations made or conduct which has occurred over a course of time will have some bearing upon the degree to which volunteers can argue that they are workers or employees. Claims may arise against the charity if, for example, an individual's contract is terminated without the charity having held a disciplinary hearing. The charity may also face substantial claims from the Inland Revenue in relation to unpaid PAYE and national insurance contributions, if it were deemed that 'expenses' paid were in fact a disguised form of salary or wages. Where accidents occur, the officers of the charity may also find themselves personally liable if employer's liability insurance has not been maintained.

It is worth considering the use of a volunteers' charter setting out the rights and obligations of volunteers working for a charity. If so, consideration of the facts set out above must take place when deciding upon what to include.

Chapter 3

AGENCY WORKERS

3.1 INTRODUCTION

Agency workers are workers who contract with an employment agency to offer their services to client organisations of the agency, such as charities. The charity pays the agency a fee for the worker's services and the agency pays the worker wages out of the fee. The position of agency workers under UK law is currently unique since it is unlikely that they are either employees of the agency or of the charity for whom they work. The staff do not have a contractual relationship with the charity, although the charity may control their activities. This means that they are unlikely to be employees of the agency either. The potential risk to charities is that some charities operate control over agency staff to the extent that an employment relationship can grow by default, especially if the charity then employs the member of staff in another capacity, for instance to provide cover at night in the provision of services, or if the charity extends some employment benefits to the member of staff.

This position is subject to change, as the UK is out of step with the rest of the European Union on this issue. In all countries in the European Union except the UK and Ireland, agency workers are treated as employees of the agency.

3.2 PRACTICAL GUIDANCE – RISK MANAGEMENT

To reduce the risk of a tribunal finding that an agency worker is either an *employee* or a *worker*, the charity should:

- not contract directly with the agency worker;
- limit the amount of control it has over agency workers and not treat them as employees;
- pay the fee directly to the agency, not the worker;
- avoid lengthy engagements.

3.3 WHAT TO INCLUDE IN A CONTRACT WITH AN AGENCY

A contract with an agency should ensure that:

- it is clearly stated that there is no employment relationship between the charity and any agency workers which are supplied;
- there is a right to refuse or terminate the engagement of any worker supplied by an agency;
- the agency will be responsible for ensuring compliance with the Working Time Regulations 1998 (WTR 1998), the National Minimum Wage Act 1998 (NMWA 1998) and the Part-time Workers (Prevention of Less Favourable Treatment) Regulations 2000 (PTWR 2000);
- the agency will be responsible for the employment or engagement of the worker generally, including pay, tax, national insurance, training, capability, disciplinary and grievance, holidays, sick pay, termination of employment, etc;
- where possible, the agency provides an indemnity for employment-related claims and any claims under the WTR 1998, NMWA 1998 and PTWR 2000;
- any fee which may be payable by the hirer to the agency is stipulated, including the amount or method of calculation of such fee and the circumstances, if any, in which refunds or rebates are payable, the scale of such refunds or rebates, and if no refunds or rebates are payable, a statement to that effect;
- a procedure to be followed if a work-seeker introduced or supplied to the hirer proves unsatisfactory is also stipulated.

3.4 ADVANTAGES AND DISADVANTAGES OF USING AGENCY WORKERS

For charities, the main advantages of using agency workers are that the administrative burden of paying the workers is taken on by the agency and they are able to find appropriate staff at short notice. Using agency workers also has advantages for charities since it is likely that the obligations imposed by an employee–employer relationship will not apply. For example, the agency worker will not have the right to make a complaint of unfair dismissal. However, the disadvantage for the charity is that agency workers are likely to show little loyalty to the charity and are more likely to leave at short notice, possibly leaving the charity short-staffed. The workers will also still have a number of rights as workers (see **1.6** for a list of those rights), unless they have been delegated to the agency.

3.5 EUROPEAN DIRECTIVE ON AGENCY WORKERS

In 2002 the European Union issued a draft directive concerning agency workers. This is intended to provide employment rights to the thousands of workers in the member states who work for agencies. It requires that agency workers should not have less favourable employment conditions than permanent workers in the client company where they are sent to work, unless this is objectively justified. At the time of writing, this right would apply from the time the worker commenced work, although the Government is lobbying for a qualification period of 3 months. Other areas of current debate relate to whether the directive will extend to all contractual terms, or just pay. The final directive is set to be issued in late 2003.

3.6 'TEMP TO PERM' REGULATIONS

One of the biggest disincentives faced by charities or businesses considering the hire of agency workers is the transfer fee many employment agencies impose if the hirer wants to offer permanent employment to the agency worker. The Government is concerned about the effect such transfer fees have on labour mobility and has been consulting widely to introduce an alternative.

The latest draft of the Conduct of Employment Agencies and Employment Business Regulations (known as the Temp to Perm Regulations) was released in July 2002. The Regulations provide that if the contract between an employment agency and a hirer does not give the hirer the option of an extended hire period as an alternative to the transfer fee, the employment agency cannot enforce the payment of the transfer fee. When hiring has ceased, the transfer fee is not enforceable from the date 8 weeks from the last day of hire (or 14 weeks after the first day of hire, whichever is later).

Consultation on the latest draft Regulations ended in November 2002 and it is likely that they will come into force during 2004.

Chapter 4

RECRUITMENT

4.1 INTRODUCTION

Recruiting the appropriate person for the job is of fundamental importance to all charities and a great deal of time and resources are devoted to the recruitment process. The process begins with a charity advertising for prospective employees; continues by interviewing and subsequently selecting prospective employees; and concludes by offering them a position. This chapter looks at some of the legal pitfalls that can occur at any of these stages during the recruitment process and offers advice as to how they might be overcome. Many of the problems that may arise relate to discrimination, even where unintentional. Therefore, this chapter ought to be read in conjunction with Chapter 7.

4.2 ADVERTISING

Charities, like all employers, are under a statutory duty to avoid discrimination in their recruitment practices. This includes an obligation to ensure that job advertisements do not discriminate against a prospective employee on grounds of sex, race or disability. From December 2003 charities will also be under a statutory duty to avoid discrimination in their recruitment practices against a prospective employee on grounds of sexual orientation, religion or belief. By December 2006 charities will also be prohibited from discriminating in their recruitment practices against a prospective employee on grounds of age. An advertisement will be deemed to be discriminatory if it indicates or might reasonably be understood as indicating an intention to discriminate unlawfully.

Unlawful discrimination can occur in two ways: either directly, by treating a person less favourably on grounds of their sex, race or disability, or indirectly.

For example, a charity should not advertise for a person of a specific sex or race. An employer also needs to take particular care when advertising for a prospective position not to discriminate indirectly. For example, an advertisement that requires an employee to be over 6 ft tall could be discriminatory against women, as fewer women than men will meet that requirement. Such a requirement must therefore be justified carefully.

4.3 PRACTICAL GUIDANCE – RECRUITMENT ADVERTISEMENTS

Charity employers should ensure that the job advertisement is clear and that it states briefly:

- the requirements of the job;
- the necessary and desirable criteria for job applicants;
- the activities and working practices of the organisation;
- the job location;
- the reward package;
- job tenure; and
- the application procedure.

4.4 INTERVIEWING AND SELECTION

Provided that the interview and selection procedures are not discriminatory, an employer may adopt any interviewing and selection procedure it wishes.

4.4.1 Interview

The current law is that during an interview an employer must not ask questions which discriminate against a person on grounds of sex, race or disability. From 1 December 2003, questions which discriminate on grounds of sexual orientation, religion or belief will also be prohibited, as will, from December 2006, questions which discriminate on grounds of age. This does not automatically mean that questions cannot be asked about those subjects. However, an employer must ensure that the reason for asking those questions could not be deemed to be 'less favourable treatment'. For example, it would not be discriminatory for an employer to include a question on an application form asking whether someone has a disability, as it does not automatically mean that that person will be treated less favourably. Indeed, if a person who is suffering from a disability is invited to attend an interview, the employer will be legally obliged to make reasonable adjustments to enable that person to attend the interview.

Under the Data Protection Act 1998 (DPA 1998), applicants are entitled to request access to copies of interview notes. Employers should ensure that during the interview process they record only information which is necessary in order to make the recruitment decision or to defend a challenge to the decision (see Chapter 14).

4.4.2 Selection

Provided that the selection is not made on a discriminatory basis, an employer is free to select whichever candidate it chooses as a prospective employee. There are, however, a number of a statutory limitations on that freedom.

(1) Children

For the purposes of the statutory provisions relating to the employment of children, a child is a person who is not over compulsory school age (at present 16 years). A detailed consideration of the legislation restricting the employment of children and young persons is beyond the scope of this work, and employers should ensure that consideration is given to the provisions restricting the employment of children as set out in the Children (Protection at Work) Regulations 1998, the Children and Young Persons Acts 1933 and 1963, and the Children (Protection at Work) Regulations 2000.

As a general rule, no child under the age of 14 years may be employed, whether paid or not, and any child between the ages of 14 and 16 may be employed only to do light work for a restricted amount of time. Under the Children and Young Persons Acts, local authorities are empowered to pass by-laws restricting the employment of children and any employer who breaches such a by-law will be guilty of a criminal offence, as will any person by whose act or default a contravention took place.

(2) Foreign employees

It is a criminal offence to employ a person who is not entitled to work in the UK under Immigration Rules. A charity found guilty of an offence is liable, on summary conviction, to a fine not exceeding £5,000.

It is, of course, important for employers to remember that the UK is ethnically diverse and that many people from ethnic minorities are British or European citizens and therefore entitled to work in the UK without immigration restrictions. The law on the eligibility of foreign workers for employment in the UK makes a distinction in the procedure between nationals of member states of the European Economic Area (EEA) and others. A detailed consideration of UK immigration law is beyond the scope of this work. However, the main provisions are summarised below.

EEA nationals

The EEA comprises the 15 member states of the European Union together with Norway, Iceland and Liechtenstein. Nationals from the EEA are free to come to England, Scotland, Wales and Northern Ireland to seek or take up employment without the necessity of first obtaining a work permit. Employers are not therefore prohibited from employing EEA nationals.

Non-EEA nationals

Non-EEA nationals who are subject to immigration control must obtain work permits in order to be able to take up employment in the UK, unless the Immigration Rules provide otherwise. Charity employers are therefore prevented from employing non-EEA nationals if they do not have a work permit allowing them to work in the UK or they are not within one of the limited categories of persons who do not require a work permit. These include business visitors, Gibraltarians, Commonwealth citizens given leave to enter or remain in the UK on the basis that at least one grandparent was born in the UK, persons with indefinite leave to remain in the UK, and persons wishing to engage in certain specified occupations.

Subject to certain conditions, non-EEA students who are studying at UK institutions are no longer required to obtain permission from a job centre to take up vacation work.

(3) ***Employer's defence***

All employers have a statutory defence to a claim that they have unlawfully employed a person who is not entitled to work in the UK, if they can demonstrate that they have checked that a potential employee is in possession of one of a range of documents verifying his or her status. Acceptable documents include:

- a documented national insurance number;
- a passport confirming that the person is a British citizen;
- a passport or identity card as an EEA national;
- a passport or identity card which shows entitlement to live and work in the UK;
- a UK birth certificate;
- a letter from the Home Office confirming that the person is allowed to work.

It is therefore important that checks are made before individuals start work. To avoid breaching race discrimination legislation, it is sensible for charities to ensure that identical checks are carried out for all applicants. Charities should also ensure that they follow the Home Office Code of Practice for employers on the avoidance of race discrimination and recruitment practice whilst seeking to prevent illegal working. The Code sets out steps that employers need to take in order to ensure they do not act in a discriminatory fashion when complying with their obligation to employ only workers who are entitled to work in the UK. Although the Code does not impose any strict legal obligations itself, failure to observe the Code is admissible in evidence in employment tribunal proceedings as evidence of an employer's poor practice.

(4) Ex-offenders

In considering whether to employ an ex-offender, charities should be familiar with the Rehabilitation of Offenders Act 1974. It is unlawful for an employer to exclude a person from any office, profession, occupation or employment by reason of a spent conviction. The length of time which must elapse before a person's conviction becomes spent depends on the nature of the sentence imposed and runs from the date of the sentence. Certain sentences can never become spent, including imprisonment or custody for life, sentences of imprisonment, youth custody or detention in a young offender institution or corrective training for a term exceeding 30 months and detention.

A person whose conviction has become spent is known as a rehabilitated person and is to be treated for all purposes in law as a person who has not committed or been charged with or convicted of the offence in question. If questions about past convictions and related matters are put during a job interview or on an application form then they may be answered by the rehabilitated person on the basis that they do not refer to spent convictions.

There are, of course, exceptions to this rule and members of certain occupations and professions are obliged to disclose any spent convictions. These professions and occupations include doctors, nurses, midwives, dentists, barristers, solicitors, accountants, teachers, police officers and directors or other officers of building societies.

There is a general exception to this rule which is pertinent to many charities and which covers any office or employment which is concerned in the provision of accommodation, care, leisure and recreational facilities, schooling, social services, supervision or training to persons under 18 years, where the holder of the office of employment would have access to such minors in the normal course of his or her duties or if the duties are carried out wholly or partly on the premises where such provision takes place. Charity employers should also be aware of their obligations in relation to employing care staff where it may be obligatory to obtain criminal records certificates (see Chapter 27 on care workers).

If during a selection process an applicant reveals previous convictions which are spent, this is not necessarily a good reason for refusing the applicant the job, unless he or she is applying for any position in a professional occupation which is excluded from the protection of the Rehabilitation of Offenders Act 1974. Such applicants must answer questions relating to previous convictions and may be refused or dismissed from employment for a conviction or for failing to disclose such a conviction.

Charities should be aware that the DPA 1998 limits the right of an employer to process data on an employee's criminal convictions without the express consent of the employee (see Chapter 14).

4.5 PRE-EMPLOYMENT MONITORING

Employers may often require prospective employees to undertake a pre-employment medical check before confirming an employee in post. In addition to Data Protection Act issues, charities also need to be aware of their obligations under the Disability Discrimination Act 1995 (DDA 1995). If only disabled individuals are sent for pre-employment health checks, it may be possible for an applicant to argue that this is less favourable treatment and therefore discrimination on the grounds of disability. Furthermore, if the results of the pre-employment health check reveal that an applicant is suffering from a disability which the applicant has not previously disclosed, charities are obliged to give consideration as to what reasonable adjustments can be made in accordance with the DDA 1995 to assist that person in performing his or her contractual duties.

The best way to process pre-employment health checks is to identify those roles where there is a good business reason for a health check to be undertaken. For example, if someone will be carrying out manual labour on behalf of the charity, it may be a requirement that an appropriate risk assessment is carried out to ensure that a prospective employee is able to fulfil the requirements of the role.

4.6 TRADE UNIONS

Employees have a right to belong to the trade union of their choice or not to belong to a trade union at all. It is unlawful to refuse a person employment on the grounds of membership or non-membership of a trade union.

4.7 OFFERING EMPLOYMENT

Once a charity has selected an applicant as a prospective employee, it should inform the employee of the terms and conditions under which he or she is to work, together with the commencement date and time.

When engaging new employees, the vast majority of charities will initially employ new employees for a probationary period. This does not affect the relationship between the employer and the probationary employee. If a probationary employee is dismissed with at least 12 months' continuous employment, he or she may bring a claim for unfair dismissal in the same way as any other employee. In circumstances where there is no qualifying period, such as dismissal for reasons relating to trade union activity, health and safety activities, pregnancy or child birth, probationary employees are able to bring claims for unfair dismissal before 12 months have elapsed. Furthermore, any probationary employee who is dismissed on the grounds of sex, race or disability may bring a claim for discrimination (see Chapter 7). Many employers will have a shorter notice period for probationary employees and this should be set out clearly in the contract of employment and appointment letter.

Charity employers should also be aware that consultation is under way in relation to a new statutory regime which establishes statutory disciplinary and grievance procedures that will apply to all workers regardless of their length of service. The statutory procedures are likely to be introduced in October 2004. The procedures will apply to all probationary employees, and charity employers may therefore need to review their approach to the discipline and dismissal of probationary employees. (See Chapters 22 and 23.)

4.8 WITHDRAWAL OF OFFERS OF EMPLOYMENT

Having made an offer of employment to a prospective employee, there may be circumstances where the employer no longer wishes to proceed with the employment. Once an offer of employment has been made and accepted, a valid contract exists although the date on which the employee commences employment may be deferred. If an employer retracts the offer or terminates the contract prior to the commencement of work, an employee has three possible remedies:

- he or she may have a claim for wrongful dismissal which can be brought before an employment tribunal or in the county court;
- he or she may have a claim for unfair dismissal if the dismissal is for an inadmissible reason where no period of qualifying employment is necessary;
- he or she may have a claim alleging that the dismissal was discriminatory on grounds of sex or race or disability.

If an offer of employment is made subject to the employer receiving satisfactory references, medical checks or criminal records checks and those are not received, the employer may not wish to proceed with offering the position to that prospective employee. In such circumstances the employee will not normally have redress. Charities should ensure that any offer is made strictly subject to the receipt of satisfactory further information and it should be made clear that a contract will not be concluded until such references are received. See Chapter 5 in respect of references.

4.9 PRACTICAL GUIDANCE

Charities should consider the following checklist of matters in relation to a recruitment process.

- Ensure that all managers and other members of staff who are involved in the recruitment process receive appropriate training including training on equal opportunities.
- Ensure that advertisements are carefully drafted and checked before they are published.
- Ensure that a job description is prepared prior to the interview and selection process in order to identify the requirements for the role.
- Identify whether the role is such that a pre-employment health check will be required, and if so, ensure that all applicants are required to undertake a health check.
- Prepare a pro forma list of questions for each interviewer to ensure consistency throughout the selection process.
- Ensure that any decisions made throughout the selection process are carefully recorded and ensure that interviewers receive appropriate training on the DPA 1998 issues to understand their obligations in relation to the recording of data.
- Ensure that offer letters are carefully drafted to avoid the creation of a contract of employment prior to the satisfaction of any additional requirements such as health checks and/or satisfactory references.

Chapter 5

REFERENCES

5.1 INTRODUCTION

The reference has long been one of the main selection and recruitment tools used by charities. In the past few years, there have been a number of developments which have turned this once informal procedure into a minefield for the unwary.

5.2 GIVING REFERENCES

5.2.1 A dual responsibility

Since the 1960s it has been assumed that an employer has a responsibility and obligation to the employer requesting the reference, when providing a reference about an existing or former employee. This responsibility means that the employer must take reasonable care when writing the reference. If he fails to do so, and the recipient suffers loss as a result, the employer may be held liable to pay damages and compensation for the loss. Employers should therefore guard against offloading troublesome employees through inaccurate references.

This is not the only duty of care which the employer owes. In the 1990s, the House of Lords decided that the employer also owes a duty of care to the employee about whom the reference is given. In this particular case, a reference was described as the 'kiss of death' to an insurance salesman's career, as it contained adverse comments on his integrity and honesty which, although claimed to have been made in good faith, could not be substantiated. To bring a legal challenge, the employee only has to show that he or she has lost a reasonable chance of employment due to the negligently written reference, and has thereby suffered; the employee does not have to show that he or she would have been employed but for the reference. There may even be cases where claims for defamation or malicious falsehood could also be brought; however, these are much more difficult to prove.

Employers would therefore seem to be stuck between a rock and a hard place, with duties owed on both sides. An easy way to avoid these responsibilities and possible risks would appear to be to avoid writing any references at all. But can it be that simple?

5.2.2 Should charities give references?

It used to be generally accepted that an employer is under no obligation to provide a reference for an employee, unless there is an express term in the employment contract or any agreement made with the employee upon termination of the employment.

However, the vast majority of charities choose to provide a reference upon request. As a result of this almost universal practice, the absence of a reference in itself speaks volumes and could well disadvantage the individual in the job market. There may well now be an implied duty in every employment contract to give a reference, particularly when it is the normal custom and practice of the employer to provide one. In particular, there is an obligation for care providers to provide a reliable reference where requested under the General Social Care Council's Code of Practice for Social Care Employers, issued in September 2002 (see Chapter 27).

In addition to these points, there are circumstances where the refusal to give a reference could lead a charity into dangerous straits. If the employee was involved in a discrimination complaint either as the complainant or as a witness giving evidence for a colleague, and was refused a reference because of this, this would amount to victimisation, a form of discrimination.

Charities should therefore bear in mind that, although there is no legal obligation to provide a reference except where there is an express contractual term, a refusal to provide a reference could cause risks in the following situations:

- where there is an implied obligation to provide one through industry standards and custom and practice within the employer;
- where the basis for refusing to provide one is that the (ex-)employee was involved in a discrimination complaint against the charity;
- where the charity is a care provider.

5.2.3 Content of a reference

The charity has a duty to both the employee and the recipient of the reference to ensure that it is written with reasonable care. The reference must be accurate in its detail and should not give an overall unfair or misleading impression, even where factually correct.

The reference does not, however, need to be full and comprehensive, as it is accepted by case law that this additional responsibility would impose too crippling a burden upon employers.

A reference should contain details such as the length of the employee's service, the position(s) the employee held, the employee's competence in the job, his or her time-keeping and attendance record, any reason(s) for leaving, and any more personal observations relating to the employee that might be relevant to his or her employability.

With regard to other details, such as disciplinary action, it may not always seem straightforward to balance the dual responsibilities to recipient and employee. The general view is that:

- if an employee was not aware that allegations had been made, or that he or she was being investigated, or if any allegations or investigations against the employee had not been resolved at the time of termination, these should not be included in any reference;
- if, however, disciplinary proceedings were completed against an employee, the referee may be in breach of his or her duty to the recipient if details of these proceedings are not included in the reference.

Charities should also be aware of the provisions of the Data Protection Act 1998 (DPA 1998) and its impact on references. On being rejected for a new job, an aggrieved and disgruntled employee, in addition to requesting any interview notes, can also request any references given to the prospective employer. Therefore, despite the reference being marked private and confidential, the employee would have a right of access to the confidential reference, once it has been received by the prospective employer, and where reasonable in all the circumstances. In addition, under the DPA 1998, the express consent of the employee is required before 'sensitive personal data', which will include details of the employee's health or union membership, is released. (See Chapter 14.)

5.2.4 An agreed reference

Where an employee signs a compromise agreement or agrees terms of settlement on termination of his or her employment, there is frequently a term that the employer will give a reference in an agreed form when asked by prospective employers.

In these situations it is tempting for the charity to cast the reference in a more favourable light than might otherwise have been the case. This is because the employer knows that by doing this money can be saved: for example, by settling an action promptly, before any legal costs have been incurred. It also appears to remove the risk associated with the employer's duty and responsibility towards the employee.

There are two potential problems with this: first, where misconduct is discovered after the reference has been agreed; and secondly, where there is the possibility of a subsequent unfair dismissal claim.

Subsequent misconduct could put the employer into a difficult position: to amend the reference could lead to a breach of contract claim, but to fail to amend could lead to a claim from the recipient for an inaccurate reference. A possible solution would be to include a disclaimer stating that the reference is 'subject to any further information coming to our attention'.

Where an employer dismisses an employee for a reason such as misconduct or lack of capability, but provides a satisfactory reference (so any severance payment will be smaller), there is a risk of a subsequent finding of unfair dismissal if the employee brings a claim. The dismissed employee could claim, successfully, that there had not been any misconduct/incapability as the employer alleged, and he or she could rely on the reference as evidence of this.

5.2.5 Disclaimer

It is generally not possible to exclude liability for the negligent misstatement of facts in a reference, where these are ordinarily within the knowledge of the employer. However, a disclaimer may be effective to exclude liability with regard to statements which relate to other matters. For example, a disclaimer may cover any comment on a person's suitability for a job of a different type, of which the employer has no particular knowledge.

Any disclaimer must be reasonable in all the circumstances. Where the charity has the requisite knowledge and the reference is very important, it is not reasonable to rely on such a disclaimer, and the court will have very little sympathy for any charity seeking to hide behind it. The disclaimer could, however, be used to ensure that the employer is not liable for any events that come to light after the reference has been provided, or to limit the reference to all knowledge, at the time it was written, in the employer's field of activity.

5.2.6 Practical guidance

Due to the risks involved in making errors, a charity should always consider its approach to references. Any approach should be adopted uniformly and consistently, ensuring that all ex-employees are treated equally. This is not to say that all employees should receive glowing references, merely that if a charity intends to refer to disciplinary procedures for one employee, it should do this in all references.

Charities should observe the following.

- References should only be prepared by the HR team or one other nominated person.
- Line managers should be told to pass any reference requests to the HR team or the nominated person.
- The charity should have a policy on whether, and if so how, to respond to written and/or oral follow-up queries.

- The charity should have a policy on whether to provide only standard references, ie dates of employment and job title only.
- The charity should have a policy on whether to include a disclaimer in any reference provided.

5.3 OBTAINING REFERENCES

The recipient of the reference owes no special duty or obligation to the employee with regard to the reference. The prospective employer should, however, consider asking for specific details in the reference, particularly details which would have a direct impact on the job. Of course, as described above, the reference provider may choose not to give any more detail than length of employment and positions held. However, a prospective employer loses nothing by asking. The recipient of a reference should also note the position under the DPA 1998 (see Chapter 14).

5.3.1 Reference checking

It is vital that references are checked. This might seem obvious, but it is an element of the recruitment process that is frequently overlooked, especially when the sense of relief at having found an apparently suitable candidate negates the inclination to investigate the candidate's past. However, it is important to ensure that the candidate is suitable at the outset, as the charity may not be able to take action later if a reference is false and was not investigated when given. There is a specific obligation on care providers to check references (see Chapter 27).

5.3.2 Practical guidance

- Write to the awarding body or institution and check the qualifications and grades.
- Do not accept the references provided if there seems to be a big gap in the employment record – be proactive.
- Try to speak directly to the individual referees.
- Check the basic facts, especially the years of employment – years can often go missing.
- Try to uncover any weaknesses in the prospective employee's CV as this could highlight any training needs.

Remember, once an offer of employment has been made and accepted, a valid contract of employment exists. Unless it is made clear that the job offer was conditional upon receiving satisfactory references (see below), retracting the offer or terminating the contract could lead to problems, even before the actual commencement of work.

5.3.3 'Subject to a satisfactory reference'

Many job offers are expressly made subject to a satisfactory reference. It has been held that 'satisfactory' in this context means subjectively satisfactory to the prospective employer. However, it has been recognised that the requirement could be an objective test instead. If the reference is clearly unsatisfactory, the job offer can be withdrawn. However, if the reference were objectively satisfactory, then the subsequent withdrawal of the job offer could lead to problems, if the withdrawal were challenged. The problems would be the same as if there had been no such condition attached initially.

As a result, it is generally advisable to withdraw only where the reference is objectively unsatisfactory. Alternatively, the employer might consider using wording such as 'subject to a reference satisfactory to us' to avoid any doubt or ambiguity.

Particular care should be taken where the reference discloses for the first time involvement in trade union activity or a disability. Withdrawing the job offer in such circumstances could lead to claims for unfair dismissal and discrimination claims in addition to any claim for wrongful dismissal.

Again, it should be remembered that a request under the DPA 1998 would probably enable the failed employee to obtain a copy of the reference.

Chapter 6

CONTRACTS OF EMPLOYMENT

6.1 INTRODUCTION

We have already considered one of the most fundamental employment law questions for charities: whether a particular staff member is an employee or not. As we have seen, an employee is a person who works for another person pursuant to a contract of employment (see Chapter 1). This chapter considers both the form and terms of the contract of employment; the legal implications of changing contracts of employment; and the position where there has been a breach of contract.

6.2 FORM OF THE CONTRACT

As a general rule, an employer and employee may agree whatever terms they wish. Therefore in the majority of cases the legal framework governing the employment relationship is that agreed between the parties themselves.

A contract of employment may be either a formal written agreement, an oral agreement based on discussion during the selection procedure, or a mixture of the two. Thus, its form may vary significantly. In any event, provided that the parties are in agreement over the essential terms of the contract, such as wages and hours, there will be a valid contract of employment enforceable by either party. The terms of the contract of employment are considered in more detail below.

There is no legal requirement for the contract of employment to be in writing. However, the law requires that every employee be provided with a written statement of particulars of certain terms of the contract within 2 months of the beginning of his or her employment. These are set out in detail below.

There may be circumstances where an employee is required to work outside the UK for more than a month, in which case the statement must be given within 2 months of the beginning of the employment and before he or she leaves the UK to begin work.

6.3 PARTICULARS WHICH MUST BE GIVEN

The written statement must contain the following information:

(a) the names of the employer and the employee;
(b) the date on which the employment commenced;
(c) the date on which the employee's period of continuous employment began (taking into account any employment with a previous employer which counts towards that period);
(d) the scale, rate or method of calculating remuneration;
(e) the intervals at which remuneration is paid (ie weekly, monthly or otherwise);
(f) any terms and conditions relating to:
  (i) holiday entitlement, including public holidays and holiday pay;
  (ii) incapacity for work due to sickness or injury, including any provisions concerning sick pay;
  (iii) pensions and pension schemes (unless established under statute);
(g) the notice period which the employee is obliged to give and entitled to receive in order to terminate the contract;
(h) the job title or a brief description of the work;
(i) the period during which non-permanent work is expected to continue, or the date when fixed-term work is due to end;
(j) the place of work or an indication of various places where the employee is required or permitted to work, together with the employer's address;
(k) any collective agreements directly affecting the terms and conditions of employment, including details of the parties by whom they were made, if not the employer; and
(l) where the employee is required to work outside the UK for more than a month, further particulars concerning that period, the currency of remuneration, any additional remuneration and benefits, and any terms and conditions relating to the employee's return to the UK.

In addition to the written particulars, the statement must include notes setting out the following information:

(a) whether a contracting-out certificate is in force for the particular employment;
(b) any disciplinary rules applicable to the employee or a reference to a document (such as a policy) which is reasonably accessible to the employee and which specifies any disciplinary rules;
(c) a person to whom the employee can apply if dissatisfied with any disciplinary decision relating to him or her;
(d) a person to whom the employee can apply with any grievance relating to his or her employment, together with details of the manner in which any application should be made.

Subject to the introduction of statutory disciplinary and grievance procedures later in October 2004 (for details of which see Chapters 20 and 22 on disciplinary and grievance issues), there is no legal requirement that a contract of employment must contain provisions in relation to all of the above matters. The legal requirement is simply to notify employees of any provisions that do exist. It is important, however, that if there are no provisions relating to any of the above, this should be stated clearly in the contract.

Although the written statement of particulars may be given in instalments during the 2-month period, certain particulars must be contained in a single document. Therefore, unless there are exceptional circumstances, it is best practice to provide the above information in a standard statement of terms and conditions, and for that to be given to the employee within one week of commencing employment.

6.4 FAILURE TO GIVE PARTICULARS

An employee has no right to claim damages from his or her charity employer for a breach of the statutory duty to give written particulars. However, an employee may make a complaint relating to the failure to an employment tribunal. If the employee succeeds, the tribunal will state the particulars which should have been given and the charity will be deemed to have given a statement including those particulars. If there has been no express or implied agreement on a particular term the tribunal cannot invent a term for the parties. A tribunal may be able to imply a term after considering all the facts and circumstances of the relationship between the charity and the employee concerned. If a charity has acted in breach of any of the terms which the tribunal states should have been given, the employee may subsequently bring an action against the charity in the county court or the High Court for breach of contract and damages arising out of that breach.

6.5 TERMS OF THE CONTRACT

As a general rule, the parties to a contract of employment are free to agree any terms they wish. In practice this usually means that the parties agree upon a set of express terms which govern the contractual relationship between the employer and employee. In addition, there may be other terms which regulate the employment relationship. These may be implied, incorporated or statutory terms, or may be contained in handbooks and policies which confer a benefit on employees.

6.6 IMPLIED TERMS

The general rule is that a term which has not been expressly set out in the contract of employment will be implied if the term is necessary to give the contract business efficacy. Terms may also be implied if they are customary in the trade or from the usual practice of the employer, provided that the custom or practice is reasonable, certain and sufficiently well known.

There are commonly implied terms as follows.

6.6.1 Both parties

To give the other party a reasonable period of notice of termination when no specific notice has been agreed

The written particulars of employment given to the employee should include the length of notice that the employee is obliged to give or entitled to receive. If, however, the notice period has not been expressly agreed between the charity and the employee, then there is an implied term that the contract may be terminated on reasonable notice. The court or tribunal will determine what amounts to reasonable notice and will take into account all the facts of each individual case. Factors that the court may take into account include the seniority, age and length of service of the individual employee. It is important to note that, whatever the express or implied contractual provision, the notice given must be at least the statutory minimum period of notice. (See Chapter 23.)

6.6.2 Employer

Not to act in a manner likely to destroy the relationship of trust and confidence between the employer and the employee

The test to determine whether an employer has acted in breach of the implied term not to act in a manner likely to destroy the relationship of trust and confidence is a severe one. Not only must the conduct be so bad as to destroy or seriously damage the relationship but there must also have been no reasonable and proper cause for the conduct. There are a number of circumstances in which it is possible for an employer to breach this implied term, ranging from a single incident of verbal abuse to an employer's unilateral reduction of the employee's hours in circumstances where the job could not be performed within the reduced hours. A breach of this implied term may entitle an employee to resign and claim constructive dismissal as a result of the breach.

CASE STUDY

The Court of Appeal considered the implied duty of trust and confidence in the case of *Gogay v Hertfordshire County Council* [2000] IRLR 703.

Ms Gogay was a care worker employed by Hertfordshire County Council. A child under her care made allegations of sexual abuse by Ms Gogay. The Council decided that the allegations needed investigating and suspended Ms Gogay, informing her that she was suspended whilst investigations of sexual abuse were conducted. She was then suspended for many months. At the end of the suspension the allegations were dropped. The Court of Appeal considered that being accused of sexual abuse was capable of seriously damaging the employment relationship and that the employer had overstated matters in saying that the reason for the suspension was an allegation of sexual abuse. The Court of Appeal held that this was a 'knee jerk' reaction to an allegation which was not well founded; and that there was no reasonable and proper cause for the Council's conduct. The Court held that the suspension and the reason given to Ms Gogay amounted to a breach of the implied term for an employer not to act in a manner likely to destroy or seriously damage the relationship of trust and confidence between the employer and the employee.

To take reasonable steps to ensure the employee's health and safety

Whilst this includes providing a safe system of work to prevent physical injury by the employee, charities should also be aware that they owe a duty to take reasonable care not to cause psychiatric harm to an employee by reason of the volume or character of work imposed on the employee. There is no legal definition of what is 'reasonable care' but the courts have found that what is reasonable depends on factors such as the nature of the relationship, the magnitude of the risk of injury that was reasonably foreseeable, the seriousness of the consequences for the employee if that injury should occur, and the cost and practicability of preventing the risk. Charity employers should ensure that they are aware of the potential risks to employees of the volume or character of the work imposed on them. Best practice suggests that appraisal and supervision sessions should address and monitor the employee's workload and concerns they have about the volume or character of his or her work. (See Chapter 18.)

Other implied terms

The above list of employers' duties is not exhaustive and case law has developed a number of other implied duties on employers. For example, in *Scally v Southern Health & Social Services Board* [1991] ICR 771 an employer was under an implied duty to take reasonable steps to bring to the employee's attention a right which he had but which he would lose unless he took certain action, in circumstances where the employee could not reasonably have been expected to be aware of the relevant contractual term unless it was drawn to his attention.

Accordingly, if charity employers become aware of a right that employees may lose they should consider whether they are under an implied duty to take reasonable steps to bring the right to the employees' attention. An example of this is the right to take paid holiday leave when on unpaid sick leave.

Another area where terms may be implied is where an employee is absent by reason of ill health. Where, for example, a contract of employment contains terms entitling an employee to benefits during a period of ill health and the receipt of those benefits is dependent on the individual remaining in the employer's employment, the courts have taken the view that a term will be implied into the contract that the employer cannot dismiss the employee while he remains incapacitated so as to deprive him of the continued receipt of those benefits. In *Aspden v Webbs Poultry and Meat Group (Holdings) Ltd* [1996] IRLR 521, the High Court formulated an implied term that the employer could not terminate the contract of employment (save for a cause other than ill health) in circumstances which would deprive the employee of his continuing entitlement to benefit under the PHI policy.

6.6.3 Employee

To comply with the duties of fidelity; obedience; due diligence and care; and not using or disclosing the employer's trade secrets or confidential information

In addition to the employee's duty to serve his employer faithfully and not to act against the interests of the employer's business, an employee is also obliged to obey the reasonable instructions of his employer.

If there is no express term in the contract setting out the location of the employee's workplace, this term will be implied. There are circumstances in which the term implied may be that the employee is required to work anywhere within reasonable daily travelling distance.

6.7 INCORPORATED TERMS

Where parties agree on certain terms of the contract by reference to a collective agreement, the terms of the collective agreement may be incorporated into the contract of employment either expressly or as an implied term of the contract deriving from custom and practice in the industry. In either case, the collective agreement will be incorporated notwithstanding, for example, that a particular employee may not approve of the term negotiated by his trade union, or may even have ceased to belong to that union. A collective agreement will not be incorporated into individual contracts of employment merely because the employer belongs to the trade union or association which negotiated that agreement. (See Chapter 15.)

6.8 STATUTORY TERMS

The law sets out standards in relation to an employee's employment, which are implied into any contract as a minimum. For example, the law sets out minimum standards in relation to pay, notice, sick pay and holiday. From the end of 2004, disciplinary and grievance procedures will be implied into all contracts of employment. (See Chapter 22.)

6.9 HANDBOOKS AND POLICIES

The vast majority of charities provide their employees with access to handbooks and policies which govern the conduct of the relationship between them. There are two particular circumstances where it is important to identify whether or not these documents have contractual effect.

First, if the policy or handbook is contractual, an employer may not unilaterally change that policy. Secondly, if a charity departs from the policy or procedure in the handbook, the employee may claim that the employer is in breach of the contract of employment. If, for example, a disciplinary policy is contractual and a charity proposes to dismiss an employee without following that procedure, the employee may seek an injunction to prevent that dismissal from taking place. If the policy is not contractual, the employee would have no such claim.

As a rule of thumb, a policy or procedure set out in a company handbook will have contractual effect if it may be regarded as conferring rights on employees. If the policy is not intended to confer rights, but is merely a statement of good practice which an employer would be expected to follow, it is unlikely to have contractual effect.

6.10 UNENFORCEABLE TERMS

Although the parties are free to agree whatever terms they like, some of those terms may be unenforceable by an employer:

6.10.1 Terms which are unlawful or contrary to public policy

If the terms of a contract are unlawful (for example, to perform an illegal act) or contrary to public policy (for example, for an immoral purpose), that contract will be unenforceable. This means that as long as the employee is unaware of the fact that the employer was unlawfully performing the contract (for example, by not deducting tax), the employee may rely on the contract for the purposes of claiming employment protection rights. An employee may still bring a claim for discrimination in circumstances where the contract itself is unenforceable by reason of illegality; a complaint of discrimination will not rely on the unenforceable contract but rather arises out of the conduct of the employer.

Example

Examples of circumstances in which the terms of a contract of employment are unlawful include a contract where a foreign employee is working illegally without a work permit or a contract which defrauds the Inland Revenue. In those circumstances, neither the employer nor the employee would be able to assert their rights under the contract of employment.

6.10.2 Restrictions on contracting out

Any attempt by an employer or an employee to contract out of their statutory rights and obligations (for example, in relation to discrimination) will be ineffective unless permitted by the particular statutes concerned.

6.10.3 Discriminatory terms

Any contractual term which is contrary to the Sex Discrimination Act 1975 or Race Relations Act 1976 or the Race Relations (Amendment) Act 2000 is void and unenforceable. When new discrimination law comes into force between 2003 and 2006, any contractual term which discriminates against an employee on the grounds of sexual orientation, religion or belief, disability or age will also be unenforceable.

6.10.4 Terms in restraint of trade

Many employers often include clauses in contracts of employment, seeking to control competing activities by employees after they leave employment. Given the nature of the work of charities, it is rare for a charity to want to restrict an employee's freedom to work after leaving employment. A charity can, however, rely on such a clause if it can demonstrate that it has a legitimate business interest which requires protecting, such as trade secrets and confidential information. If it cannot, any term which purports to restrict an employee's freedom to work after he or she leaves employment will be unenforceable. Charities sometimes consider these clauses for senior members of staff. There are four common types of terms restricting behaviour after termination of employment:

(a) non-solicitation covenants, which prevent a former employee from soliciting the custom of clients of the employer;
(b) non-dealing covenants, which prevent a former employee from dealing with clients of the employer;
(c) non-competition covenants, which prevent a former employee from engaging in a competitive activity;

(d) non-solicitation of other employees, which prevents a former employee from recruiting his or her colleagues.

It is most likely that, of these clauses, a non-solicitation clause could be of practical benefit to charity employers particularly in circumstances where the charity has invested its funds and resources into maintaining a team of skilled staff. A detailed consideration of the validity of terms in restraint of trade is beyond the scope of this work, and advice should be taken in relation to the drafting of appropriate non-solicitation clauses.

6.10.5 Restrictions on industrial action

Unless the contract of employment expressly or impliedly incorporates the terms of a collective agreement relating to strikes, any provision in a collective agreement which purports to restrict the right to take industrial action will not form part of an individual employee's contract of employment.

6.10.6 Unfair contract terms

The Unfair Contract Terms Act 1977 may render certain types of contractual term unenforceable unless inclusion of the term was fair and reasonable in the circumstances and was, or ought reasonably to have been, known to or in the contemplation of the parties when the contract was made. Accordingly, any contractual term which purports to exclude or restrict liability for death or personal injury resulting from negligence will usually be void.

6.11 CHANGES TO THE TERMS OF CONTRACT

As a general rule, an employee's contractual terms may not be changed without consent. The employee can expressly agree to the change orally or, preferably, in writing. If there is no express consent, it may be possible to imply consent by the employee if the employee continues to work for the employer without protest for a significant period of time whilst aware that the change to terms and conditions has taken place.

If the charity has expressly reserved the right to vary the terms of a contract by including such a right in the contract itself, the term must be clear and unambiguous in creating a power to alter unilaterally the terms of the contract. The term must not go further than allowing an employer to vary the contractual provisions and the rights of the employee under the contract must not be affected. This right is therefore likely to be limited.

Any change in terms which is not agreed with the employee or permitted in accordance with the contract is, on the face of it, a breach of the contract of employment. An employee may resign following the unilateral variation and, if able to show that the change was significant, could claim constructive dismissal. (See Chapter 23.)

An employee may, however, continue to work under protest. This would prevent a charity employer from arguing that the employee had impliedly consented to the change and would leave a charity open to a potential claim for breach of contract. It is not necessary for an employee to leave employment in order to bring a claim of this nature.

In the absence of any agreement by the employee, if the change in contractual terms is of importance to the employer, the only course of action is to enforce the change, or to terminate the original contract of employment and offer new terms. In these circumstances, the charity should ensure that it has good objective business reasons requiring the change and should consult with the employees regarding the reasons requiring the change and also the details of the proposed changes. A charity should then give reasonable notice of when the change will come into effect. As a rule of thumb, notice should be as long as the notice one would give to the employee to terminate employment.

6.12 BREACH OF CONTRACT

If a term of the contract of employment is breached, either party may have a potential claim.

6.12.1 Employer's options on taking action

There are five possible remedies for a charity if an employee acts in breach of the contract of employment:

Withholding or deduction of wages

If an employee does not perform or refuses to perform the full range of his or her contractual duties, he or she will not be entitled to the full contractual wage. For example, an employee is not entitled to be paid for days when he or she is either absent from work without good reason, or refuses to perform contractual duties in breach of the contract of employment. In such circumstances, a charity can deduct an amount equivalent to a day's wages from salary and may be able to take further action to recover any financial loss suffered as a result of the employee's breach.

This remedy should be exercised with caution as any deduction from wages which is not required or permitted by a statutory or contractual provision, or one to which the employee has given prior written consent, will be unlawful. Ideally, a charity should include an express term in the contract to deduct wages where an employee fails or refuses to comply with his or her contractual obligations. In order for a charity to argue that there is an implied contractual term which permits the deduction of wages in these circumstances, the charity must be able to demonstrate that it acted reasonably in deducting sums from the employee's wages. As a general rule, this should be done only where there is an express refusal by the employee to perform duties. It should not, for example, be used in circumstances where the charity suspects that an employee is feigning illness in order to avoid performing his or her contractual duties.

Acceptance of fundamental breach

If the employee breaches one of the fundamental contractual obligations, a charity may accept that breach and bring the contract of employment to an end. As a rule of thumb, such a fundamental breach would ordinarily consist of a major failure to carry out the work required of the employee, such as failing to attend work at all without any explanation. The charity should include wording in the contract allowing itself to accept such a breach, in certain circumstances.

Damages

A charity employer may bring proceedings against an employee for damages for breach of contract. In practice, such claims are rare.

Injunction or specific performance

It is common for charities to enquire whether they can force an employee to carry out work by obtaining an order of the court. However, a court will never grant an injunction or order specific performance of an employee's contractual duties.

Account of profits

In exceptional circumstances where the normal remedy of damages does not provide an adequate remedy, the court may order an employee to account for any profits made as a result of acting in breach of contractual duties. It is unlikely that this remedy would be relevant to the majority of breaches by employees of charities.

Example

An example of when a charity may consider seeking an order for an employee to account for profits may be where an employee is strictly prohibited under contract terms from using confidential information about the charity. While still in employment, the employee breaches that obligation and publishes a best-selling book about the charity which uses that confidential information. The charity may not be able to demonstrate the loss it has suffered as a result of the employee writing the book; in which case, the court could order the employee to account for the profits he or she makes from publishing the book.

6.12.2 Employee's options on breach of contract

An employee may bring proceedings in either the county court or the High Court for sums due under the contract of employment and for damages in circumstances where an employer acts in breach of the contract of employment. An employee can bring such a claim while remaining in employment. However, if the charity's breach of contract is sufficiently serious, an employee may resign and bring proceedings for his or her prospective loss in addition to any sums outstanding at the date of the dismissal.

Employment tribunals may hear claims for breach of contracts of employment but only where such a claim arises (or is outstanding) on the termination of the employee's employment and does not exceed £25,000. The employment tribunal does not therefore have jurisdiction to consider a claim which is made by an employee while remaining in employment and the employee must sue for that type of breach in the county court or High Court.

An employee need not actually have commenced duties in order to be able to bring a claim. Therefore, if an employee has accepted an offer of employment, there is a valid contract of employment even if the start date is postponed. If the contract is terminated before the actual start date, the employee will have a claim for breach of the contract, which will be for the salary and benefits he or she would have received during the notice period in the contract (see Chapter 4).

Damages

If an employee is summarily dismissed without notice, the measure of damages is the sum which the charity would have had to pay in order to bring the contract to an end lawfully. This would be the sum payable in respect of the notice period, assessed as being the net salary and benefits the employee would have received during the notice period. If an employee is able to show that he or she was contractually entitled to go through a disciplinary or other procedure prior to dismissal, he or she may be able to claim the lost wages for the time during which the disciplinary or other procedure would have taken place. Damages include loss of pension rights that would have accrued had the employee not been dismissed summarily.

Damages for the loss of the chance to claim unfair dismissal

In circumstances where, had an employee been given contractual notice, he or she would have been employed for 12 months, thereby accruing unfair dismissal rights, the employee may be able to claim damages for the loss of the chance to claim unfair dismissal. In these circumstances, the employee may recover the loss of the value of the chance of bringing that claim. These damages are usually assessed at a notional figure of £250.

Damages for loss of reputation

If an employee is able to demonstrate that it was reasonably foreseeable that the breach of contract by the charity would cause the employee to suffer a loss of reputation (and provided that the employee has taken steps to mitigate that loss), an employee may be able to recover damages for loss of reputation.

Damages for the manner of dismissal

An employee is not able to recover damages for the manner of a dismissal and, accordingly, there is no right for an employee to recover damages for injury to feelings caused by the actual dismissal.

Injunctions

In limited circumstances, the court may grant an employee an injunction to restrain the charity employer from taking action which would be in breach of contract. This may be used in circumstances where an employer is proposing to dismiss an employee without following a contractual disciplinary procedure. In these circumstances it will be necessary for the employee to show that the procedure itself is contractual; unless he or she is able to do this, the remedy will not be available. Charities should of course be aware that, once the statutory disciplinary and grievance procedures are in force at the end of 2004 (for details of which, see Chapters 22 and 23), if there is a proposal to dismiss an employee without reference to the statutory procedures, an employee may be able to seek an injunction to restrain the employer from dismissing him or her without following the appropriate procedure.

6.13 PRACTICAL GUIDANCE

Charities should draft standard terms and conditions which, as a matter of best practice, should be given to the employee within one week of employment commencing. These terms and conditions should include the following:

- the names of the parties;
- the date when employment commenced (and date of continuous employment if different);
- details of remuneration and when it is paid;
- the hours of work;
- details of any terms and conditions regarding holiday entitlement, absence from work due to sickness or injury, and pensions and pension schemes;
- the notice that the employee is obliged to give and entitled to receive;
- the job title or a brief description of the work;
- for temporary work, the period to which the work is expected to continue, or for fixed-term work, a date when it is due to end;
- the place or places of work, together with the employer's address;
- details of any collective agreements directly affecting the terms and conditions of employment;

- details of any period where the employee is required to work outside the UK for more than a month;
- details of any disciplinary rules or policies;
- details of any grievance policy or procedure;
- whether or not the pension scheme is contracted in or out of SERPS/SSP;
- specific clauses that will be relevant to the employee in question, such as covenants protecting intellectual property, or restrictive covenants;
- a clause allowing the charity to deduct wages where an employee does not perform the contract, or on termination when the employee owes money to the charity – for example, where there is an outstanding loan;
- a clause allowing the charity to terminate employment where the employee does not perform his or her duties at all – for instance, when the employee fails to turn up for work;
- a clause permitting the charity to deduct an amount from the employee's final salary in respect of any holiday that has been taken in excess of the employee's annual entitlement (see Chapter 11);
- a clause confirming the employee's consent to the processing of personal data by the employer (see Chapter 14);
- any clauses relating to enhanced entitlements to holiday or sick pay which differ from the statutory rules (see Chapters 11 and 12).

Chapter 7

DIVERSITY WITHIN THE WORKPLACE

7.1 INTRODUCTION

Although the legal framework governing discrimination and equal pay has now been in place for more than 30 years, implementation for all employers, including charities, has been a slow and arduous process. This has not been assisted by a sometimes inconsistent and overly complex interpretation of the law.

There is clear evidence to suggest that discrimination is not just detrimental for individuals, but for all employers, including charities. Discrimination leads to poor performance and absence, which has a palpable effect upon the functioning of the charity. A more diverse workforce will help promote and improve the image of the charity and improve performance and retention of staff within it. Government statistics show that the average cost of each employer implementing a diversity policy will be £157, but cost savings in the long run will be between £102 and £567 million for the workforce in view of the reduction in turnover of staff and increased productivity. A number of large organisations which operate a diversity policy report gains in productivity which they argue would not have occurred had they not implemented the policy. Those organisations report an increase in creativity and innovation, improved service delivery, and better recruitment and retention of staff.

Apart from the business reasons for diversity there is also an incentive from the Charity Commission, which requires charities to consider diversity in the constitution of their Boards and for the composition of each Board to reflect the diversity of the charity's beneficiaries.

Those charities which carry out public services may also be obliged to consider the impact of the Race Relations (Amendment) Act 2000 and the general and specific duties imposed upon those providing public services to promote equality of opportunity and good relations between different racial groups.

It therefore is advisable for economic, regulatory and legal reasons that all charities seriously consider implementing a diversity policy.

The law imposes a basic set of benchmarked standards upon employers to prevent discrimination in the workplace. These form the legal framework for equality of opportunities and diversity in the workplace.

7.2 CURRENT LEGAL FRAMEWORK.

Discrimination law is governed by six statutory provisions:

- the Equal Pay Act 1970 (EPA 1970);
- the Sex Discrimination Act 1975 (SDA 1975);
- the Race Relations Act 1976 (RRA 1976);
- the Disability Discrimination Act 1995 (DDA 1995);
- the Part-time Workers (Prevention of Less Favourable Treatment) Regulations 2000;
- the Fixed-term Employees (Prevention of Less Favourable Treatment) Regulations 2002.

By the end of 2006 the following three areas of discrimination will become unlawful by virtue of new regulations:

- sexual orientation;
- religion or belief;
- age.

There is a large and complex body of case law from both national and European courts; and Codes of Practice for the SDA 1975, RRA 1976 and DDA 1995 are designed to provide an interpretation of those statutes.

This chapter is not aimed at guiding the reader through the detailed nuances of statute and case law, but seeks to outline those provisions governing the five main heads of discrimination, which are sex, race, disability and discrimination against part-time and fixed-term employees.

7.3 MATTERS COMMON TO SEX AND RACE DISCRIMINATION

7.3.1 What does discrimination mean?

Discrimination is defined by the SDA 1975 and RRA 1976 as taking three forms:

- direct discrimination;
- indirect discrimination; and
- victimisation.

Direct discrimination

Direct discrimination means treating somebody less favourably than another on the grounds of sex or race, where as a result of such treatment the person suffers a detriment: for example, appointing to a position a man in preference to a woman, or a person who is African instead of one who is African Caribbean, when in each instance both are equally qualified to do the job. The employer's intention is irrelevant. Discrimination can occur without the employer being consciously aware of it and so case law has found that the intention and motive are irrelevant. Moreover, it is extremely rare for an employer to admit to having discriminated against an individual. Tribunals therefore draw inferences from witness evidence during the course of proceedings.

Indirect discrimination

The definition of indirect discrimination under sex and race discrimination is slightly different. The test of indirect discrimination will be satisfied if it can be shown that:

- the charity has a 'provision, criteria or practice';
- with which, in the case of sex discrimination, a considerably smaller proportion of persons of one sex as opposed to another can comply, and which cannot be shown to be justified by the requirements of the job;
- which, in the case of race discrimination, places individuals of a particular race or ethnic origin at a particular disadvantage, and which cannot be shown to be a proportionate means of achieving a legitimate aim; and
- not being able to comply is to the person's detriment.

Example

An example would be where an advertisement states that job applicants are required to have a GCSE in English Language. Here the employer is seeking to impose a requirement which fewer non-British as opposed to British applicants will be able to comply with; it is therefore indirectly discriminatory on the grounds of race if it cannot be shown to be a proportionate means of achieving a legitimate aim. If the advertisement had stated that a GCSE *or* equivalent would be acceptable, then this would not be indirect discrimination.

Victimisation

Victimisation is defined as less favourable treatment of an individual because he or she has taken legal action of some kind under the SDA 1975, RRA 1976 or DDA 1995, or has been involved in such action. For example, where a person makes a complaint of sexual or racial harassment, and is dismissed unfairly or is made redundant because of having made that complaint, victimisation has occurred.

7.3.2 Sexual and racial harassment

Although not defined under the SDA 1975, it is now well recognised that harassment on the grounds of sex or race will amount to discrimination.

From 17 July 2003 harassment on the grounds of racial, natural or ethnic origin is unlawful, and the UK will introduce regulations no later than October 2005 to implement the same principles in the SDA 1975. For the first time, a binding EU-wide definition of harassment is being set out in UK law. It is likely to cover intimidatory conduct, bullying, physical or verbal abuse carried out against a person because of his or her sex or race or ethnic origin. Any behaviour which is sex-based may not be unlawful unless the conduct 'occurs with the purpose or effect of violating the dignity of a person, and of creating an intimidating, hostile, degrading, humiliating or offensive environment'.

There is ongoing debate as to whether a single act of harassment will meet the definition or whether there will need to be a continuing act. It seems likely that it will be a matter of degree.

In practice it is unlikely to be the charity itself which commits an act of sexual or racial harassment. However, under the legislation an employer remains liable for the wrongful acts of an employee committed during the course of employment. Where an act of this nature has taken place during the course of employment, the charity has a defence if it can establish that it took such steps as were reasonably practicable to prevent the act from occurring. In practice this means being able to show that an Equal Opportunities Policy is in place and distributed to all workers, and that equal opportunities training is also given, particularly to managers or those in positions of responsibility. If a charity cannot show such a policy or training, the charity is likely to be found liable for discrimination, even where it was unaware of any such harassment by one worker against another.

7.4 REQUIREMENTS NECESSARY FOR A MEMBER OF STAFF TO BRING A DISCRIMINATION CLAIM

An individual may bring a claim for discrimination even if he or she is not an employee, but merely a worker or a person defined as engaged in a contract to provide services (save under the Fixed-term Employees (Prevention of Less Favourable Treatment) Regulations 2002). A volunteer will also be able to bring a claim if his or her status can be described as that of a worker (see Chapters 1 and 2). The intention is that all workers, except those genuinely engaged as self-employed, are entitled to bring a claim for discrimination.

The right to bring a claim for discrimination arises from commencement of employment. There is no need for the worker or the employee to show that he or she has been employed or contracted to work for a given length of time. The individual has 3 months from the date of the last act of discrimination to bring a claim. In certain cases a claim may be brought outside the 3-month time-limit where it would be 'just and equitable' to allow it, or where the time limit can be extended because the discrimination can be viewed as a continuing act. The claim can be against an employer and against named individuals. A person bringing a claim for disability discrimination can bring a claim only against an employer with 15 or more employees.

The claim is heard by the employment tribunal. It is a claim for compensation which is technically unlimited, but awarded on the basis of the individual's financial loss as a result of the discrimination, and the injury caused to his or her feelings.

Under the Employment Act 2002 all employers will be contractually obliged to implement statutory disciplinary and grievance procedures from autumn 2004, and all employees who wish to pursue a claim for discrimination will have to pursue an internal grievance using the new procedure before proceeding with a claim, or risk it being struck out. This means that complaints of discrimination are likely to form a large proportion of complaints made under grievance procedures and will also need to be dealt with in accordance with the new legislation. For further information, see Chapter 20.

7.5 EQUAL PAY

The EPA 1970 gives an individual a right to the same contractual pay and benefits as a person of the opposite sex in the same employment where a man and a woman are doing:

(a) like work; or
(b) work rated as equivalent under an analytical job evaluation scoring; or
(c) work proved to be of equal value.

The employer can defend a claim where there is a material reason unrelated to sex for the difference in pay and benefits between men and women.

The EPA 1970 does not give a right to fair pay, but is a form of sex discrimination legislation.

7.6 DISABILITY DISCRIMINATION

7.6.1 The meaning of 'disability'

This subject is also dealt with in Chapter 12. The legal framework of the DDA 1995 is set out in this chapter. The DDA 1995 came into force in 1995. The Government helpfully issued Guidance Notes to the law at the time, which are still helpful assistance for employers.

Under the DDA 1995, a person is defined as disabled if he or she:

> 'has a physical or mental impairment which has a substantial and long-term adverse effect on his or her ability to carry out normal day-to-day activities.'

This definition comprises the following elements.

- The impairment may be physical or mental. For example, a person with a clinically recognised mental illness, such as depression, may be protected. A person suffering solely from stress will not generally be disabled for the purpose of the Act.
- The effect must be substantial. This term is further defined by the Guidance Notes as meaning more than minor or trivial.
- The effect must be long term. This is defined in the Guidance Notes as meaning likely to last for 12 months or more, or for the rest of the person's life. This includes past disability. For example, a person who previously suffered from schizophrenia, who is now seeking to apply for a job, may still be able to claim a disability under the Act, even though at the date of the job application he or she was not suffering from the illness.
- The effect must be on normal day-to-day activities. The person is not regarded as disabled if suffering from an impairment which merely limits exceptionally strenuous activities, unless that is part of the job.
- The effect of any medical treatment is ignored. It is therefore necessary to look at what the symptoms would be if the person was not actually under any course of treatment. For example, a person suffering from cancer may not have his or her normal day-to-day activities affected when under medication. However, if the symptoms cannot be controlled without medication, and as a consequence normal day-to-day activities are affected, then the individual could be disabled for the purpose of the Act.

7.6.2 The meaning of disability discrimination

Less favourable treatment

The definition of direct discrimination under the DDA 1995 is similar to that under the SDA 1975 and the RRA 1976, ie treating a disabled person less favourably than others who are not disabled and in this case doing so for a reason related to that person's disability. The employer's intention is irrelevant. In order to ascertain whether a person has been treated less favourably, the tribunal will need to compare the treatment that the disabled person has suffered with the treatment of a person who was not absent from work and not disabled. Using this type of comparator will almost always produce a result that the person concerned has been discriminated against, if that person is treated less favourably on the grounds of the disability. However, the charity could still escape liability if it could be argued that the discrimination was justified (see below for an explanation of justification).

Reasonable adjustments

Under the DDA 1995, an employer is under a duty to take steps that are reasonable in all the circumstances to prevent the disabled person from being placed at a substantial disadvantage compared with other staff. Examples of such steps are allowing an individual with a long-term absence to work from home temporarily to help ease him or her back into full-time employment, making adjustments to premises, allocating some of the disabled person's duties to another person, changing his or her working hours, arranging for training, acquiring or modifying equipment, and allowing time off for treatment of the disability.

7.6.3 What if the discrimination is justified?

Even where a charity is found to have discriminated against a disabled employee, the charity can avoid liability under the DDA 1995 by showing that the treatment was justified. This is a defence which will not be available following the introduction of amendments to the DDA 1995 (probably to be implemented in October 2004). In discussing employers' duties in respect of promotion and transfer, the Code of Practice for the Elimination of Discrimination in Employment defines justification as 'both material to the circumstances of the particular case and substantial when the reason relates to the individual circumstances in question and is not trivial or minor'. The Code then goes on to provide a number of examples where discrimination would not be justified. One of the examples given describes a factory worker who has a mental illness and is sometimes off work because of it. However, when compared to other employees, his level of absence is relatively low. Under the circumstances his dismissal for reasons of his disability would be discriminatory and could not be justified.

Some examples of cases where discrimination was justified include where:

- the demands of the job were such that the individual could no longer carry out the role;
- the individual failed to co-operate with the employer's efforts to meet to discuss the employee's absences or to comply with its attendance policy;
- the absences themselves had been lengthy and there were no adjustments which could be made to improve attendance;
- operational difficulties would arise from having to make adjustments;
- there was no indication of when (if ever) the individual would have returned to work;
- to provide temporary cover for the absent individual's role would not have been appropriate;
- the individual concerned was a key worker who could not be replaced on a temporary basis.

Examples of cases where discrimination was not justified include where:

- the employer had made assumptions about an individual's ability to do a certain job without the benefit of medical evidence;
- the duration of the employee's sick leave was no more than the average compared to the rest of the workforce, and the individual was not a key worker who needed to be replaced.

7.7 PART-TIME WORKERS

Under the Part-time Workers (Prevention of Less Favourable Treatment) Regulations 2003, from 1 July 2002, part-time workers gained protection from discrimination.

7.7.1 To whom do the Regulations apply?

The legal definition of a 'part-time worker' is someone who is 'not identifiable as a full-time worker'. Whilst in most cases common sense would dictate that any contractual hours in excess of, say, 35 hours per week would be regarded as full time, disputes may arise if the same employer also employs others on, say, a 42-hour week.

7.7.2 What are a part-time worker's rights?

A part-time worker's rights under the Regulations are to be treated not less favourably than a comparable full-time worker, unless such treatment can be justified on objective grounds. The DTI Guidelines state that the less favourable treatment must be to achieve a legitimate objective (for example, a genuine business objective), that it must be necessary to achieve that objective and that it must be an appropriate way to achieve that objective.

7.7.3 Salary and benefits

Part-time workers are entitled to receive the same rate of pay, promotion and training opportunities, sick pay and maternity rights, access to occupational pension schemes, entitlements to holiday, health insurance and the like, and parental leave and career break schemes.

A part-time worker is not entitled to the same overtime rate as a full-time worker until he or she has worked the same number of hours as a full-time worker would have worked in order to qualify for overtime. This is important: it means that a part-time worker exceeding his *part time* hours is not entitled, by virtue of having done so, to an overtime payment.

7.7.4 Full-time worker returning part time

If a full-time worker returns to work part time he or she will be able to compare the new terms and conditions with the previous package, which is particularly helpful to women returning from maternity leave. It is not necessary for the worker to identify a full-time employee with a similar job as a comparator in this situation. In all other situations, however, the full-time comparator must be engaged in the same or broadly similar work.

7.7.5 Written statement of reasons for less favourable treatment

A part-time worker is entitled to call for a written statement of the reasons for less favourable treatment. A failure on the employer's part to reply entitles a tribunal to draw the inference that the employer has infringed the rights in question.

7.7.6 Occupational pension schemes

Insofar as discrimination against part-time workers who have been denied membership of an occupational pension scheme is concerned, the Regulations provide that any compensation must be limited to 2 years before the date of the complaint. This provision may well be attacked, following a recent ruling by the European Court of Justice in the case of *Preston and Others v Wolverhampton Healthcare NHS Trust* (Case No 78/98) that a 2-year limit for backdated membership of a pension scheme is incompatible with EU law.

7.8 FIXED-TERM EMPLOYEES

The Fixed-term Employees (Prevention of Less Favourable Treatment) Regulations 2002 ('the Regulations'), which came into force on 1 October 2002, grant fixed-term or temporary employees the right not to be treated less favourably than permanent employees. This right does not apply to the larger category of 'workers'.

7.8.1 To whom do the Regulations apply?

A 'fixed-term employee' means an employee who is employed under a fixed-term contract, and a 'permanent employee' means an employee who is not employed under a fixed-term contract.

A 'fixed-term contract' is a contract which will terminate:

- on the expiry of a specific term;
- on the completion of a particular task; or
- on the occurrence or non-occurrence of any other specific event.

In order to make a claim for less favourable treatment under the Regulations, a fixed-term employee may make a comparison with a 'comparable permanent employee'. Both employees must be employed by the same employer, and be engaged in the same or broadly similar work having regard, where relevant, to whether they have a similar level of qualification, skills and experience. The comparable employee must work or be based at the same establishment as the fixed-term employee, or, where there is no comparable employee working or based at that establishment, be an employee who is employed by the same employer but works or is based at a different establishment, yet still satisfies the requirements regarding work and skills.

For the purpose of the Regulations the comparison can either be made between the package of the fixed-term employee and the package of the comparable permanent employee as a whole, or on a term-by-term approach.

7.8.2 Benefits

Fixed-term employees are entitled to be treated as favourably as permanent employees in relation to provisions on statutory sick-pay, guarantee payments, payments on medical suspension, pension and so forth. Where there is a qualifying period for a particular benefit, such as access to an occupational pension scheme, it should be the same for fixed-term and permanent employees, unless different qualifying periods can be objectively justified. The Regulations indicate that less favourable treatment on one element of a worker's terms and conditions will be justified where the fixed-term employee's employment package is not less favourable 'as a whole'. It is therefore possible that a higher salary could be paid to compensate the employee for being ineligible for membership of a pension scheme.

7.8.3 Objective justification

Less favourable treatment can be defended by employers if it can be objectively justified.

7.8.4 Written statements

Fixed-term employees will be able to request a statement from their employer, giving reasons for any less favourable treatment suffered. The employer will have 21 days in which to provide the statement.

7.8.5 Redundancy payments

For new fixed-term contracts of 2 years or more, it will no longer be possible for employees to waive their right to a statutory redundancy payment. Waiver clauses agreed before the Regulations come into force will remain in force, but any waiver inserted into a fixed-term contract that is agreed, renewed or extended after 1 October 2002 will not be valid.

7.8.6 Permanent vacancies

The Regulations provide for fixed-term employees to have the right to be informed by the employer of 'available vacancies' in the establishment.

7.8.7 Successive fixed-term contracts

The Regulations state that if a fixed-term employee has been continuously employed for 4 years or more, the contract will be regarded as a contract of indefinite duration. However, employers will be able to use fixed-term contracts beyond this point where:

- this is objectively justified; or
- collective agreements or workforce agreements modify this limit.

7.8.8 Remedies

A fixed-term employee may bring a complaint before an employment tribunal in relation to the infringement of certain rights. The tribunal may make a declaration, an order for compensation or a recommendation to reduce the adverse effect of such infringements.

Compensation is unlimited, having regard to the employee's loss, subject to the duty to mitigate. No award will be made for injury to feelings.

7.9 POSITIVE DISCRIMINATION AND POSITIVE ACTION

The promotion of diversity implies that a charity employer should be able to recruit from specific groups of individuals, taking what is sometimes called 'affirmative action'. However, unlike other European countries, there is no provision in law in the UK that allows an employer to discriminate in favour of one sex or racial group as opposed to another. There are, however, very limited circumstances under which a charity can discriminate positively. It is also lawful to undertake positive action, in the following circumstances.

Under the RRA 1976, one can act positively to the extent of providing specialist training to remedy under-representation and of encouraging people in under-represented groups to apply for jobs.

In addition, charitable trusts may in effect undertake positive action under the SDA 1975. This effectively permits charities to discriminate on the grounds of sex in relation to the provision of benefits to persons of one sex only where such provision is provided for in a charitable instrument. So, if the charity's purposes are exclusively charitable, and the power to take positive action is provided for within a charitable instrument, then positive action may occur.

The SDA 1975 also permits a charity to discriminate in relation to the provision of 'communal accommodation' for one sex only, for reasons of privacy and decency or because of the nature of the sanitary facilities available. When seeking to provide communal accommodation for one sex only because of the nature of the facilities available, the circumstances to be taken into account include supply and demand between the two sexes, and how (if at all) it is reasonable for the charity to alter or extend the accommodation or provide an alternative.

Example

A charity runs a nurses' home which is equipped primarily for female nurses. It may be that few, if any, male nurses ever ask the charity to provide accommodation. If they do, the charity could argue that it is not worth its while to alter the home because the demand for men's accommodation is so small. The charity would have to make some form of payment to the male nurse to compensate him for the fact that he has not been provided with accommodation. Furthermore, if demand for accommodation for male nurses increases, the charity would have to reconsider the possibility of changing its arrangements to provide for accommodation for both males and females.

Corresponding provisions relating to race are contained within the RRA 1976.

The DDA 1995 permits a charitable instrument to confer benefits on a particular group by reference to mental or physical capacity. However, the charity can do this only if the group being treated more favourably is one with whom the charitable purposes of the charity are connected, and the more favourable treatment is in pursuance of those purposes. So, for example, a disability charity would only be permitted to discriminate positively in favour of individuals with a disability, and not in favour of any other groups.

Both the SDA 1975 and RRA 1976 allow different treatment of individuals where there is a genuine occupational qualification (GOQ) that the job requires a specific type of worker.

Unlawful discrimination on the grounds of sex is therefore permitted in the following circumstances:

(a) where the essential nature of the job requires that it be performed by one sex as opposed to the other, eg dramatic performances (for example, where an actress is required to play the part of Juliet in a stage production of *Romeo and Juliet*);
(b) where decency or privacy requires it, such as assisting a beneficiary with personal care;
(c) domestic service involving close personal contact, in prisons or in homes of beneficiaries;
(d) if living accommodation is provided and cannot be separately equipped for both sexes;
(e) if the job involves working in a country where the law or custom requires one sex as opposed to the other.

A GOQ under the RRA 1976 covers situations in the following circumstances:

(a) where the job involves participation in a dramatic performance and it is necessary for an individual of a particular racial group to carry out the job;
(b) where the job involves modelling in a work of art, and it requires a person of a particular racial group to carry out the job;
(c) where the job involves working where food and drink is served and for reasons of authenticity a person of a particular racial group is required, eg a Chinese man serving in a Chinese restaurant;
(d) where the job provides personal services in promoting welfare to people of a particular racial group, and those services can most effectively be provided by a person of the same racial group.

Circumstances in which charities sometimes find themselves relying on GOQs usually fall within the personal services paragraph at (d) above.

Under the new Race Relations Act 1976 (Amendment) Regulations 2003, any job which is advertised as having a GOQ must meet the test that the requirement that an employee/worker is of a particular race, nationality or ethnic group is a 'genuine and determining occupational requirement' and it is proportionate to make that requirement. This overriding obligation does not apply to filling posts with persons of a particular sex.

So, if a charity wishes a person of a particular race to fill a post it must show either that it is necessary for that job, or that it can rely on one of the GOQs set out above.

7.9.1 Positive action

It is still possible in any event for a charity to take positive action to increase the diversity of the workforce, provided it does not overstep the mark and discriminate against individuals or groups of individuals (see 'Implementing diversity' at **7.16.4**).

In addition, the proposed legislation on sexual orientation and religion or belief provides that positive action can be undertaken in relation to access to facilities and training.

7.10 DISCRIMINATION ON THE BASIS OF RELIGION OR ETHNIC GROUP

The RRA 1976 prohibits discrimination on the grounds of colour, race, nationality, or ethnic or national origins. In the same way as the SDA 1975, it makes unlawful direct and indirect discrimination and victimisation. In order to satisfy the definition of 'ethnic group' an individual will need to establish that he or she belongs to a community with a shared history and culture. Thus, Jews, Sikhs, English, Scots and Irish persons will satisfy the definition, but Rastafarians will not, on the basis that they do not possess a particular history or have any distinct culture in the way that other ethnic groups do.

This is set to change in December 2003, upon the implementation of regulations making unlawful discrimination based on 'religion or belief'. It is anticipated that some of the more 'unusual' groups (such as pacifists or vegans) whose views are founded on a commonly held religious or moral belief will be able to gain protection, although the position is unlikely to become clear until cases are brought before the courts.

7.11 RACE RELATIONS (AMENDMENT) ACT 2000

This legislation came into force in 2001 and, while it amends the RRA 1976, it is treated separately, partly because it introduces revolutionary new concepts to employment law.

The law states that all public sector bodies listed in the Act shall have due regard to the need to:

- eliminate unlawful racial discrimination; and
- promote equality of opportunity and good relations between persons of different racial groups.

In addition, a number of *specific duties* have been set out in the legislation to assist public authorities in meeting the general duty, including:

- identifying policies which deal with race discrimination, and how and why they are relevant;
- setting out arrangements for assessing, monitoring and consulting on the impact of those policies; and publishing the results of such assessments and evaluations;
- setting out arrangements for the training of staff in connection with the general duty.

The bodies listed as public authorities include local authorities and government departments, and the Charity Commission, as well as numerous other bodies with quasi-governmental functions.

There is no statutory duty imposed upon charities to comply with this Act, but, as public authorities have an obligation to promote equality, many authorities include provisions in contracts with charities requiring them to comply with the Act in part or in its entirety.

For example, a charity could be bound by any contract it enters into with a public authority to carry out a number of *general duties* to promote race equality by tackling race discrimination, promoting equality of opportunity, and harmonising relations between people from different racial groups.

It is less usual for charities to be asked to comply with specific duties than with the more vague general duty.

7.12 CIRCUMSTANCES IN WHICH DISCRIMINATION CAN OCCUR

Discrimination can occur without any intention whatsoever on the part of the employer. This does not mean that a charity would have a defence to a claim, and charities should be alert to the possibility of discrimination occurring in their organisations and take steps to protect themselves.

Discrimination could potentially arise in the following areas.

7.12.1 Recruitment and selection

There is a specific prohibition of discriminatory advertising in both the SDA 1975 and the RRA 1976. For example, any advertisement which uses terminology with a gender-based connotation such as 'waiter' or 'salesgirl' will be taken as exhibiting an intention to discriminate under the SDA 1975 unless the advertisement contains an indication to the contrary. Likewise, any advertisement for recruitment or promotion which makes reference to colour, race, or ethnic origins could also be contrary to the RRA 1976. Charities should also be wary of indirect discrimination, For example, using complicated application forms or aptitude tests that require a higher standard of English than is necessary could constitute unlawful indirect race discrimination (see Chapter 4).

7.12.2 Promotion opportunities

Opportunities for promotion, training, and the provision of benefits, facilities and services could be affected by, often unwitting, discrimination. Grievance procedures can also be operated in a discriminatory way, often without intention. Criteria used for promotion may work against race and sex.

Example

Studies have shown that ethnic minorities tend to score less in an appraisal system when being evaluated for team communication. In particular, a large institution looking at diversity discovered that the competencies in which ethnic minorities received low scores were highly valued in its appraisal system. As a result of this discovery, the organisation reconsidered the values placed on certain skills and re-evaluated the manner in which appraisals were performed, including providing more focused guidance to managers.

7.12.3 Dismissal

A charity's decision to dismiss can sometimes be perceived as discriminatory, including discriminatory selection for redundancy. In addition, any treatment contrary to legislation against race, sex and disability discrimination may well amount to a constructive dismissal if it is serious enough to bring the employment contract to an end.

7.12.4 Failure to make reasonable adjustments

The charity has an obligation to make reasonable adjustments to the workplace to enable disabled employees to carry out their jobs. Examples include changing a person's hours, allowing time off for treatment, or installing a piece of equipment which would enable the employee to carry out his or her role.

7.13 POST-EMPLOYMENT DISCRIMINATION

The current position is that workers are not permitted to bring claims for discrimination in respect of acts that are alleged to have occurred following termination of their employment. However, the regulations bringing in discrimination provisions on the basis of sexual orientation, religion or belief and age between December 2003 and 2006 all allow claims to arise after termination of employment. At the time of writing, it is possible to bring a claim for sex and race discrimination only in relation to acts of post-employment victimisation, following cases reported recently. The best example of this is where an employee who has brought a claim for sex discrimination during her employment is refused a reference as a result of the litigation after her employment ends.

7.14 OTHER FORMS OF DISCRIMINATION: PROSPECTIVE LEGISLATION

7.14.1 European Anti-discrimination Framework Directive

The scope and coverage of discrimination law in the UK is set to change dramatically over the next 3 years. The European Anti-discrimination Framework Directive requires EU member states to introduce regulations prohibiting discrimination on the grounds of:

- sexual orientation (by 2 December 2003);
- religion or belief (by 2 December 2003);
- disability (by 4 October 2004);
- age (by 2 December 2006).

7.14.2 Sexual orientation discrimination

The current provisions of the SDA 1975 covers only discrimination on the grounds of a person's gender, gender reassignment or marital status. They do not cover a person's sexuality. The regulations are designed to remedy this defect.

The regulations define 'sexual orientation' as an orientation towards persons of the same sex (this covers homosexual men and lesbians); the opposite sex (this covers heterosexual men and women); or both sexes (this covers bisexual men and women). It does not extend to sexual practices and preferences (eg sado-masochism).

The regulations outlaw direct discrimination, indirect discrimination, victimisation and harassment on grounds of an individual's sexual orientation. The definitions used are the same as for the Race Regulations.

The regulations prohibit discrimination not only during employment but also after the employment relationship has ended.

The regulations provide for various exceptions where the discrimination is a genuine occupational requirement for the job, where benefits are granted on the basis of marital status, and where the employer operates a positive action programme designed to achieve equality. Most controversially, they allow certain religious organisations to discriminate against persons of certain sexual orientation on doctrinal grounds.

7.14.3 Religion or belief discrimination

At present the RRA 1976 protects workers against religious discrimination only to the extent that they belong to an ethnic group (see 7.10). The new regulations will make the following changes. They will render it unlawful to discriminate on grounds of religion, religious belief or similar philosophical belief in employment (covering direct discrimination, indirect discrimination, victimisation, harassment and post-employment discrimination).

'Religion or belief' is defined as being a religion, religious belief or similar philosophical belief. The courts may consider a number of factors when deciding what is a 'religion or belief' (eg collective worship, clear belief system, profound belief affecting way of life or view of the world).

The regulations are similar to those for race and sexual orientation in that they also provide for exceptions (where being of a particular religion or belief is a genuine occupational requirement for a post and in respect of positive action programmes designed to prevent or compensate for disadvantages linked to religion or belief).

7.14.4 Disability discrimination

The regulations will make changes to the DDA 1995. They will ensure that treatment amounting to 'direct discrimination' against disabled people cannot be justified and will expressly prohibit harassment against disabled people on the grounds of their disability. The prohibition will extend to all employers and not only, as at present, to those with at least 15 employees.

Again, discrimination after the employment contract has terminated will also be prohibited.

The scope of indirect discrimination will be extended to cover performance-related pay, pensions and insurance, and employers will also be obliged to make reasonable adjustments to avoid the scope of indirect discrimination.

The new legislation is likely to affect charities who employ disabled people. Until the new law is published, it is difficult to predict the new legislation and its effect on working practices.

7.14.5 Age discrimination

There is a continuing debate as to how laws prohibiting age discrimination will work in practice. At the moment it remains quite difficult to determine the nature and effect of the provisions on age discrimination. However, the main features of the proposed legislation will deal with the following:

- the question of whether to exclude mandatory retirement from the legislation;
- the circumstances in which direct age discrimination will remain lawful; and
- how indirect age discrimination laws will operate.

7.15 PROCEDURE FOR DEALING WITH DISCRIMINATION CLAIMS

If a worker or an applicant for employment feels that he or she has been discriminated against, he or she has the right to bring a claim against the charity complaining about the alleged discrimination within the charity. What should an employer do in such circumstances?

7.15.1 Questionnaires

A usual precursor to any litigation is a request under the appropriate legislation to the employer to complete answers to various questions set out in a questionnaire. The usual format of questions is:

> 'I, [
>
> (i) *the Complainant*],
> (ii) Consider that you may have discriminated against me contrary to the [*inserts relevant discrimination Act*] because:
> [*Sets out reasons*]
> (iii) I consider that this treatment may have been unlawful because:
> [*Sets out legal reasons*]

(iv) Do you agree that the statement in (ii) is an accurate description of what happened? If not, in what respect do you disagree, or what is your version of what happened?

(v) Do you accept that your treatment of me was unlawful discrimination by you against me?

If not:

- Why not?
- For what reason did I receive the treatment accorded to me? How far did my sex or marital status affect your treatment of me?'

The respondent (usually the employer) then gets an opportunity to respond by completing another questionnaire.

A charity cannot be forced to answer such questions; however, if it does not, its refusal can be taken into account in any future tribunal action.

7.15.2 Tribunal claims

If a worker/employee is unable to seek satisfactory redress through the grievance or questionnaire process, the next course is to appear before an employment tribunal.

Claims can be brought in addition to other claims. It is not uncommon for a claim for discrimination to be brought in addition to a claim for unfair dismissal.

It is not necessary for the individual who brings a claim for discrimination to leave the employment of the charity in order to do so. This can lead to difficulties in the office; an employer should not seek to redress matters by treating the complainant member of staff differently from others, but may wish to ensure that the employee is in a position where no further potential discrimination can occur.

Complainants have 3 months from the last act of discrimination in which to bring a complaint for sex, race or disability discrimination. They have 6 months to bring a claim under the EPA 1970 for a breach of the contract.

For further discussion on tribunals, see Chapter 24.

7.16 PRACTICAL GUIDANCE

In order to protect the charity's interests regarding diversity, the following guidance should be observed.

7.16.1 Equal opportunities policy

It is essential for all charities to have an equal opportunities policy. It is difficult to defend any claim for discrimination without one, and having such a policy is good practice in any event.

The policy must set out the definitions of all forms of discrimination. There must be an equal opportunities policy statement which makes it clear that positive steps will be taken by the employer to promote good relations. The charity should ensure that employees are aware of the statement and that active steps are taken to promote and implement equality of opportunity. Care providers have specific obligations to have an equal opportunities policy and to provide equal opportunities training. For further information, see Chapter 27.

The policy must also set out the steps that the charity will take in order to ensure that the equal opportunities objective is maintained. These could include:

(a) ensuring that job specifications relate to the requirements of the performance of the job;
(b) providing equal opportunity training such as the charity considers is appropriate to enable workers to implement equal opportunities;
(c) ensuring that the ethnic and gender composition of the workforce is monitored and monitoring carried out in accordance with accepted practices recommended by the equal opportunities bodies or good human resources practice;
(d) ensuring that all monitoring will be used only for the purpose of equal opportunity monitoring and will be anonymous.

In the case of disability, it is important to consider what steps may be taken to ensure that disabled individuals are not disadvantaged in the charity's workplace.

7.16.2 Harassment policy

Charities should consider the use of a harassment policy. The harassment policy should contain a policy statement confirming that any form of harassment, whether based on sex, race, disability, sexual orientation, age, or religion or belief, will not be tolerated. A definition of harassment and some practical examples of what could constitute harassment should also be included.

A harassment procedure should also be set out, making it clear the steps which the charity has agreed to undertake should a complaint be made. The steps should include formal stages; investigation and decision making; and the sanctions that could be imposed should the complaint be upheld. It is also important to make sure that the policy itself is properly implemented for staff at all levels. Failure to do so could lead to a successful claim against the charity.

7.16.3 Training key staff

In addition to providing employees with the appropriate policies it is also important to provide proper training on how to implement equal opportunities. In the event that a claim is made against the charity on the basis that it is vicariously liable for the acts of one employee against another, a defence to a discrimination claim may not succeed if training has not been given. This may in fact be the case even if a policy is in place and has been distributed to staff. The logic behind this approach is clear. Some charities will have appropriate policies in place, but many workers may not be able to understand the implication of equal opportunities and how the issues work from a practical viewpoint, without training. As a minimum, it is recommended that training is carried out for managers, although ideally all workers should be provided with some training.

7.16.4 Implementing diversity

If a charity has business reasons, such as poor recruitment or retention levels, it could consider implementing a diversity policy. On recruitment, this may have the effect of widening the pool from which employees are recruited. In addition, many charities consider it is a good policy in any event.

- Consider expanding the use of monitoring statistics for diversity and the publication of those statistics. This creates a transparency to any commitment to diversity – a recruitment tool in itself.
- Consider recruitment methods with a view to targeting particular groups, eg working mothers, people from a particular community, or people of a particular age.
- Consider promotion and appraisal processes with a view to widening the basis of recruitment. For example, an emphasis on evening work may make a job less attractive to mothers who are less able to assist in evening work.
- Audit any public sector contracts for obligations under the Race Relations (Amendment) Act 2000.

CASE STUDY

Jane and Sarah are employed by 'Good Aid'. Theresa was employed by the charity until 2 months ago.

Jane has been the victim of offensive sexual remarks made by male colleagues. Men have constantly asked her out, pinched her bottom and put up 'page 3' pin-ups in areas where she works. The charity carried out an investigation into her allegations of harassment 6 months ago, but no subsequent action was taken against the men, despite the fact that the investigation concluded that the allegations were true. Since the investigation, the harassment has stopped.

Theresa was downgraded 4 months ago; as a result, her earnings were reduced by £80 per week. The reason given by the charity for the downgrading, was the need to reduce costs, but only female staff have been downgraded. As a result of the restructure, Theresa has resigned.

Sarah was recently turned down for the post of international co-ordinator. The job was given to Kumlesh. In the immediate vicinity of Good Aid's offices, 40% of the inhabitants are Asian, although the number of Asians employed by the charity is about 5%. Sarah was turned down for the job because Personnel told her it was only open to members of ethnic minorities.

What action, if any, could Jane, Theresa and Sarah take against the charity?

The Position of the Three Individuals

All parties may have potential discrimination claims against Good Aid.

Jane

Jane may be able to claim direct sex discrimination on the grounds of her sex. Provided she can show that the harassers concerned would not have treated another man in the same way, then it is likely that she will be able to show that the conduct occurred because of her sex. Jane will also need to show that she suffered a detriment as a result of the harassment. The conduct judged objectively could be said to be causing her a detriment as, despite her complaints, and the investigation, the charity has done nothing further. Her claim, however, may be out of time (if she has failed to present her claim to the tribunal within 3 months from the date of the last act of discrimination) as we are told that since the investigation the conduct has stopped. She will need to show that there are continuing acts of discrimination. Since no action has been taken and she also fears that the harassment may be repeated, then she may still be able to bring her claim out of time.

Theresa

On the face of it, Theresa would also appear to be the victim of sex discrimination. Only women have been downgraded. A difference in gender and a difference in treatment will often point to discrimination. However, it is debatable whether the reduction in salary can be seen as a continuing act if, like Jane, she has failed to present her complaint within 3 months of the act. Unless she has complained about it and Good Aid have refused to act on the complaint, then it remains unlikely that it will be viewed as a continuing act of discrimination and her claim will not succeed as it is out of time.

Sarah

Sarah has been rejected for a job as international co-ordinator. The job is given to Kumlesh. The RRA 1976 allows an employer to encourage employment from a racial group where there are no members of that group doing the work, or the numbers are small in relation to the population in the area in which the recruitment takes place. The proportion of Asians living in the area in which the office is situated is 40%, but Asians make up only 5% of Good Aid's workforce. If the area where the office is situated is the only area in which Good Aid recruit, there would appear to be an imbalance. If, however, the area of recruitment is much wider, it would be necessary to look at the racial mix of the inhabitants to see if the RRA 1976 could apply.

Even if the area of recruitment is restricted, in the absence of having a charitable instrument that permits positive action in favour of certain racial groups, Good Aid could be in breach of the RRA 1976. It appears, however, that Good Aid are doing much more than taking positive action in that they appear to have imposed a condition that any applicant must be a member of an ethnic minority. On this basis Sarah can argue that she has suffered indirect discrimination on racial grounds as the charity were imposing a condition that all of her race could not comply with and because she cannot comply with the condition she has suffered a detriment in being refused the job.

Chapter 8

PAY

8.1 THE NATIONAL MINIMUM WAGE

8.1.1 Introduction

When the Labour Party took up office in 1997, it stated its commitment to the establishment of a national minimum wage (NMW). In particular, the proposal was to target women, part-time workers, young people, workers from ethnic minorities and home workers. Indeed, the Third Report from the Low Pay Commission (2001) confirmed that 70% of women have benefited from the introduction of the NMW, and of these, two-thirds of part-time female workers benefited. Whether the introduction of the NMW has had a negative impact on business is debatable as supporters and dissenters of the legislation disagree on its impact. However, the Low Pay Commission has stated that most businesses have adapted to the increase in costs by raising prices, reducing expenditure and increasing productivity. This chapter looks at the obligations of employers under the NMW laws and their duty to pay people fairly.

8.1.2 The legislation

The National Minimum Wage Act (NMWA 1998) and the National Minimum Wage Regulations 1999 (NMWR 1999) set out the obligations on employers to pay the NMW. The law guarantees a minimum level of pay for workers when they are working, and not when a worker is absent from work (a worker may nonetheless qualify for statutory sick pay or paid holiday entitlement). The minimum wage level was set from 1 October 2003 at £4.50 per hour for adults (those aged over 21 years) and £3.80 per hour for youth workers (those aged between 18 and 20). There is no minimum rate applied to those aged under 18 years.

Who should receive the NMW?

The NMW applies to any worker ordinarily in work in the UK. The term 'worker' is defined as including apprentices (excluding those aged under 26, who are employed under a contract of apprenticeship, and those who, within the first 12 months after commencement of that employment, have not attained the age of 19). 'Worker' also includes those who personally perform work for another (who is not a customer of a business carried on by the worker). Home-workers and agency workers are covered by the term 'worker' and are entitled to be paid the NMW. Charities should consider whether any of their volunteers might be considered workers under this legislation (see Chapter 2).

A large number of workers are excluded from the right to be paid the NMW. These include:

- au pairs;
- family members engaged in family businesses; and
- those engaged in specific training.

A rate of pay lower than the NMW may be paid to adults for the first 26 weeks of employment if that period includes at least 26 days' 'accredited training'.

What counts as NMW pay?

To identify whether a worker's pay is in line with the NMW, it must be calculated in a particular way. This is often complicated, since a worker's pay may be made up of various components. The NMWR 1999 set out which elements of pay may be included in the calculations and it is important that, when calculating the NMW pay, charity employers make sure that this is carefully checked. Wrongly including an element of pay that does not count could end up with the worker not, in fact, being paid the NMW.

What components can be included?

The starting point is that the calculation should be based on the worker's *gross* pay (ie before the deduction of tax and national insurance). Gross pay will not include any payment that is a loan, an advance of wages, pension payments, redundancy payments or a reward under a staff suggestions scheme, but will include sick pay, holiday pay and income guarantee pay. In addition to the basic pay that a worker receives, there are other elements of pay that may be included in the NMW calculation. These include:

- payments made as part of an incentive, merit or performance-related pay scheme;
- bonus payments;
- tips paid through the payroll;
- accommodation provided by the employer up to a maximum of £24.50 per week (from 1 October 2003).

What components cannot be included?

The NMWR 1999 specify a number of components that must be deducted from the worker's gross pay on the basis that they do not count towards NMW pay. These include:

- benefits in kind, such as meals, luncheon vouchers, fuel, car and medical insurance;

- premium payments: if a worker receives a premium payment (eg an enhanced hourly rate) for working overtime or particular duties, the premium element will not count as NMW pay;
- allowances over and above standard pay (eg London weighting) unless the payments are consolidated as standard pay;
- tips or gratuities that are paid directly to a worker and not through the payroll;
- expenses;
- accommodation over and above the maximum of £24.50 per week.

Charities may therefore benefit by consolidating payments into basic pay, where they are able to do so.

It is important for charities to ensure that the calculation of NMW is carefully checked and that all the appropriate elements of pay are included. The Guidance from the Department of Trade and Industry sets out the following useful summaries:

> 'Summary of what counts as NMW:
>
> - gross pay
> - incentive pay
> - bonuses
> - tips paid through payroll
> - income tax and employee's NI contributions
> - deduction or payment of a penalty
> - deduction or payment to repay a loan
> - deduction or payment to repay an advance of wages
> - deduction or payment to refund accidental overpayment of wages
> - union subscription
> - worker's pension contribution
> - any deduction made by the employer but not for his use or benefit
> - accommodation up to the limit specified in the NMWR 1999
> - unforced payments by the worker for goods and services from the employer'
>
> 'Summary of what does not count as NMW:
>
> - loans
> - advance on wages
> - pension payment
> - lump sum on retirement
> - redundancy payment
> - reward under a staff suggestions scheme
> - premium payments
> - allowances that are not consolidated into pay
> - expenses
> - refund of money spent on work
> - deductions or payment for tools, uniforms, etc
> - deductions or payment for the employer's own use or benefit
> - payments made by the worker to another person connected with the job

- accommodation over the limit specified in the NMWR 1999
- benefits in kind'

Types of work

The NMWA 1998 sets out four different categories of work.

(1) Time work – this is work paid wholly by reference to time spent working.
(2) Output work – this is measured wholly by reference to output. Output work may be paid by reference to hours worked or a 'fair estimate' of the hours worked.
(3) Salaried hours work – this is work in respect of which wages are paid in equal instalments, regardless of fluctuations in hours worked.
(4) Unmeasured work – this is defined as any other work that is not time work, salaried hours work, or output work, including work when there are no specified hours and the worker works only when needed, or when work is available. Unmeasured work is calculated as the total number of hours which the employee works during the pay reference period (which will be one month, or, in the case of a worker who is paid wages by reference to a period shorter than one month, that period), except where there is in place a prior written agreement 'determining the average daily number of hours the worker is likely to spend in carrying out the duties required of him'.

8.1.3 Difficult issues

Unfortunately, applying the NMW legislation in practice has proved to be extremely difficult and it has not been easy to identify which category of work best describes what an individual worker does.

Two cases have recently been considered by the courts which are directly relevant to charities: one involves a care worker and the other nursing bank staff.

CASE STUDY 1

In *Walton v Independent Living Organisation Limited* [2003] All ER (D) 373, the Employment Appeal Tribunal (EAT) was asked to determine whether a care worker was a 'time worker' or whether she was undertaking 'unmeasured work' within the meaning of the NMWR 1999, and hence whether she was being paid the statutory minimum wage by her employer.

The applicant worked as a carer, looking after an epileptic for 3 days at a time. When on duty she was required to be continually in residence day and night, but would spend the following 3-day period off work. Her remuneration was agreed at £31.40 per day, and there was a signed assessment by which the employer and employee agreed that in a working period of 24 hours on duty the employee would spend an average of 6 hours and 50 minutes in active caring, the balance of the day being available to react to untoward situations and keeping her charge company. The employee brought a claim that her employer had failed to pay her the remuneration to which she was entitled under the NMW laws.

At first, the employment tribunal rejected the employee's contention that she was engaged in time work which would have meant that she should have been paid £31.40 for working 14 hours a day (under the NMWR 1999). Instead the tribunal found that she was employed on 'unmeasured work' and that there was a 'daily average agreement' permitted by the NMWR 1999, so that the employee was paid at an hourly rate which fell within the minimum wage provisions.

The employee appealed to the EAT, which also dismissed her claim. The EAT confirmed that the employee was engaged in unmeasured work because the daily rate was not a time-computed figure, and the number of hours to which it could refer was so uncertain. The tribunal found that the scope of unmeasured work matched the duties undertaken by the employee in her 72-hour stints, and the employer could point to the existence of a 'daily average agreement' which showed that she worked 6.83 hours a day on active care duties. Thus, the EAT ruled that the applicant was not engaged in 'time work': even though her pay was expressed to be by the day, the evidence clearly showed that she was engaged in 'unmeasured work'. This meant that her daily pay of £31.40 was to be calculated with reference to 6.83 hours, therefore her hourly rate was above the minimum wage.

On 26 February 2003 the employee appealed to the Court of Appeal, which agreed with the decision of the employment tribunal and the EAT. The Court of Appeal agreed that the live-in carer was engaged in 'unmeasured work and not 'time work', and that she did not spend 24 hours a day carrying out her contractual duties.

CASE STUDY 2

In *British Nursing Association v Inland Revenue* [2002] IRLR 480, the Court of Appeal was asked to determine when a worker is 'working' for the purposes of applying the NMWR 1999 and found that a worker was 'working' even when not actually engaged in work but merely awake and awaiting telephone calls at home.

British Nursing Association (BNA), a charity, operated a 24-hour telephone service for the supply of bank nursing staff in homes and other institutions on an emergency basis. The booking service was provided 24 hours a day. During the day, the booking service was operated by employees working at the charity's premises. During the night, the work was transferred to telephone operators who worked from home between 8 pm and 9 am. The telephone operators were all qualified nurses, and their role involved answering diverted phone calls and responding to requests for nursing staff. There was no provision for specific periods of sleep during shifts but they could sleep or carry out other activities while waiting for calls.

The Inland Revenue took the view that those employed on the night-shift were entitled to be paid the minimum hourly rate for the hours they were on duty. The charity contended that the telephone operators were not entitled to the national minimum wage for all the hours they were on duty as they were not actually working throughout the shift; and that although the operators were required to be available to deal with telephone calls, they could spend part of their shifts doing other activities, such as reading or watching television.

When asked to look at whether the bank nursing staff were 'working' for the purposes of applying the NMWR 1999, the Court decided that the telephone operators were working throughout their shifts notwithstanding that they could undertake other activities; they were therefore engaged on 'time work'. The Court gave the following guidance on the factors to be taken into account in determining the time when an employee is working:

- the nature of the work and the extent to which the employees' activities are restricted when not performing the particular task;
- whilst the way in which the parties approached their mutual obligations, and the way in which remuneration was calculated, was not conclusive, calculation of pay by reference to a shift provides some illustration of the nature of the obligation for which remuneration is being paid;
- the extent to which the period during which work is being performed is readily ascertainable; and
- whilst working at home, the telephone operators were not, as is the case for some home-work, available to pick and choose the periods of time during which to answer calls – there was a continuing obligation to be available throughout the night.

8.1.4 Practical guidance

- **Review all staff contracts to ensure that workers over the age of 21 are receiving £4.50 per hour or its equivalent.**
- **Review the contracts of employment of all staff working nights or on an 'on-call' basis.**

- Ensure that appropriate records are kept of the hours worked if the employee is based at home while on call.
- Assume that sleep-in and on-call duties will count towards the NMW calculation.
- If paying for the whole period for which the employee is on call is to be avoided, consider whether it is practical to ensure that specified periods for sleep and facilities are included in the contracts of employment of all staff who are required to be on call at the premises and that there are adequate levels of staffing to cover any rest periods.
- For new employees, consider whether entering into a daily average agreement which provides a measure of the hours of work to be performed is necessary (remember that this must be entered into before the terms and conditions of employment are agreed between employer and employee).

8.1.5 Travelling time and rest breaks

For the purposes of the legislation, hours of work do not include:

- time spent travelling to and from work, and
- rest breaks provided for under the Working Time Regulations 1998.

However, there are some exceptions. Time that constitutes hours of work includes:

- time spent travelling, waiting and/or training where such activity is work related and has been approved by the employer;
- time when a worker is awake and available at or near a place of work, other than his or her home, for the purposes of doing work and is required to be available for such work.

8.1.6 Zero hours contracts

Zero hours contracts do not guarantee or lay down the hours which the employee will be required to work at any one time. They typically cover circumstances where an individual waits to see if he or she is needed by the employer. Workers engaged on zero hours contracts must only be paid the NMW for the hours when they are actually working, and not when they are waiting to see if they will be required to work.

8.1.7 Enforcement

The NMWA 1998 provides workers with a contractual right to any shortfall between their wages and the NMW. This right can be enforced either:

- by a claim for breach of contract by the employee; or
- by a claim for unauthorised deduction from wages by the employee; or
- by enforcement by the Inland Revenue Pay Compliance Officers.

8.2 DEDUCTIONS FROM WAGES

8.2.1 Lawful deductions

Case law has confirmed that an employee's failure to perform his or her duties under the contract of employment can justify an employer making deductions from the employee's pay packet. An example of when an employer may lawfully reduce an employee's wages is where an employee fails to attend work or perform the agreed tasks between some or all of the stated times in the contract. In these circumstances, the employer has an option either to refuse to pay for any of the work offered and thereby avoid payment altogether, or to accept the work offered and reduce pay on a pro rata basis. An employer may also refuse to pay any of the wages in respect of a period of defective or part performance of the contract where the employer has made it clear in advance that it will not accept partial performance. Employers are often keen to invoke such rights during periods of industrial action.

8.2.2 Statutory protection against unfair deductions from wages

As stated above, the failure by an employer to pay a qualifying worker the NMW entitles the worker to bring a claim for unlawful deductions from wages and recover the difference between what the worker was paid and the NMW. A failure to pay wages is held to constitute a deduction.

Under ss 13–15 of the Employment Rights Act 1996 (ERA 1996) an employer must not make deductions from the wages of a worker unless:

- the deduction is required or authorised by law or contract, or
- the worker has previously given his consent in writing to the deduction in his contract, and has a copy of that contract or has been told of its effect.

Additional protections against unfair deductions from wages exist for those working in the retail trade, which may affect charities with trading subsidiaries.

A failure to pay any of the following types of wages (amongst others) in whole or in part will amount to a deduction:

- any fee, bonus, commission, holiday pay or other emolument referable to employment;
- statutory sick pay;
- statutory maternity pay;
- a guarantee payment;
- any payment for time off;
- remuneration or suspension on medical grounds;
- any payment of a sum in pursuance of reinstatement or re-engagement.

Chapter 9

PENSIONS

9.1 INTRODUCTION

A pension can be defined as a regular payment to a (usually elderly) person either in return for past services or payments, or gratuitously. In the UK, pensions are paid by the state, by companies to their former employees and their dependants, and by financial institutions (for example, insurance companies) to people who take out pension policies with them.

A charity employer will not usually pay pensions directly to its former employees. Instead, it normally sets up a pension scheme a long time before the pensions actually become due for payment. The charity, and often the employee, pay money regularly into the scheme, which the scheme invests and eventually uses to pay the pension.

Pension schemes do not only provide pensions. They also often pay out lump sums, for instance to an employee (or former employee) who is retiring in addition to or in lieu of part of his or her pension entitlement, and to the family of an employee who dies.

9.2 DIFFERENT TYPES OF UK PENSION ARRANGEMENTS

9.2.1 State pensions

The state pension is divided into a basic flat rate pension, and a supplementary earnings-related pension. A person is eligible for the full basic pension only if he has paid national insurance contributions as either an employed or a self-employed person for about 40 years. If he has not, the pension is reduced.

9.2.2 State Earnings Related Pension

The State Earnings Related Pension (SERPS) is additional to the old age pension. The level of benefit is based on earnings over a period, and it is possible to buy the pension from the Government (via increased national insurance contributions) or through an occupational or personal pension. If SERPS is bought from the Government, this is known as 'contracting-in', and if the pension is bought privately by an occupational or personal pension, it is known as 'contracting-out'.

All contracts of employment must state whether the occupational scheme is 'contracted in' or 'contracted out'.

9.2.3 State Second Pension (S2P)

From April 2002 SERPS was replaced by the State Second Pension (S2P). The principles are very similar to SERPS, and the S2P operates as a replacement for SERPS (ie as a second-tier state pension), with revised national insurance contracted-out rebates.

9.3 DOCUMENTATION

9.3.1 Trust deed and rules

The basic documents governing an occupational pension scheme are the trust deed and rules. The trust deed sets out the powers of the charity employer and the trustees, and the rules set out details of the benefits the scheme is to provide.

The law of trusts has developed in court cases over many years, and cannot be found in a single statute. However, partly as a result of the Maxwell scandal in the early 1990s, a number of statutes have been implemented which govern and affect pensions law. These are: the Pension Schemes Act 1993; the Pensions Act 1995; the Employment Rights Act 1996; the Data Protection Act 1998; the Income and Corporation Taxes Act 1998; the Welfare Reform and Pensions Act 1999; the Child Support, Pensions and Social Security Act 2000; the Financial Services Act 1986, as supplemented by the Financial Services Market Act 2000; and the Trustee Act 2000.

9.3.2 Members' explanatory booklet

An explanatory booklet is usually sent to the members of the scheme. This gives a summary of the benefits provided by the scheme. Although the explanatory booklet is not a governing document of the scheme, it can create member expectations and therefore must be carefully drafted. The document is also used to provide the minimum information the trustees of the scheme are legally obliged to provide to members.

9.4 OCCUPATIONAL PENSIONS

The benefit structure under an employer's occupational pension scheme will be either a defined benefit scheme or a defined contribution scheme. Both defined benefit and defined contribution schemes receive generous tax breaks, provided that they have undergone approval by the Inland Revenue.

Both defined benefit and defined contribution schemes can be contracted-out of SERPS. All Inland Revenue approved occupational pension schemes are required to allow their members to make additional voluntary contributions if they so wish (subject to Inland Revenue limits) and to establish arrangements under which such contributions can be paid.

9.4.1 Defined benefit schemes

These schemes are otherwise known as final salary schemes.

Most UK pension schemes have traditionally been defined benefit schemes. Almost all defined benefit schemes are based on a final salary formula. A scheme typically pays an employee, upon reaching normal retirement age (usually 65) 1/60th of whatever salary the employee is receiving when or close to when he or she leaves the employment of the charity employer (ie goes to work for another company or retires) for each year he worked for the charity employer and was a member of the scheme.

A key issue about a defined benefit (or final salary) scheme is that, as and when an employee's salary increases, this increases both the employee's pension in relation to the employee's future years of service, and the employee's pension in relation to his or her past years of service.

Under a defined benefit scheme, a charity employer will pay such contributions into the scheme as are estimated to be necessary to pay benefits from the scheme when they fall due, and the amount of contributions needed will fluctuate from time to time depending on how well the scheme investments do. Employees may or may not have to pay contributions, but, if they do, their contributions will usually be fixed (unlike the charity employer's).

There has been a marked movement away from this type of pension scheme in recent years because of the nature of the unlimited liability that can arise.

9.4.2 Defined contribution schemes

These days, more and more schemes are defined contribution (also known as money purchase) schemes. Each member has a notional pot into which money is paid, and that money is then invested on the member's behalf and the investment returns are added to the member's pot.

On retirement, the scheme usually uses the pot of money to buy the member a pension (an annuity) from an insurance company. It is sometimes possible for a member to defer buying an annuity until the age of 65 and in the meantime draw income directly from the pot.

Under a defined contribution scheme, a charity employer will pay a fixed rate of contribution into each employee's pot (sometimes varying according to age). The member may also be required to pay contributions, and the minimum figure for such contribution is usually a fixed amount.

9.4.3 Senior executives/directors

A charity employer may also have a special pension scheme for its senior executives and/or directors as a top-up to the main charity employer's scheme or alternatively as the executive's/director's sole pension arrangements. Often a senior executive's/director's pension plan is designed to attract and retain high calibre employees.

9.4.4 Local Government Pension Scheme

Many charities are members of the Local Government Pension Scheme (LGPS) as a result of their provision of public services. Charities become members by completing an Admissions Agreement to the LGPS, which sets out the basis on which a would-be member becomes an admitted body.

The LGPS is a statutory, funded pension scheme. As such, it is very secure because its benefits are defined and guaranteed in law. The LGPS is contracted out of SERPS and must, in general, provide benefits at least as good as most members would have received had they been members of SERPS. Key features of the benefits provided by the LGPS are:

- a tax-free lump sum upon retirement;
- a guaranteed pension based on final pay;
- the ability to increase one's pension by paying extra contributions;
- voluntary retirement from the age of 60;
- retirement from the age of 50 with employer's consent;
- an ill health pension from the age of 50;
- redundancy cover from the age of 50;
- a death-in-service lump sum of two times final pay;
- a widow's or widower's pension;
- children's pensions; and
- the index-linking of benefits to ensure that they keep pace with inflation.

In addition, the contributions paid by employee members of the LGPS will attract tax relief at the time they are deducted from the employee's pay. An employee will also pay lower national insurance contributions between the lower and upper earnings limits, unless the employee has opted to pay the married woman's/widow's reduced rate of national insurance.

9.5 PERSONAL PENSION PLAN

A personal pension scheme is a scheme which must be approved under the relevant taxes legislation. To be a member of a personal pension scheme, an individual must be self-employed, or in non-pensionable employment, or employed but not a member of an occupational pension scheme (except a death-in-service only arrangement). Personal pension plans are usually defined contribution schemes.

A charity employer, instead of sponsoring an occupational pension scheme, could put its name to a personal pension plan sold by a particular financial institution and, for employees who take out personal pension plans with that provider, arrange for the personal pension plan contributions deducted from the employee's salary to be paid directly to that provider.

9.6 STAKEHOLDER PENSION PLAN

This is the newest type of personal pension plan. Stakeholder pension schemes were introduced as a way of encouraging more private pension provision, particularly amongst moderate earners. A stakeholder scheme can be established either under a trust or via contracts between the provider and the member. From 8 October 2001, most employers (including charity employers) have been required to provide their employees with access to a pension scheme, which must be at the very least a stakeholder scheme.

The requirements are that:

- the employer must choose, or designate, a stakeholder scheme, having first consulted with the employees (and their unions if any);
- the employer must allow the designated scheme to be suitably publicised; and
- where an employee so requests, the employer must deduct contributions on the employee's behalf from his or her remuneration and then pay the contributions within stated time-limits to the designated scheme. However, there is no requirement for the employer itself to contribute anything to the scheme.

Some charities will not need to provide stakeholder access to their employees. Charities which do not need to provide a scheme are:

- employers with fewer than five employees;
- employers who already offer a suitable occupational pension scheme or a suitable personal pension scheme.

A charity employer has to provide access to a stakeholder pension scheme for 'relevant' employees only. The types of employees who are not relevant include those whose earnings have been below the lower earnings limit at any time during the last 3 months or those who have completed less than 3 months' continuous service with the employer.

Employers are also required to maintain records of the payments made to a designated stakeholder scheme.

9.7 ISSUES FOR THE CHARITY EMPLOYER

9.7.1 Defined benefit and defined contribution schemes compared

The use of final salary schemes is lessening and an increasing number of employers, charities included, are closing their defined benefit schemes and switching to defined contribution schemes, which are seen as a cheaper, less risky option: a charity employer is required only to meet its fixed rate contributions. Thus, if the investments perform poorly, there is no redress for the employee against the charity; it is just bad luck. Recent research by the pension fund partnership states that employees pay on average about 5% of their wages into defined benefit schemes, while employers on average pay more than 14% of their final bill into defined benefit schemes. In defined contribution schemes, the contribution rate by employers was only just over 7%.

9.7.2 Making the switch from the final salary scheme

The change-over process from a defined benefit to a defined contribution or stakeholder scheme is legally complex and requires careful consideration of both pensions and employment law. Often a charity can legally terminate a defined benefit scheme as it will have reserved the power to do so in the pension scheme trust deed and rules. This means that, from a pensions perspective, a charity may be able to close its scheme for future accrual as well as to new members.

The employer may then choose to set up a less costly defined contribution or stakeholder scheme instead. However, that is not the end of the story. A change to pension arrangements for existing staff has major employment law implications, as the charity is making a major change to the benefits of its employees. Even with an express contractual provision allowing the charity to switch schemes, a charity may not be able to do so without the consent of employees, as it will amount to a change to terms and conditions of employment.

It is possible for an employer to argue that there is no breach of contract if its defined benefit scheme is terminated in circumstances where:

- the employer has reserved for itself the power under the trust deed to trigger closure of the scheme;
- the terms and conditions of employment contain a statement that the employee may be eligible to join the company's pension scheme, details of which can be found in the members' booklet;

- there is a statement in the members' booklet that the employer 'reserves the right to terminate the scheme without necessarily providing a replacement'; and
- no subsequent announcements have been made which might conflict with this.

This means that the employee is contractually entitled to participate in the scheme, and that participation is subject to the express right of the employer to terminate the scheme. Having said that, an employer must always act reasonably and in some circumstances it is not possible to terminate a generous benefit without legal ramifications.

It is important to remember that every pension scheme is different and an employer should check thoroughly the balance of powers in the scheme documentation, and the contracts of employment of all employees before taking action. Best practice includes consulting regularly with employees and their representatives, as well as lawyers, as this is likely to reduce potential costly disputes.

Chapter 10

WORKING HOURS

10.1 INTRODUCTION

Hours of work are mainly a matter for agreement between charity employers and their workers. However, there are minimum requirements set out by law which regulate the hours of work of an individual.

The Working Time Regulations 1998 (WTR 1998) regulate hours of work, night work, breaks and holidays for all workers, including employees working under a contract of employment, and other individuals who personally perform work or provide services for an employer. This chapter considers the rights given to workers in relation to their working time. Chapter 11 considers the rights given to workers in relation to holidays.

10.2 MODIFICATION OF RIGHTS BY AGREEMENT

There are a number of cases, which are dealt with in more detail below, where the WTR 1998 permit modifications to workers' rights if there is an agreement to cover the situation. The type of agreement is either a collective agreement, a workforce agreement or a relevant agreement.

10.2.1 Collective agreement

A collective agreement is an agreement made by or on behalf of one or more independent trade unions and one or more employer or employers' association.

10.2.2 Workforce agreement

A workforce agreement is an agreement between an employer and its workers or their elected representatives, which satisfies certain conditions. The conditions are as follows:

- the agreement is in writing;
- the agreement has effect for a specified period of no more than 5 years;
- the agreement applies to all the relevant members of the workforce or a particular group;

- the agreement has been signed by representatives of the workforce and, in circumstances where the employer has workers numbering 20 or less, the agreement has been signed by appropriate representatives of the majority of workers;
- before the agreement was signed, the employer provided all workers with copies and guidance in order to enable them reasonably to understand the terms of the agreement.

10.2.3 Relevant agreement

A relevant agreement is any agreement in writing which is legally enforceable between the worker and employer. This includes any written contract of employment.

10.2.4 Opt-out agreement

An opt-out agreement is any agreement in writing which may be withdrawn by a worker giving at least 7 days', and no more than 3 months', notice, and which excludes the 48-hour working week (see below).

10.3 MAXIMUM WEEKLY WORKING TIME

10.3.1 What is working time?

One of the first things that charity employers must do when dealing with issues relating to the working hours of their employees, is identifying which hours constitute 'working time' for the purposes of the WTR 1998. Although this is likely to be a very straightforward process for those employees who work standard contractual hours (eg 9 am to 5 pm with an hour's break for lunch), the position is slightly more complicated where individuals work for 'on-call' or 'sleeping-in' periods.

The European Court of Justice has twice considered the issue of on-call time in *SIMAP v Conselleria de Sawidad y Consumo de la Generalidad Valenciana* [2000] IRLR 845 and most recently in *Landeshauptstradt Kiel v Jaeger* (C-151/02). Both these cases involved doctors who were required to be at the hospital for the duration of their 'on-call' shift; the entire shift was held to be 'working time'. If, however, individuals are not required to be physically present at their place of work and are free to pursue other activities while waiting to be called upon to work, this would not be 'working time'.

Activity	*Working time?*
Working lunches	✓
Business travel time	✓
Job-related training	✓
Non job-related training	✗
Time spent working abroad for a UK employer	✓
Travel outside normal working hours	✗
Travel from home to work	✗
Rest breaks where no work is done	✗
On-call duties when based on site	✓
On-call duties where based at home	✗

10.3.2 The law

Charities are required to take all reasonable steps to ensure that every adult worker works no more than 48 hours in each working week, averaged over a period of 17 weeks. The limit for young persons' working hours is 8 hours per day and 40 hours per week.

The 48-hour weekly maximum will not apply if the worker provides written agreement, by way of an opt-out agreement, to exceed these hours. Opt-out agreements must be entered into voluntarily and it is unlawful for any employer to victimise or dismiss a worker for refusing to sign an opt-out agreement.

In addition, if an employee is in a position of management and the duration of the employee's working time is not measured or pre-determined, or can be freely determined by the employee, then the 48-hour weekly maximum will not apply.

Charities must maintain up-to-date records of all workers who have signed an opt-out agreement, and charities are required to keep records for 2 years to show that they have complied with the provisions on maximum weekly working time in respect of each of their workers.

10.3.3 Practical guidance

Charities should check:

- what constitutes working time;
- the amount of working time each worker spends;
- whether hours can be reduced if they exceed 48 hours or whether an opt-out agreement can be agreed;
- what records should be maintained.

10.4 NIGHT WORK

10.4.1 The law

Charities are required to take all reasonable steps, to protect workers' health and safety, to ensure that night workers' normal hours of work do not exceed 8 in each 24 hours, averaged over a 17-week period.

A 'night worker' is an individual who works at least 3 hours during night time (which is a period of at least 7 hours including the period between midnight and 5 am). Before assigning an adult worker to night work, the charity employer must ensure that the worker has the opportunity of a free health assessment.

The maximum hours of night work may be exceeded or modified if there is a collective or workforce agreement in place.

If, during the course of employment, a charity employer is advised by a registered medical practitioner that a worker is suffering from health problems which are connected with night working, the charity is required to transfer the worker, if possible, to work which does not qualify as night work.

Charities are required to keep up-to-date records for 2 years which are adequate to show compliance with the provisions on length of night work and health assessments.

10.4.2 Practical guidance

Charities should check:

- the number of night workers employed;
- the amount of working time night workers normally work;
- whether this can be reduced if it exceeds more than 8 hours a day;
- whether the work done is particularly hazardous;
- what health assessments, if any, must be carried out and how often;
- whether any night workers should be transferred to day work;
- adequate records are kept.

10.5 REST PERIODS

Workers are entitled to daily and weekly rest periods totalling 90 hours per week and to rest breaks during the working day. A rest period is defined as a period which is not working time, other than a rest break or statutory annual leave.

10.5.1 Daily rest periods

Adult workers are entitled to a rest period of at least 11 consecutive hours in each 24-hour working period. It is not necessary for the 11 hours to fall within the same calendar day provided they are consecutive. This would obviously be satisfied by allowing a worker a rest period overnight.

Where shift workers change shift and cannot take an 11-hour rest period between shifts, this rule will not apply provided that compensatory rest is offered or appropriate protection is in place to safeguard health and safety.

10.5.2 Weekly rest periods

Adult workers are ordinarily entitled to an uninterrupted rest period of at least 24 hours in each 7-day period of working. This may be arranged as two uninterrupted rest periods of not less than 24 hours in each 14-day period or one uninterrupted period of not less than 48 hours in each 14-day period.

The minimum weekly rest period should not run concurrently with any part of a daily rest period except where this is justified by objective or technical reasons or reasons concerning the organisation of work.

Where shift workers change shift and cannot take a weekly rest period between shifts, this rule will not apply provided that compensatory rest is offered or appropriate protection is in place to safeguard health and safety.

10.5.3 Rest breaks

After a working period of 6 hours an adult worker is entitled to a rest break. In the absence of any collective or workforce agreement determining the length of the break and any conditions relating to it, the break should be an uninterrupted 20 minutes, which the worker may take away from the work station.

In addition to these specific obligations, an employer must ensure that workers are given adequate rest breaks where the work pattern puts workers' health and safety at risk.

10.5.4 Practical guidance

Charities should check:

- whether workers can take appropriate time off and/or rest breaks;
- whether any exceptions or flexibilities apply;
- the different entitlements that apply for young workers.

10.6 RIGHT TO REQUEST PART-TIME WORKING

From 6 April 2003, employees have the right to request to work flexibly, changing their hours, times or place of work. An employee may request this if he or she has a child under the age of 6 (18 if disabled), and the employer will be able to refuse such a request for one of a list of specified reasons. For more details of this, see Chapter 16.

10.7 ENFORCEMENT AND REMEDIES

Working time-limits are enforced by either the Health and Safety Executive or local authorities. In the case of charities, the majority of establishments will be monitored by the local authority. In circumstances where weekly working time, length of night work, health assessments for night workers and transfers to day work, rest breaks, record keeping, and compensatory rest in relation to night work are not satisfied, the employer will be guilty of an offence, which is punishable on summary conviction by a fine not exceeding £5,000. On conviction on indictment, the punishment is an unlimited fine.

Individuals may also make claims before the employment tribunal if their rights to daily rest, weekly rest, rest breaks, annual leave, compensatory rest, and payments in respect of annual leave have been breached. If a worker is successful in his or her claim, the tribunal will make a declaration to that effect and may make an award of compensation which is just and equitable in all the circumstances.

CASE STUDY

Adam is employed on a working week of 8 hours each day and does overtime of 12 hours each week for 10 weeks, followed by no overtime for 7 weeks. His employer Does Good UK calculates his total hours as follows:

17 weeks of 40 hours and 10 weeks of 12 hours' overtime:

$(17 \times 40) + (10 \times 12) = 800.$

The average weekly working time that Adam spends is therefore:

$800 \div 17 = 47.1$ hours each week.

In these circumstances Does Good UK is complying with the average limit of 48 hours per week.

Does Good UK wants to increase the amount of overtime that Adam does and asks him to sign an opt-out agreement consenting to work more than an average of 48 hours a week. Does Good UK sets out in the letter that, unless Adam agrees to sign the opt-out, his wages will be reduced by the amount of overtime that he was carrying out. Adam does not sign the opt-out agreement but notices that he is still rostered to work for 40 hours a week and 12 hours' overtime for each week of the 17-week period. Adam raises this with Does Good UK, which says that it is entitled to increase his hours as there is an opt-out agreement in place.

Adam makes a complaint to his local employment tribunal, which finds that there is no valid opt-out agreement as Adam has not agreed to opt out.

Adam returns to work following the decision and in his subsequent pay packet notices that his pay has been reduced for the overtime he has been working.

Adam makes a further complaint to his local employment tribunal, which finds that Does Good UK has subjected him to a detriment for refusing to sign an opt-out agreement and orders Does Good UK to reimburse Adam for the difference in his pay.

Chapter 11

HOLIDAYS

11.1 INTRODUCTION

The majority of charities give their staff paid holiday from work. It is recognised that not only is this beneficial to an employee's health and well-being but it is also beneficial to employers as it can increase productivity and promote good employment relations.

Until 1998 employees had to rely on their employers recognising the benefit of paid annual leave as there was no statutory right to paid holiday leave. The first legal recognition that holidays are important for staff, and assist an employer in complying with the duty to take care of the health and safety of its staff, came in 1998 when the UK implemented the Working Time Regulations 1998 (WTR 1998).

Under the WTR 1998, a worker is statutorily entitled to 4 weeks' paid leave in each leave year (including bank holidays). All workers, including those who are employed but are absent from work due to long-term sick leave or other reason, will accrue holiday entitlement during the leave year. Paid leave will start to accrue from the first day of employment, and employers cannot limit the right to annual leave to workers with a specified period of continuous service.

In addition to the entitlement to statutory annual leave, charity employers may also allow employees additional paid leave. In the case of enhanced entitlements, employers are permitted to set out such rules and procedures as they feel are necessary. In most cases, it may be necessary to distinguish the rules that may apply to enhanced entitlements in the contract of employment.

Charity employers cannot restrict the statutory amount of leave to which staff are entitled and cannot discharge their liability to pay holiday pay by unilaterally reducing an employee's contractual rate of pay.

Example

Adam was employed on 30 November 1997 as project worker for Does Good UK. He was paid £5 per hour to work in the Does Good UK shop on Oxford Street for 35 hours per week. Although he was permitted to take 4 weeks' leave per year he was not paid for that leave. Does Good

UK's wage bill for Adam was for 48 weeks a year at a rate of £175 per week, totalling £8,400 per year.

Following implementation of the WTR 1998, Adam received his first monthly payslip and realised that his rate of pay had been reduced to £4.61 per hour. He had not discussed this with Does Good UK and they had not informed him of this change in advance. When he raised the reduction with Does Good UK, Adam was advised that from 1 October 1998 he was entitled to be paid for his 4 weeks' annual leave. Adam was delighted that he was now receiving paid annual leave but was concerned that his hourly rate had been reduced without his consent. When he did some arithmetic, he realised that his average pay for a 35-hour week at £4.61 per hour would be £161.35.

Adam made a complaint to his local employment tribunal, which found that this was a breach of the WTR 1998, as Does Good UK had unilaterally reduced Adam's contractual rate of pay. It awarded him a payment of 4 weeks' paid leave at a rate of £5.00 per hour, which amounted to £700.

One option for a charity is to negotiate an agreement with workers for their pay to include rolled-up holiday pay. While workers remain entitled to take annual leave, provided that the contract specifically identifies an element of pay which is expressly stated to be an advance on holiday pay, there should be no requirement to pay the worker an additional sum when annual leave is in fact taken. In *Marshalls Clay Products Ltd v Caulfield* [2003] IRLR 552, the EAT gave guidance as to how rolled-up holiday pay could be used without breaching the WTR 1998. In order to pay rolled-up holiday pay, charity employers should:

- ensure that rolled-up pay is clearly incorporated into the contract of employment and expressly agreed;
- clearly identify the percentage or amount of pay that is payable in respect of holiday (either in the contract or, preferably, on the wage slip);
- ensure that the additional payment amounts to a true addition to the contractual rate of pay;
- ensure that records are kept of holiday taken and take reasonable steps to ensure that workers take their holiday entitlement before the end of the leave year.

Example

Following the decision of the employment tribunal, Does Good UK negotiated an amendment to Adam's contract and increased his contractual rate of pay to £5.42. The new contract that was issued clearly set out that the additional 42p was an advance on holiday pay to which Adam was entitled. The result of this was that Adam's weekly pay packet increased to £189.70 per week but he did not receive a payment in the weeks in which he was taking his annual leave entitlement. His annual salary for Does Good UK was therefore £9,105.60, which was the near-equivalent of the charity paying Adam for 52 weeks a year at a rate of £175. Adam was happy to agree for this element of pay to be an advance on holiday pay and signed up to the amendment to the contract.

A charity cannot unilaterally vary an employment contract to apportion part of the pay as holiday pay: it must obtain the worker's agreement. Neither can it rcplacc lcavc with a payment in lieu of holiday pay. The reason for this is that the law is drafted to ensure that staff take time off from work.

A payment in lieu of holiday may be made only in circumstances where the employment is terminated and the worker has outstanding leave which has not been taken. In circumstances where a worker has taken more paid holiday than he or she has accrued, an employer does not have a statutory right to recover excess holiday pay that has been paid unless specific provision to do so is made in the terms of the contract of employment.

11.2 NOTICE

In order to take leave, a worker must give notice of the dates on which he or she intends to be absent. That notice must be equivalent to at least twice the period of leave intended.

Example

Adam decides he would like to take a 2-week break from 24 June to 5 July inclusive. He checks Does Good UK's annual leave policy and sees that he must give notice that is equivalent to at least twice the period of leave he is proposing to take. As he is proposing to take 10 working days' leave, he must give at least 20 working days' notice of his leave. He hands his notice of the proposed dates to his manager on 27 May 2002.

Although an employer can serve a counter-notice postponing leave, an employer may not use this as a method to refuse paid holiday altogether. An employer may, however, require employees to take all or part of their leave on certain dates by giving them notice of that requirement, which must be at least twice the period of leave that it requires them to take. Provided that the same amount of notice is given, an employer may also specify certain dates on which an employee may not take leave.

11.3 BANK HOLIDAYS

If a charity decides to allow its employees paid leave only in accordance with the WTR 1998, then the 4 weeks' leave to which they are entitled *includes* bank holidays. Charities may, however, wish to be more generous than the statutory provisions and to permit their staff to take at least 4 weeks' annual leave plus bank holidays. Charities may wish to give special consideration to circumstances where an additional public holiday is announced (as happened in 1999 for the Millennium and in 2002, the Royal Jubilee year).

11.4 HOLIDAY ON SICK LEAVE

The EAT has recently considered whether an employee who is absent from work on long-term sick leave can claim for holiday pay in relation to a period of employment throughout which he or she has been absent. An employee whose entitlement to sick pay has ceased may give notice to the employer that he or she wishes a certain period of the sick leave to be treated as annual leave for which there is paid entitlement. The EAT held that the WTR 1998 give an entitlement to paid holiday leave if the person claiming is or has been a worker during the whole or part of the leave year. No work need have been done in order to be a worker, nor, indeed, need attendance at work have occurred. Although it has not been tested by the courts, it is likely that entitlement to holiday leave will also continue to accrue during other absences from work while the contract of employment subsists, such as maternity or paternity leave.

11.5 HOLIDAY PAYMENTS ON TERMINATION OF EMPLOYMENT

Under the WTR 1998, a worker is entitled to receive a payment in lieu of any outstanding holiday that has accrued but has not been taken at the time of the termination of employment. Conversely, there is no statutory right for an employer to recover payment for excess holiday that has been taken but has not yet accrued unless there is specific provision permitting that recovery in a written agreement with the worker. Charities will need to ensure that, if they wish to be able to recover payment for excess holiday, they include this provision in the contracts signed by their workers.

11.6 PART-TIME WORKERS

Charity employers should be aware that if they grant full-time employees an enhanced holiday entitlement over and above the statutory entitlement, unless any variations can be objectively justified in accordance with the Part-time Workers (Prevention of Less Favourable Treatment) Regulations 2000, part-time workers are also entitled to receive, pro rata, an enhanced entitlement to annual leave (see Chapter 7).

11.7 REMEDIES

A worker may complain to an employment tribunal if a charity refuses to allow him or her to take annual leave or fails to pay him or her in respect of leave that is taken. Such a claim must be brought within 3 months of the act complained of, although the tribunal may extend time if it considers that it was not reasonably practicable for the worker to submit a claim within 3 months. If the worker is successful in his or her claim the tribunal may make an award of compensation which it considers to be just and equitable in all the circumstances, having regard to the employer's default in refusing to permit the worker to exercise his or her rights.

11.8 PRACTICAL GUIDANCE

Charities should:

- carry out a careful audit of all staff contracts to ensure that workers are receiving the correct entitlement to paid annual leave and consider provisions dealing with holiday leave while on sick leave;
- ensure that they have proper contractual provisions to reclaim any monies due from an employee who has taken more than his or her pro rata entitlement;
- audit the contracts of employment of part-time and fixed-term workers to ensure that they are receiving the equivalent pro rata amount of holiday;
- ensure that any rules that apply to enhanced entitlements and which differ from the statutory regime are clearly set out in the contracts of employment.

Chapter 12

DEALING WITH SICKNESS ABSENCE

12.1 INTRODUCTION

When a new employee starts work, the presumption will be that he or she is in good health; it is not anticipated that there will be short-term, let alone long-term, absences. However, working days lost because of sickness absence continue to rise in number each year, particularly in 'stress' cases, where an employee's absence can be for periods of months and sometimes years. Stress is now one of the main causes of workplace absenteeism, accounting for 6.5 million days, at a cost of £1.2 billion. Trade union figures show a twelve-fold increase in the number of claims involving stress being made against employers between 2000 and 2001, with figures rising from 516 cases to 6,428.

Finding solutions to employee absence is not easy; there are many different reasons why somebody is off work 'sick'. The reasons will be genuine in some cases, and may be due to work-related causes, whereas in other cases, factors such as domestic or personal problems will be the true cause.

This chapter considers how employers should seek to deal with sickness absences and the ultimate sanction of dismissal for persistent short-term absences or chronic long-term absence.

Where an employee has been absent from work for a lengthy period this can start to have an adverse effect on the business. For example, it may be necessary to hire a temporary replacement at extra cost, particularly if the charity has had to use an agency. The more senior the employee, the more difficult it is to find a replacement on a temporary basis. It may be seen as a waste of resources to train a new person to do the absentee's job, only to dismiss the trainee when the absentee eventually returns to work. The charity may also be making payments in respect of sick pay in addition to temporary costs.

12.2 SICK PAY

Most employees are entitled to be paid Statutory Sick Pay (SSP). The majority of charities also pay contractual sick pay.

SSP is payable to an employee who fulfils the following criteria:

- is over the age of 16 and under the age of 65 on the first day of their period of absence from work;
- has been continuously sick for 4 or more calendar days in a row; and
- has average earnings at least equal to the lower earnings limit (currently £77 per week).

SSP is currently paid at a rate of £64.35 per week, up to 28 weeks in a spell or linked spells of sickness absence (they are linked if there is less than 8 weeks between them).

Contractual sick pay is payable at a charity's discretion and it is difficult to identify a sector-wide level of pay.

An employee can claim 'contractual' sick pay only where this is provided for in the contract of employment. This is to be distinguished from a right to claim statutory sick pay which all employees have, subject to service.

12.3 SHORT-TERM ABSENCES

No matter how justifiable short-term absence may be, the fact remains that persistent short-term absence can cause the same problems as long-term absence both in terms of the profitability and accountability of the charity and its effects on staff morale. Many employers feel powerless in the face of a document completed by an employee self-certifying absence due to sickness. A doctor's certificate is even more difficult to challenge. Charities may often suspect employees of 'skiving' or 'taking a sickie' and, whatever the circumstances, charities should not be shy of dealing with staff with an unacceptably high level of sickness.

12.3.1 Practical guidance

There is ample material published on this subject to assist the HR manager, including the CBI 'Focus on absence' report, the Cabinet Office publication, *Managing Absence in the Public Sector: Putting Best Practice to Work*, and the ACAS advisory handbook, *Discipline at Work*.

It is recommended good practice for charities to have and to operate a sickness absence policy; HR professionals and managers should be trained to use the policy and it should be applied consistently throughout the organisation. Care should be taken to ensure that there are no inconsistencies between the provisions in this policy and those in the disciplinary policy. The following points should be considered when constructing a policy document.

- Employees should be told when and how they are expected to contact their employer with details of their absence from work. For example, it may be useful to say that they must phone in before a certain time on the first day of the absence and must speak to their line manager direct rather than leave a message with another member of staff.
- It should be made clear for what period of time a self-certificate will be acceptable. It may be appropriate to ask for a doctor's certificate after a few days or where the absences fall persistently on Mondays or Fridays, or after a bank holiday. A doctor may not agree to provide a certificate for short periods of illness, and in such circumstances the charity should be prepared to pay the GP for such a certificate.
- It should state that the doctor's certificate does not provide conclusive proof of the illness.
- Provision should always be made for the charity to require examination by a GP or specialist subject to the Access to Medical Records Act 1988 (see **12.9.1**).
- There might be a requirement for regular medical screening and the completion of a medical certificate.
- Reference should be made to the company's disciplinary procedure, in respect of the withholding of sick pay, or recovery of sick pay improperly received, in circumstances where the employee breaches or is found to have exploited the sick pay rules.
- All absentees should be subject to a 'back to work interview': HR professionals and managers should be trained in asking probing questions, without appearing insensitive to any genuine illness. In all cases, the employees should be told what improvement in attendance is expected and what the likely consequences will be if this is not achieved.
- The policy should state that if there is no improvement then the charity will need to consider dismissal by taking into account some of the factors outlined in **12.4.1**, but in particular considering the employee's age, length of service, likelihood of change in circumstances, and the availability of options to accommodate the employee's continuing sickness, such as suitable alternative employment.
- If the charity suffers from a widespread problem of short-term sickness absences it is worth considering what other reasons there are for absences, including organisational reasons. For example, there could be internal problems concerning the manner in which employees are being managed. Are they being undervalued or, even worse, are they subjected to bullying or harassment? The charity should consider the patterns of sickness within the organisation to see whether problems arise in a particular department or unit. It could even be that the contractual sick pay which the charity offers is too generous. It is an unfortunate fact that many employees have the notion that paid sick days should be treated as an alternative form of paid holiday. The charity should also consider whether its policy is being correctly implemented and whether it is sufficiently robust to withstand exploitation: does it include the provisions suggested above?

- There could be problems unconnected with the workplace, such as domestic problems caused by a relationship breakdown or debt. Where absences arise from temporary domestic problems, the charity should decide whether there is likely to be an improvement in attendance before taking appropriate action.

12.3.2 Dismissal for short-term absences

It is extremely rare to dismiss an employee for short-term absences without a prior warning, whether it be oral or written. A system should be in place (preferably linked to the disciplinary procedure) which empowers the charity to issue written warnings in appropriate circumstances of short-term absence. It will not be appropriate to issue warnings in cases of long-term chronic absence or where the person is suffering from a serious medically recognised condition which may require absence for short intermittent periods.

There should be a right of appeal against any decision to dismiss. The individual assigned to deal with an appeal should not be the same person who made the decision to dismiss at the original disciplinary hearing. This will ensure that the process is conducted in an objective manner.

An employee can bring claims against any dismissal due to ill health (outlined below).

Ultimately, it may be necessary for a charity to terminate the employment of an individual as a result of sickness. This is often where the relationship reaches its crunch point, and the charity faces its greatest legal risks. If the dismissal is not carried out properly, the charity exposes itself to potential claims for unfair dismissal and disability discrimination.

Establishing the correct reason

The principles concerning fair dismissal are dealt with more fully in Chapter 23; however, it is useful to outline some of the points that relate to dismissals for short-term absences.

There are three potentially fair reasons for the dismissal of an employee on short-term sickness absence: 'capability', 'conduct', and 'some other substantial reason'. Establishing the correct reason is crucial: the charity employer's failure to assess the employee's condition properly is likely to render a dismissal unfair and so the employer must consider the reason for the dismissal carefully before reaching a decision on what route to take.

The most likely reason for dismissal due to ill health is the lack of capability shown by an employee who is unable to carry out the tasks of the job adequately.

When dismissing an employee for incapability, it is always important to ensure that the correct procedure is followed. Charities who embark on this route with an employee for short-term absences must anticipate that the procedure will take time to complete.

12.4 LONG-TERM ILL HEALTH

Whether an employee is on sick leave regularly with short gaps or for a long-term absence, the effect on the charity will still be felt. It is therefore sensible to consider a situation where an employee has or is likely to have a period of long-term ill health.

12.4.1 Practical guidance

When dealing with long-term absence it is important to ascertain the true position. The charity should therefore consider the following.

(a) Investigate the nature and length of the illness. The charity will be required to obtain the employee's consent to be medically examined by a suitably qualified GP or a specialist consultant. There should be a clause in the contract of employment requiring the employee to give consent in such circumstances; unless there is an express contractual provision, the employee cannot be forced to consent, and to do so may constitute a repudiatory breach of contract. If the employee does refuse to co-operate, the charity is entitled to make a decision on the facts available to it. The charity should require the consultant to prepare a medical report, dealing with the following points:
   (i) the nature of the illness – whether the employee is suffering from a medically recognised condition, whether the employee is disabled for the purpose of the DDA 1995;
   (ii) the likely length of the illness, and when it is expected that the employee can return to work. If the charity decides to dismiss at some further stage, it is likely to be an unfair dismissal unless the medical report states that the employee is unlikely to return to work in the foreseeable future;
   (iii) if the employee is currently unable to perform the job that he or she is employed to do because of the illness, whether it will be possible for the employee to undertake any other job within the charity;
   (iv) whether there is anything the employee can do (eg undertake therapy) to improve his or her prospects of a return to work.

(b) Remember that it is not appropriate to issue verbal or written warnings where the illness is genuine.

(c) Assess the impact on the business: the more important the employee is to the business the more likely it is that the situation will not be able to continue for a long period. It is also relevant to consider the additional costs of overtime pay.

(d) Assess the impact on the other employees, ie an increase in their workloads. If the effect on other employees is great, the situation will not be able to continue for long.
(e) Consider alternative work. In any future case brought by the employee for unfair dismissal or disability discrimination, the employer will be expected to have considered this option.
(f) Take account of the employee's length of service and any Permanent Health Insurance (PHI).

12.4.2 Dismissal for long-term ill health

Subject to satisfying a number of statutory requirements (including the requirement that the employee has been in continuous employment for one year), an employee may be able to bring a claim for unfair dismissal if dismissed for long-term ill health. In order to avoid such a claim, the charity will need first to establish a potentially fair reason for the dismissal and, secondly, to show that it acted reasonably in treating it as a sufficient reason for dismissing the employee.

The charity may be able to show that it has a fair reason to dismiss on the grounds of the employee's 'capability', ie if the sickness absence relates to the capability of the employee in performing work of the kind that he or she was employed to do. Capability is assessed by reference to an employee's skill, aptitude, and physical and mental health. Ultimately, if an employee is dismissed for long-term ill health, the charity will have to show that the employee's capability was such that he or she was unlikely to return to work in the foreseeable future.

If it transpires that the employee was untruthful about his or her state of health, the reason for dismissal will be treated as one of misconduct rather than capability, although this is more likely to occur with short-term absences. The charity, however, should be careful not to jump to conclusions. In *McMaster v Manchester Airport plc* [1998] IRLR 112, an employee took a day trip to France whilst off sick. The EAT took the view that the trip itself was taken with the idea that it might have improved the employee's condition. In the circumstances the employer was wrong to have treated it as a misconduct offence, and the employee's claim for unfair dismissal succeeded. This is to be contrasted with the case of *Hutchinson v Enfield Rolling Hills* [1981] IRLR 318, where it was held that an employee who was signed off sick but travelled to Brighton to participate in a trade union demonstration was fairly dismissed even though he had been signed off as sick by his doctor.

If the charity has consulted and considered all possible options with the employee it will have acted as fairly as could be expected and will be able to show it has acted reasonably.

12.5 PRIVATE HEALTH INSURANCE

If the employee is entitled to benefit from a PHI policy, it is important that the charity takes all necessary steps to ensure that the employee receives the appropriate benefits. There are other pitfalls about which the charity should be aware. The charity will need to ensure that a claim does not arise from the dismissal of an employee who might otherwise be entitled to benefit from such a scheme. For example, dismissing a sick employee for incapability after an absence of 4 months, who is entitled to claim under the policy after 6 months' paid sick leave, is a breach of contract. A dismissal of a sick employee for reason of misconduct or redundancy or where he or she has failed to comply with the rules of the scheme will not be a breach. However, in these circumstances the charity could be faced with some evidential difficulty in proving that the dismissal was indeed for a reason other than the employee's illness.

Whether or not the employee is actually entitled to receive the benefit of PHI will ultimately depend upon the decision of the insurers. If the insurers take the decision not to award the benefit to any employee, will the charity still be liable to the employee for breach of contract? In these circumstances, the position will be governed by what the contract of employment actually says: if the contract does not refer to an entitlement being subject to the insurers' decision, then the charity itself will be liable to every employee to make a payment that represents what would have been paid had the insurance payment actually been made. It is therefore extremely important for the charity to limit its liability to the terms of the insurance policy or the insurers' willingness to pay. However, this does not exonerate the employer completely. In those circumstances the charity will need to take legal action against the insurance company to obtain payment for the employee rather than paying out itself. It also means that the charity will be able to recoup the costs of any such action that it needs to take on behalf of the employee from the employee.

It should also be noted that where there is a conflict between the terms of the contract and the insurance policy, the contract will prevail. For example, in a recent case (*Pioneer Technology (UK) Ltd v Jowitt* [2003] EWCA Civ 411) the employer undertook to provide two-thirds of the employee's salary after 26 weeks' continuous absence, provided the employee was unfit to work. The insurance paid out only if the employee was not following any other occupation. The court applied the term of the contract and not that of the insurance policy.

12.6 CONSULTATION

In order to dismiss an employee fairly for capability in a case of long-term sickness, the charity will also need to consult with the employee and keep him or her informed of steps being taken. It is vitally important for the charity not to take any decisions about an employee's employment without having first consulted with him or her, taking into account any suggestions he or she may have. It is therefore suggested that an employer consults with an employee throughout any long-term period of ill health. All meetings must be carefully documented, and any representations made by the employee must be taken into consideration. However, the ultimate decision to dismiss the employee must lie with the charity. All copies of relevant letters and other correspondence, including medical reports, should be disclosed so that the employee has an opportunity to make representations upon what has been said.

12.7 DISABILITY DISCRIMINATION

This is also dealt with in Chapter 7. It should be noted that a person who is dismissed or treated 'less favourably' may have the right to claim disability discrimination, provided certain criteria are met. It is also important to note that such a claim can be made by a worker, and there is no requirement that the person has been continuously employed for one year, as there is with unfair dismissal.

The following criteria must be met in order to bring a claim.

- The charity must have more than 15 workers. From 2 December 2006 (or possibly even by 1 October 2004, as the Government intends at the time of writing) this requirement will be removed so that every organisation, regardless of size, will be required to comply.
- The worker must be disabled, as defined by the Disability Discrimination Act 1995 (DDA 1995). Effectively this means that a person must have a physical or mental impairment which has lasted or is expected to last for a period of more than one year and has a substantial and long-term adverse effect on a person's ability to carry out normal day-to-day activities (which are listed in Guidance to the DDA 1995). This is a medical issue and should be addressed in any correspondence with the doctor instructed to prepare a report.
- The worker must either have been dismissed or be treated less favourably as a result of his or her disability, or must show that the charity has failed to comply with its duty to make reasonable adjustments.

Not all sick members of staff will be disabled for the purposes of employment law, but the circumstances under which a DDA 1995 claim can be made are much wider than for unfair dismissal. For example, the charity could be deemed liable for a failure to make reasonable adjustments where a consultant has recommended that the person concerned should be allowed time off work for treatment, say, one day per week, or that a particular piece of equipment be installed which would enable that person to carry out his or her job properly, and the charity does not follow that advice. Discrimination may also occur where an employee is made redundant because of his or her attendance, or is refused a promotion on the grounds of his or her disability. In cases of long-term ill health, a dismissal will usually be a detriment and, if it is as a result of the disability, likely to be related to it.

The charity may use the defence that the discrimination was justified, in the circumstances. This defence will not be open to employers after the proposed introduction of amendments to the DDA 1995 in October 2004. The justification defence could be used in circumstances where, for example, it could be established that the cost incurred by the business by installing a particular piece of equipment would outweigh the overall effect of assisting the employee to perform his or her role. The use of this sort of justification defence depends on the size and resources of the charity: the larger the charity, the less likely it will be that this defence will succeed.

12.8 PERSONAL INJURY CLAIMS

Another claim sometimes threatened by an employee dismissed due to ill health is that his or her injury has been caused or exacerbated by the acts of the employer. In order to bring such a claim, the employee must show that the charity breached its duty to look after the employee's health and safety and as a result he or she suffered injury to health. This is more difficult to prove than it appears.

12.9 MEDICAL RECORDS AND EXAMINATION

12.9.1 Access to medical records

Under the provisions of the Access to Medical Records Act 1988, an employer may gain access to medical reports, which have been prepared or supplied by a medical practitioner for employment purposes. The report will include notes that have been created by the employee's GP, and any other documentation supplied to or from a hospital where the employee has been treated and/or from a consultant or specialist responsible for the clinical care of the employee. An employer will not be able to gain access to an employee's medical records unless the employee has been notified of the right and consent is given. A method by which the employee's consent is obtained is for the employee to sign a form of authority.

The Act allows an employee access to his or her own medical reports, provided the medical practitioner agrees, and the employee can challenge any findings and correct inaccuracies. Equally, information may be withheld from the employee if, in the view of the medical practitioner, disclosure would be likely to cause serious harm to the employee or others, or would reveal information about a third party. The charity must treat the information in confidence, but can use it as evidence upon which to consider alternative employment/dismissal as appropriate.

12.9.2 Medical examinations

The charity cannot require an employee to consent to a medical examination, unless he or she agrees. The contract of employment should therefore contain an express provision stating that the employee agrees to be examined in appropriate circumstances. This is express consent.

12.9.3 Employee's refusal to give consent

An employee's refusal to consent to a medical examination without justification for doing so may constitute misconduct. It also presents a difficulty for the charity, which will be forced to make a decision about the employee's future without the benefit of medical evidence. The employee should be told of the charity's right in this respect when he or she refuses consent. In the absence of a justifiable reason for refusing consent, one would fully expect a tribunal to take an adverse view of an employee's refusal when assessing a claim for unfair dismissal or disability discrimination.

CASE STUDY

Wishbone is a registered charity campaigning on issues concerning the protection of the environment. It is a large charity employing around 500 people in the UK. The office has recently experienced a large number of employees being absent from work due to sickness. In particular, the charity is unsure how to deal with the following problem which has arisen. James is an employee at Wishbone who has worked there for 2½ years. He called in sick due to stress about a month ago and has since sent in a medical report which says he is sick due to 'stress/debility'. Over the last year, he has had five periods of sick leave.

Although there is no sickness absence policy contained within the contract of employment, there is a clause which confirms that James has agreed to be medically examined by the charity's occupational therapist. The HR manager, Julia, suspects that his illness may not be genuine. She reported that approximately a week ago, on a day on which he took sick leave, she saw him driving along the road that runs past her house. On returning to work after his last absence, Julia asked him to sign a form of consent allowing his medical records to be released to the occupational therapist, but he refused.

Answer

James has worked for the charity for more than a year and so he has the potential right to bring a claim for unfair dismissal against Wishbone. He does not appear to be suffering from any form of illness which could be classed as a disability. It is still advisable, however, for the charity to obtain a letter from his GP or an occupational health doctor in order to ascertain the true medical position.

As Wishbone wishes to dismiss him, there are two potentially fair reasons open to the charity on which to dismiss: incapability on the basis that his illness is genuine, or misconduct on the basis that it is not. The fact that he was spotted by the HR manager, during business hours, driving near the area in which he lives could be explained: for example, he could have been visiting his local GP.

Wishbone should be advised to set up an initial meeting as investigation for a potential disciplinary hearing, to ascertain why he was seen out and about during business hours. If the charity is satisfied that he was not genuinely ill, then his behaviour should be treated as a misconduct offence and dealt with in accordance with the disciplinary policy.

If, on the other hand, Wishbone is satisfied that the illness is genuine, then it must be treated as a capability issue. The terms of any relevant policy should be followed. The fact that James has refused to consent to the release of his medical records may constitute a misconduct offence, but that in itself is unlikely to be viewed as gross misconduct warranting immediate dismissal. Again, it will be necessary for Wishbone to carry out a separate disciplinary hearing to deal with this aspect. If James still refuses to consent, then Wishbone will be forced to take a decision without the benefit of medical evidence. Provided Wishbone is fair and reasonable in connection with all other aspects of the dismissal it is unlikely that this aspect in itself would necessarily render the dismissal unfair.

Chapter 13

CONFIDENTIALITY, VICARIOUS LIABILITY AND INTELLECTUAL PROPERTY

13.1 DUTIES OF CONFIDENTIALITY OWED BY VOLUNTEERS AND WORKERS

During the course of volunteers' engagement with a charity they are likely to view or have access to confidential information held by the charity. This may include data concerning the financial status of the charity, details of donations, and other information which is not within the public domain. Provided a volunteer cannot be deemed an employee (see Chapter 1), the charity will need to ensure that the volunteer is made aware that he or she should not disclose any confidential information while engaged with the charity and also after leaving the organisation. This principle applies equally to workers and, in both cases, a simple letter setting out what amounts to confidential information and the penalties that could be imposed upon disclosure should suffice. Again, this is something that can be included in a volunteers' charter.

Care should be taken in carrying out the formalities of this procedure: a charity will not want to formalise the relationship so as to indicate an 'employment relationship' as a result of the existence of such documentation. This is to be contrasted with the position of employees, who are impliedly bound not to disclose confidential information during the course of their employment. A charity could find itself in the invidious position of ensuring that it is protected against the consequences of a harmful disclosure, only to create a situation where a volunteer or a worker could acquire the status of an employee, particularly if some or all of the other factors outlined in Chapter 1 are present. For example, should a volunteer breach an express agreement to maintain confidentiality during the engagement, the charity may wish to discipline the person concerned by issuing a written warning. An act of this nature would be consistent with treating this person as an employee, and not as a volunteer or a worker.

13.2 VICARIOUS LIABILITY OF THE CHARITY FOR THE ACTS OF WORKERS AND VOLUNTEERS

The general principle is that a charity will not be liable for the acts of its volunteers or workers. This is to be contrasted with the position of employees, who are not personally liable for their acts during employment, unless the act was one causing injury or damage to a third party and was carried out wilfully, or, in some cases, where the employee has been grossly negligent. Given the fact that employers should be insured against such eventualities, there are clear policy reasons why charities should be liable for the acts of their employees, but not for their volunteers.

Generally speaking, a charity will not be vicariously liable for the acts of individuals unless they are employees or are deemed to be so. There are, however, a number of exceptional circumstances where a charity could be liable: for example, if it authorises a wrongful or unlawful act executed by a volunteer or worker. As the lines between employees, workers and volunteers have become more blurred, the more difficult it has become to distinguish the situations in which a charity could be vicariously liable. Nevertheless, the general principle remains the same.

As far as board members and trustees are concerned, the position is a little more complex. There are no decided cases on this point. However, guidance can be drawn from the case of *Moores v Bude-Stratton Town Council* [2000] IRLR 676. In this case, the EAT considered whether the council could be vicariously liable for the acts of one of its councillors, who was accused of verbal abuse and of dishonesty against one of the council's employees. The EAT held that councillors were under a duty not to engage in conduct likely to undermine the trust and confidence required in employment contracts, even though there was no actual employment relationship between the council and individual councillors.

On the basis of the reasoning set out in *Moores*, there may be circumstances in which a charity may be vicariously liable for the acts of its volunteers. This would depend upon the following factors.

(a) Did the volunteer receive remuneration from the charity?
(b) Were the activities undertaken by the volunteer carried out for the direct benefit of the charity?
(c) Was the act which is the subject of complaint incidental to the duties of the volunteer?
(d) Was the charity in a position of control, not only to order what was to be done, but also how it was to be done?
(e) Was the charity in a position to suspend or stop the activity which is the subject of the complaint?
(f) Was the act done expressly or impliedly authorised by the charity? For example, if the charity was aware or could be deemed to have

been aware of what was going on, then it could be said to have authorised the act of the volunteer.

No single question or answer is likely to be determinative, but together the answers should provide an overall picture from which the charity should be able to judge whether vicarious liability exists.

The charity could be vicariously liable for any act of sex, race or disability discrimination carried out if the perpetrator is an employee or a worker, but is unlikely to be liable if the individual is a volunteer. As referred to in Chapter 1, the threshold for establishing status as a worker is lower than that of an employee.

The charity could potentially find itself liable for an act of discrimination over which it has no control, unless it can establish that it took all reasonable steps to prevent the act occurring in the first place. Claims of this nature are most likely to arise where a worker or employee harasses another on the grounds of his or her sex or race, and often in circumstances of which the charity is completely unaware.

A charity should be able to defend any action for discrimination provided it can show that it had an Equal Opportunities Policy, had trained its staff, and sought to investigate and deal with complaints promptly and fairly.

CASE STUDY

Taurus is a Registered Charity representing the interests of people with mental health problems. The charity employs around 25 individuals, all of whom have been provided with contracts of employment and are paid a monthly salary. They are regarded by the charity as an integral part of the business.

Around 200 other individuals perform a variety of different roles as volunteers. They are paid expenses and are not required to attend an office because they work from home; the charity has provided each of them with a mobile phone and computer. Several months ago the charity decided it would introduce a contributory pension scheme for all staff, including volunteers.

Volunteers are not required to work set hours or produce timesheets showing the hours worked in any given week. All volunteers are left to their own devices to perform their roles, which can include campaign management, recruiting other volunteers, and preparing and presenting seminars to outside bodies.

There is no written contract or other documentation between Taurus and each volunteer. Volunteers are, however, formally appraised by the HR director on a monthly basis.

Maria has issued a claim against Taurus for unfair dismissal and sex discrimination. Taurus have asserted that she is a volunteer, and therefore not able to bring either of these claims. What is the legal position?

Maria's position

A variety of different factors need to be taken into account in assessing Maria's actual status. If she is deemed to be an employee then she can bring a claim for sex discrimination and, provided she has worked for the charity for one year, she can also bring a claim for unfair dismissal. If, on the other hand, she is deemed to be a worker, then her claim will be confined to sex discrimination only.

There appears to be a high degree of flexibility over how and when volunteers perform their roles. They are not required to work set hours, or produce work within a certain time frame, and they are not paid for what they do (which is to be contrasted with the position of employees). On that basis, no control is exercised by the charity, save for the appraisals from Head Office. There also appears to be minimal mutuality of obligation between the charity and its volunteers.

On the other hand, Taurus provides some of the tools and equipment necessary for them to perform their role. Furthermore, like the employees, volunteers now benefit from a pension, and they are described by Taurus as being an integral part of the business. All of these factors point towards them being workers or employees.

Although the factors seem to be evenly balanced, it is unlikely that Maria would be deemed an employee of the charity because she does not receive a salary or wage. However, it remains unlikely that her status is simply one of a volunteer. Given the mix of factors present, her status is more likely to be that of a worker, in which case she would have the right to bring a claim for sex discrimination.

13.3 OWNERSHIP OF INTELLECTUAL PROPERTY

13.3.1 Employees

If a person is genuinely deemed to be an employee then the position regarding the ownership of intellectual property will be governed by a variety of lengthy and complex statutory provisions. Intellectual property is a generic title, covering things such as patents, trade marks and design rights. In general, inventions, creations and works of copyright belong to the employer, if they were carried out during the course of the employee's normal duties, or in the course of duties specifically assigned to the employee, or whilst carrying out specific instructions at the request of the employer. It is therefore advisable to include within the employee's contract of employment a job description which makes clear what the normal duties are and gives a broad definition of such duties in order to prevent disputes arising in the future.

Inventions made outside normal working hours will not automatically fall outside the employer's scope if, for example, the employee was provided with facilities to work from home.

13.3.2 Workers and volunteers

A worker or a volunteer is not bound by the same statutory obligations as an employee. For example, if the charity anticipates that a volunteer or worker may be engaged in the type of design work whereby a logo may be created, which could then become used as a trade mark for the charity, it would be advisable either to make the individual an employee or to enter into a separate agreement which confirms that any patent, invention, trade mark or copyright will belong to the charity. However, clauses in such an agreement cannot override the statutory provisions that might be applicable in the given circumstances.

Chapter 14

PRIVACY

14.1 INTRODUCTION

Whilst privacy is generally regarded as a fundamental right in the UK, the word is rarely specifically defined. Nevertheless, it is clear that privacy, whenever it is used in a legal context, refers to an interest that underpins human dignity and other key values such as freedom of association and freedom of speech. In this chapter, we look at the legal boundaries in existence in the workplace and remedies which exist for employees whose privacy is interfered with.

The key pieces of legislation which set out the boundaries are:

- the Human Rights Act 1998 (HRA 1998);
- the Data Protection Act 1998 (DPA 1998);
- the Regulation of Investigatory Powers Act 2000 (RIPA 2000).

We will also look at other matters which delineate the boundaries of privacy in the context of the employment relationship.

14.2 LEGISLATION

14.2.1 Human Rights Act 1998

The HRA 1998 came into force on 2 October 2000. This Act gives statutory effect to the European Convention for the Protection of Human Rights and Fundamental Freedoms (European Convention on Human Rights).

Although the HRA 1998 makes it unlawful for a 'public authority' to act in a way which is incompatible with the Convention, it may nevertheless be of relevance to other employers in the following ways.

- Any employer whose functions include public functions will be caught; it is clear that this can include charities. Whilst the employment decisions of these quasi-public bodies will probably not be directly covered by the Act, it will certainly have an indirect impact on them.
- A court or tribunal – which is a public authority – is obliged to interpret the law in the light of the Convention rights, in order to give effect to those rights. In adjudicating upon a dispute between a

charity and an employee, therefore, the court or tribunal must ensure that the employee's Convention rights are protected.

The HRA 1998 identifies each of those rights which are protected by the Convention. The most relevant rights in an employment situation are as follows:

- *Article 6: right to a fair trial.* Everyone is entitled to a fair and public hearing within a reasonable time by an independent or impartial tribunal established by law. It is reasonable to assume that the principles of the right will be considered by a tribunal in considering whether an employer has dealt fairly with its employee in any internal group disciplinary proceedings, although it is unlikely that a tribunal would require a disciplinary hearing to have been held in public.
- *Article 8: right to respect for private and family life.* Everyone has the right to respect for his or her private and family life, his or her home and his or her correspondence. Caveats to this right include where interference is in the interests of the prevention of disorder or crime, for the protection of health or morals, or for the protection of the rights and freedom of others.
- *Article 10: freedom of expression.* Everyone has the right to freedom of expression. The right shall include freedom to hold opinions, and to receive and impart information and ideas without interference by the public authority, and regardless of frontiers. This right may be interfered with where it is for the prevention of disorder or crime; for the protection of health or morals; for the protection of the reputation or rights of others; or for preventing the disclosure of information received in confidence.

There has been an instructive case (decided before the introduction of the HRA 1998) in relation to the right to respect for private and family life. The case of *Halford v United Kingdom* (1997) IRLR 471 was a case arising from a complaint by Alison Halford against the Merseyside Police. During the course of her complaint, it became apparent that the police had been intercepting her telephone calls from her office, and it was alleged that telephone conversations made from her home had also been intercepted (although, in the event, there was insufficient evidence to rule on that). The European Court of Human Rights held that the interception by her employers of calls made on her office telephones was a violation of Article 8 of the European Convention on Human Rights. The argument of the UK Government that an employer should, without the prior knowledge of the employee, be able to monitor calls made by the employee on telephones provided by the employer, was not accepted. The same arguments must apply equally to home telephone use. An award of £10,000 compensation was made, together with reimbursement of Ms Halford's personal expenses on attending the hearing.

The Home Office issued a circular in 1999 entitled 'Interception of Non-public Telecommunications Networks' which was addressed to all government departments and Chief police officers. The circular detailed the requirements for complying with the *Halford* judgment and those were summarised as follows.

- *Expectation of privacy.* If the person making the communication is fully aware that monitoring or tape recording of communications may take place then an expectation of privacy can, in principle, no longer exist. However, warnings to this effect may not, on their own, be sufficient to dispel the legitimate expectation of privacy. It is not reasonable to expect that employees will never be contacted on a domestic matter in work time, or that the employee will never have reason to make personal calls from the office. One way of addressing this problem is through the provision of pay phones.
- *Adequate warning that interception may take place.* Where written consent can be obtained, this is clearly the best way to give adequate warning. In the absence of that, an employer could seek to rely on implied consent. The onus is on the operator of the network to ensure that the message is advertised clearly enough to ensure that users are left in no doubt that interception may take place. This can be achieved by including a clause in the contract of employment that interception could take place. It will also be good practice for operators to make every reasonable effort to inform all potential users that not only speech, but also any other form of communication passing over the network, may be monitored or recorded.
- *Monitoring should only be used where necessary, the level of intrusion must be proportional to the offence being investigated, and monitoring should be the appropriate method of investigation.* For instance, if an employer suspects that an employee has been misusing the office telephone to make a large number of personal calls, evidence of this activity can be gathered simply by obtaining an itemised bill.

This guidance, although directed at telephone monitoring, will, in principle, be relevant to other forms of monitoring.

Individuals are free to contract out of the protection of the HRA 1998, although care should be taken to ensure that any contracting out is expressly agreed. It is also not clear whether such contracting out will be effective.

14.2.2 Data Protection Act 1998

The DPA 1998 is also legislation with its origins in Europe. This legislation, more than any other, was borne out of a general desire to prevent over-zealous surveillance by the state and employers of private citizens. The European Directive 95/46/EC on the Protection of Individuals with regard to the Processing of Personal Data and on the Free Movement of Such Data and UK legislation provide individuals with wide-ranging protection and a right of access to data held about them.

The DPA 1998 provides for protection of personal data and sensitive personal data held about individuals. Both personal data and sensitive personal data are defined in the Act.

'Personal data' means any data which relates to a living individual who can be identified from those data or from those data together with other information in the possession of, or which is likely to come into the possession of, the data controller. The data controller is the person who decides how and why the data are processed. 'Personal data' includes any expression of opinion about the individual and any indication of the intentions of the data controller or any other person in respect of the individual. The individual is called a data subject: in the context of this chapter, this will be an employee or other worker, but data subjects can also include a charity's service users.

The 'processing' of data is also defined by the Act. Processing effectively covers all uses of data. It is limited by the principles and the conditions put upon the processing. Data is any information held on computer or paper-based filing systems.

'Sensitive personal data' is defined as personal data consisting of the following information concerning the data subject:

(a) his or her racial or ethnic origin;
(b) his or her political opinions;
(c) his or her religious beliefs or other beliefs of a similar nature;
(d) whether he or she is a member of a trade union;
(e) his or her physical or mental health or condition;
(f) his or her sexual life;
(g) the commission or alleged commission by him or her of any offence; or
(h) any proceedings for any offence committed or alleged to have been committed by him or her, the disposal of such proceedings or the sentence of any court in such proceedings.

If a charity wishes to process sensitive personal data, it must have explicit consent to do so or it must rely on one of the other limited grounds set out in the Act. The likely relevant grounds are:

- where the processing is carried out in the course of the legitimate activities of any body or association which is not established or conducted for profit and exists for political, philosophical, religious or trade union purposes;
- where the processing is necessary to protect the vital interests of the data subject; or
- where the processing is necessary in relation to legal proceedings.

The condition relating to charities existing 'for political, philosophical, religious or trade union purposes' also requires, amongst other things, that data processing be 'carried out with appropriate safeguards for the rights and freedoms' of the data subject. The data can only relate to individuals who belong to, are members of, or have regular contact with the charity, and there are further conditions attached to any disclosure of the sensitive personal data by the charity to a third party.

Only 'consent' is required for processing personal data. It is understood that this includes implied consent but that implied consent can be withdrawn at any time. Alternatively, a charity can seek express consent or may rely on one of the other grounds set out in the Act, including where the processing is necessary for the purposes of legitimate interests pursued by the charity – a ground which is expected to be construed widely.

Employees also have the right to have all data held by the data controller processed within the DPA 1998 principles. The standards which must be met if the requirements of the DPA 1998 are to be complied with, can be summarised as follows:

- fair and lawful processing;
- processing for limited purposes and not in any manner incompatible with those purposes;
- adequate, relevant and not excessive processing;
- holding of accurate data;
- data not being kept for longer than is necessary;
- processing in accordance with the individual's rights;
- keeping data secure; and
- not transferring to countries without adequate protection.

Employees have various rights under the DPA 1998, including the right to have access to the data held on them and a right to information about the processes used. Both these rights are wide-ranging and potentially provide administrative headaches for charities.

An employee must make a written request and must send a fee of not more than £10 (unless the charity waives the fee). The charity must then comply with the request within 40 days and provide:

- information about whether the employer is processing personal data;
- a description of the personal data, the purposes for which the data are processed, and the persons, or classes of persons, to whom the data may be disclosed; and
- in an intelligible form the information held by the charity and any information as to the source of the information.

There are a number of exceptions to an employee's right of access to personal data. These are as follows:

- employees are not entitled to have access to any references given or to be given.
- employees are not entitled to personal data which disclose information relating to another individual, unless that other individual has consented or the data can be anonymised effectively.
- personal data which are processed for the purposes of management forecasting or management planning.
- access rights are modified for charities who are involved in education, health or social work: essentially, disclosure can be denied where the disclosure is likely to cause serious harm to the physical or mental health or condition of the data subject or any other person.

The Act also provides an employee with various remedies. The remedies include the right to ask for correction of data; the right to ask the Office of the Information Commissioner to take action; and the right to take an employer to court to rectify, block, erase or destroy those data which are inaccurate, or to access data. In very limited circumstances, an employee may be entitled to damages where distress is caused by a breach of the Act.

The Office of the Information Commissioner has the power to issue enforcement notices, where it considers that there has been a breach of one or more of the data protection principles.

Codes of Practice relating to data protection

The Office of the Information Commissioner (see website at www.dataprotection. gov.uk) has issued a Code of Practice on CCTV use and an (as yet incomplete) Employment Practices Data Protection Code of Practice. These Codes of Practice, whilst not having legal effect, are persuasive guidance for courts and tribunals in considering and finding what is good practice, and charities ignore their provisions at their peril. The Employment Practices Data Protection Code will finally have force once all its parts are issued as a whole. At the date of writing, three parts have been issued in what is expected to be their final form; whilst one other part has yet to be drafted. The date for publication of the Code is unclear.

Parts 1 and 2 of the Code are concerned with recruitment and selection, and employment records, respectively; Part 4 deals with medical data; Part 3 is entitled ‘Monitoring at Work’. Part 3 of the Code does not prohibit monitoring but it does set out some principles for monitoring. In particular, charities should note the following:

- Workers should be aware of the nature, extent and reasons for any monitoring.
- Rules and standards expected by the charity should be set out clearly in a policy, and workers should be aware of the policy.

Charities will also have to decide whether the benefit of monitoring justifies the adverse impact on employees. This is what is termed as an 'impact assessment' in the Code. An impact assessment will be a conscious decision-making process for each identifiable form of monitoring. The Code gives some indication of the factors to be considered and the weight to be given to each factor. Charities should record their decision-making in writing.

The Code also requires employers to have a written policy for the use of electronic communications – primarily email and internet use. The policy should make clear, amongst other things, the extent and type of private use allowed, the restrictions on material to be viewed or copied, and the purpose and extent of any monitoring.

14.2.3 Regulation of Investigatory Powers Act 2000

The RIPA 2000 came into force on 24 October 2000. There are also Regulations under the Act issued by the Department of Trade and Industry entitled the Telecommunications (Lawful Business Practice) (Interception of Communications) Regulations 2000 (known as 'the Lawful Business Practice Regulations').

The RIPA 2000 implements the Telecoms Data Protection Directive. It requires member states to ensure the confidentiality of communications on public telecommunications networks. It is specifically stated that this requirement extends to all types of electronic communication made 'by means of a public telecoms network' including, for example, fax and email. The requirement also extends to communications on private networks (eg office telephone networks or email systems), which will travel or have travelled on a public network. The key provisions of the RIPA 2000 are as follows.

- The Act creates offences of unlawful interception on public telecommunication systems, and a tort of unlawful interception on a private telecommunications system by the operator of that system.
- The Act authorises the interception of communications in all cases where the inceptor has reasonable grounds to believe that both the sender and the intended recipient have consented to the interception.
- The Act provides the Secretary of State with the authority in certain circumstances to intercept communication, by means of warrants issued to organisations such as security intelligence agencies and the police. In September 2003, it was proposed that the Charity Commission should be one of those organisations. The Act itself states it will be an offence for a person 'intentionally and without lawful authority ... to intercept, at any place in the United Kingdom, any communication in the course of its transmission by means of a private telecommunications system'. The definition of 'private telecommunications system' would include a charity's use of external

email and the internet. Interception of communications is authorised if the communication is one which (or which a person has reasonable grounds for believing) is both 'a communication sent by a person who has consented to the interception; and a communication the intended recipient of which has so consented'. Interception is also lawful where it is preventing a criminal act, for example, protecting a network against viruses or hackers, or combating or investigating fraud or corruption.

A charity is entitled to interfere with communications where that interference is lawful, and the Lawful Business Practice Regulations detail what is lawful. Interference by a charity can also be lawful where it occurs *with consent* which means that:

- the employer has the consent of the sender and the recipient to the interference; or
- the employer has reasonable grounds for believing that both the sender and the recipient consent to the interference.

A charity employer can lawfully intercept communications *without consent* where the interception is:

- to establish the existence of facts relevant to the business (eg keeping records of transactions and communications);
- to ascertain compliance with regulatory or self-regulatory rules or guidance (eg financial services call this monitoring);
- to ascertain or demonstrate standards, which are, or ought to be, achieved by persons using the system in the course of their duties (eg training);
- to prevent or detect crime (eg to prevent fraud or corruption or to detect inflammatory or obscene material);
- to investigate or detect unauthorised use of telecommunications systems: this can cover both internal use (eg monitoring to ensure that there is no breach by employees of the employer's procedures) or external use (eg to check for viruses or inflammatory content);
- to ensure the effective operation of the system.

It is, therefore, vital for charities to establish one of those reasons set out above – and to do so requires a clear identifiable decision-making process. Charities should consider dealing with these issues in a written policy.

The Lawful Business Practice Regulations also authorise businesses to monitor (but not to record without consent) in the following cases:

- to determine whether the communication is relevant to the business (the DTI's example is the opening of emails when staff are absent);
- monitoring communications to confidential anonymous counselling services or support helplines (eg monitoring calls to protect or support helpline staff).

These are the requirements for the monitoring to be lawful. The monitoring must be necessary and relevant to the business. This is quite a wide remit, but employers should act with circumspection. Also, employers must make every reasonable effort to inform those involved that interception may take place.

14.2.4 Other legal rights to privacy

Implied into all contracts of employment is a term that the employer will not act in any way which will undermine the trust and confidence between employer and employee. Invasion of an individual's privacy, for instance, in the form of monitoring hours of work, should be done carefully and with consideration.

Conversely, employees must act with loyalty to their employer. Furthermore, the concept of vicarious liability for the actions of its employees may make a charity liable for such things as racial harassment through email misuse. There are, therefore, compelling business reasons for employers to seek to protect themselves. However, in light of the comments in the draft Data Protection Code (see **14.2.2**), charities will need to establish those reasons carefully. The lines to be drawn must be capable of standing up to scrutiny.

14.3 PRACTICAL GUIDANCE – PRE-EMPLOYMENT MONITORING

14.3.1 References

As referred to in Chapter 5, employers often obtain references on applicants for employment. Charities will now need to have regard to the DPA 1998 and the Data Protection Code, as and when it is published.

The key standards in relation to pre-employment monitoring will be that the charity must:

- establish the specific business purpose for which the monitoring is to be introduced;
- assess the impact of the monitoring on the privacy, autonomy or other legitimate rights of staff (in making this assessment it is suggested that the relevant trade unions or other employee representatives be consulted); and
- not use the personal information collected for the purposes other than those for which the monitoring was introduced but inform the prospective employee that the reference will be sought.

Charities should have no difficulty in fulfilling the above standards but should remind themselves of these requirements when processing references.

14.3.2 Medicals

Again, the DPA 1998 and the Data Protection Code are pertinent. Charities need to consider the business needs for pre-employment vetting. Part 4 of the Code has not yet been issued (see **14.2.2**).

Charities should consider any specific business needs and then tailor the medical checks to identify any conditions which would impinge on business needs. This would also be an opportunity to consider what the employer could do by way of reasonable adjustments under the Disability Discrimination Act 1995 (DDA 1995). Should pre-employment vetting disclose a disability within the meaning of the Act, then charities need to be aware of their obligations under the Act.

Checks should be proportionate to the risks faced by an employer and should be likely to reveal information which would have significant bearing on the employment decision.

All charities also need to have regard to the HRA 1998 and the implications of obtaining information which may infringe the individual's right to a private life. The charity needs to consider whether the business need overrides the potential employee's rights.

Finally, charities must be aware that the medical information obtained will be sensitive personal data under DPA 1998 and will need to satisfy one of the requirements under the Act to use the information. Ideally, the charity should have the individual's express written consent to use the information.

14.3.3 Psychometric testing and other interviewing

The interviewing and shortlisting of job applicants is likely to involve the processing of personal data whether or not there is any automatic element. Shortlisting must therefore have regard to the data protection principles. This means that shortlisting must be fair to individuals, and employers should also be careful of any unwitting unlawful discrimination.

The DPA 1998 has a particular impact on the shortlisting process if it involves an element of automatic decision making. If a decision is based solely on the valuation of attributes of an applicant by automated means, there is a specific requirement that the applicant's interests must be safeguarded. Furthermore, an automated system must process information about individuals fairly. When using selection testing, a charity must note the following:

- it must use only methods of selection testing that can be demonstrated to produce results that are objective, consistent and fair;
- it must ensure that psychological and other complex tests are only used and interpreted by those who have received appropriate training;

– where the result of an automated test is used as a sole basis for a decision to reject an applicant or to take another significant decision in the recruitment process, the applicant must be informed that an automated system is used and be given the opportunity to make representations and consider these representations before a final decision is reached.

14.4 PRACTICAL GUIDANCE – MONITORING DURING EMPLOYMENT

Whilst charities will be operating in a wide range of fields which this chapter cannot consider in detail, certain monitoring may be considered necessary by employers during the course of employment, and below are some of the issues more likely to be relevant.

14.4.1 Policies

Charities should put in place policies regarding the use of equipment and software such as telephones and email or internet use. The policy should take account of the requirements of the Data Protection Code of Practice and should set out what monitoring of staff the charity undertakes.

14.4.2 Email/internet use

In light of the requirements under Part 3 of the Data Protection Code, and the RIPA 2000, a charity should consider its grounds for monitoring email and internet use very carefully. Charities will need, first and foremost, to establish the reasons for monitoring and consider whether they are entitled to interfere with the individual's expectation of privacy.

Charity employers will generally have good grounds for wanting to monitor – many issues ranging from the dissemination of obscenities and discriminatory material into the charity through to time-wasting can arise through email and internet use. Employers will be aware of the potential liabilities, discrimination claims, defamation claims, and workforce disharmony.

Accordingly, in limiting the legal risks, the charity must make staff fully aware of what is acceptable in the workplace. The issues that will need to be addressed are:

– what is acceptable (for instance, limited personal use or not, business use);
– what is not acceptable (for instance, visiting, displaying, printing, downloading or disseminating material from inappropriate websites or disseminating discriminatory material);
– details of what monitoring the charity employs;

- email etiquette; and
- enforcement – linked to the charity's disciplinary procedure.

These matters should be set out in a policy, as required by the Code. The policy must be publicised – most obviously through the induction process, but also by making it available generally.

14.4.3 Hours of work

Where an employee's hours of work are monitored, then consideration of the DPA 1998 and Part 3 of the Data Protection Code will again apply. Depending on the way the monitoring is carried out, there will need to be information about the monitoring; covert monitoring is very unlikely to be acceptable.

In this context, it should be noted that employers have a duty under the Working Time Regulations 1998 to keep such records as are sufficient to show compliance with these Regulations on working hours and night workers. Clearly, such information must be processed in accordance with the DPA 1998.

In the event of disciplinary action being taken on the basis of the information gathered on an employee's hours of work, care should be taken in relation to the relevance of the information, whether it is excessive.

14.4.4 Sickness/other absence

Great care must be taken in relation to sickness and other absence in light of the DDA 1995. Employers needs to consider whether the sickness or other absence is related to a disability.

Information in relation to a medical condition is sensitive personal data for the purposes of the DPA 1998. Accordingly, it must be processed in accordance with the conditions set out in the Schedule to the Act.

14.4.5 Medical testing

Medical testing includes drug testing, alcohol testing, HIV/AIDS testing and genetic testing, as well as more general medical testing.

Testing carried out manually, without a record being made of details, may not fall within the scope of the DPA 1998. However, if details are recorded or the analysis is undertaken by automated equipment, it is likely that personal data are processed within the terms of the Act.

Consideration should be given by employers to the Code of Practice. Medical testing is particularly intrusive and the information obtained will be sensitive personal data.

Furthermore, charities should be careful what they do with the information obtained, particularly with regard to the DDA 1995, the HRA 1998 and the DPA 1998.

14.5 PRACTICAL GUIDANCE – POST-EMPLOYMENT MONITORING

Once a contract of employment has terminated, for whatever reason, the individual has no special status with a charity, unless there are provisions in the contract which exist after termination of employment, such as restrictive covenants. Whilst a discussion of restrictive covenants is outside the scope of this chapter, charities will need to have regard to data protection implications of enforcing such covenants.

CASE STUDY

A charity which operates a homeless hostel has CCTV cameras at the front door to the hostel for security purposes. A manager becomes concerned about an employee's timekeeping whilst working night shifts and asks to see video footage from the camera.

Issues relating to CCTV coverage

As video tapes or other means of recording CCTV images will contain images of people's faces etc, they will therefore be recognisable, and therefore this information constitutes personal data within the meaning of the Data Protection Act 1998. The person who controls the CCTV is also deemed to be a data controller.

The Office of the Information Commissioner has published a Code of Practice in relation to CCTV. Fundamentally, the recorded images must be processed in accordance with the data protection principles.

The charity should consider the following actions for CCTV:

(1) establishing which particular person is responsible for the system;

(2) documenting the reasons for holding this system and assessing the appropriateness of the system in the light of those reasons;

(3) notifying the Information Commissioner it has this system and also the purpose for which the system is used;

(4) ensuring that the equipment monitors only those places which are necessary to comply with the given reason for having the equipment. On this basis, both the person responsible for the system, and those who operate the system must be aware of the reason for having the system;

(5) placing signs so that the public and employees are aware they are entering a zone which is covered by surveillance equipment. These signs should be clearly visible and legible to members of the public.

The code of conduct recommends a A4-sized sign at or near the entrance to the building identifying the fact that the surveillance is taking place, the identity of the person or organisation responsible for the CCTV, the purposes of the CCTV (eg crime prevention and public safety) and details of who to contact regarding it.

Any recorded information must not be retained except for the prevention or detection of criminal activity, and apprehension and prosecution of offenders. If there is a sound recording facility, this should not be used to record conversations between members of the public.

Images should not be retained for longer than necessary and should be erased regularly.

Access to recorded images should be restricted to those staff who need to have access in order to achieve the goal of maintaining security at the hostel. All access to the medium on which the images are recorded should be documented and disclosure of recorded images to third parties should only be made in limited and prescribed circumstances, eg for the prevention and detection of crime.

Any editing company in relation to a CCTV system is a data processor and therefore there should be a contractual relationship between the data controller and the data processor. The person responsible for the system should be aware of the data subject access rules.

As the CCTV camera is in use for security purposes, and if employees are unaware that their time-keeping could be monitored then, to use the footage to discipline a member of staff for time-keeping may be a breach of the DPA 1998 and the Codes of Practice.

Chapter 15

CONSULTATION OBLIGATIONS AND THE RELATIONSHIP WITH TRADE UNIONS

15.1 INTRODUCTION

The law in relation to trade unions can be broken down in to three general areas: representation, consultation and recognition. It is important that charity employers are aware of their employees' rights in respect of each of these areas since a failure to ensure that their rights are respected may prove expensive and time-consuming to remedy.

15.2 REPRESENTATION

Charities may be surprised to learn that there is in fact no general right for an employee to be represented by a trade union. Under UK law, it is the right of any employee to have membership of a trade union under UK law and it is unlawful to refuse a person employment because he or she is not a member of a trade union. However, the UK courts have held that a right to membership does not extend to the right to enjoy the benefits of being a member in the workplace. This means, rather strangely, that the employee can take advantage of the benefit of being a union member provided that this does not affect the employment relationship. This may change in the near future, as the European Court of Human Rights has held that it is a breach of the European Convention on Human Rights if the rights to membership of a trade union do not extend to a right to be represented in the workplace.

Workers have the specific right to be accompanied by a trade union official if they are called to attend a disciplinary or grievance hearing by their employer. However, as explained in Chapter 20, this is not a right to representation, and there is no right to formal involvement in individual workplace matters beyond formal disciplinary or grievance hearings.

15.3 CONSULTATION OBLIGATIONS

There is currently no general obligation on charities to consult on matters affecting their relationship with their employees. The only exceptions to this rule are particular rights provided by statute, which oblige an employer to consult on certain matters. These include situations where redundancies are proposed (discussed in detail in Chapter 25); where it is proposed that a transfer of the employer's staff under the Transfer of Undertakings (Protection of Employment) Regulations 1981 (TUPE) take place (see Chapter 26); and in relation to health and safety matters. The new Information and Consultation Directive will have far-reaching effects on the consultation obligations of all employers, including charities, once it comes into force. International employers are also obliged to set up and operate workplace consultation with Works Councils in certain circumstances.

In addition, many charities choose to recognise unions for the purposes of general consultation. This means that they will consult (seek the views of) trade unions on various issues: for instance, changing terms and conditions of employment, salaries and benefits, redundancies, TUPE transfers, for the purposes of health and safety, and restructures. Consultation, where the views of the union are considered in good faith, but agreement is not required, is not the same as negotiation, where consultation takes place and changes are agreed with the union. Any relationship between a union and a charity should be set out in a recognition agreement (see Practical Guidance at **15.8**).

15.4 HEALTH AND SAFETY CONSULTATION

Consultation on health and safety matters is complicated by the fact that there are two separate sets of regulations; which set applies will depend upon whether the employer has recognised a trade union.

If there is a recognised trade union, the union may appoint what are known as 'safety representatives', who are to be consulted by the employer. As far as is reasonably practical, the safety representatives must have been employed by the employer for at least 2 years before their appointment as safety representatives, or must have had at least 2 years' experience in similar employment.

If there is no recognised trade union, then the employer has a choice whether to consult with all the employees directly or, alternatively, with representatives elected by the employees. If representatives are elected by the employees, then they will be known as 'employee representatives'.

15.4.1 The duty to consult on health and safety

Safety representatives

The Health and Safety Act 1974 states that the duty upon the employer to consult with safety representatives is 'with a view to the making and maintenance of arrangements which will enable him and their employees to co-operate effectively in promoting and developing measures to ensure the health and safety at work of the employees and in checking the effectiveness of such measures'. Employers are obliged to consult with safety representatives with regard to the introduction of any measure at the workplace which may substantially affect the health and safety of the employees whom the safety representative represents. Any consultation must be made in good time. This means that the employer must provide sufficient time and information for the safety representatives to consult employees as necessary and to respond in reasonable detail to the issues being discussed.

If at least two safety representatives make a request in writing then an employer must set up a safety committee to review measures to ensure the health and safety at work of employees.

Safety representatives have the following rights and powers:

- to investigate potential workplace hazards;
- to examine causes of accidents and investigate health and safety complaints; and
- to make an inspection of the workplace, or any part of it, upon reasonable notice.

Employee representatives

The functions of employee representatives are not as broad as those of safety representatives. They have no power to carry out independent investigations of accidents or complaints of employees. They are entitled to make representations regarding potential hazards and on general matters affecting health and safety at work. They must also be consulted on any general matters affecting health and safety in the same way as safety representatives.

15.5 CONSULTATION ON REDUNDANCIES

There are two parallel sets of obligations which apply when a charity is required to make redundancies. One is the general obligation to consult with the individual concerned to establish if there are any alternatives to redundancy, and especially to consider suitable alternative employment. The other is the specific obligation to consult with 'appropriate representatives' of the affected employees if the charity is proposing to make 20 or more employees redundant at any establishment within a 90-day period. The charity must consult for at least 30 days if it makes between 20 and 99 employees redundant, and 90 days, if it proposes to make 100 or more redundant, in a 90-day period.

Appropriate representatives are either representatives of a recognised union which represents the affected employees or, if there is no relevant recognised union, elected representatives of the employees affected by the redundancy. These can be either those elected for a separate, but comparable, purpose which gives them implied authority to be consulted, or those elected specifically to be consulted regarding the redundancy programme.

The charity should disclose the following in writing to the appropriate representatives:

- the reasons for the proposals;
- the number and descriptions of the employees whom it is proposed to make redundant;
- the total number of employees of each description employed at the relevant establishment;
- the proposed method of selecting employees for redundancy;
- the proposed method of carrying out the dismissals; and
- the proposed method of calculating any payment in excess of the statutory minimum.

See Chapter 25 on redundancy for further detail regarding the consultation requirements.

15.6 CONSULTATION ON TUPE TRANSFERS

Charities increasingly find themselves involved in transfers of staff, whether upon the acquisition of care homes or on transferring part or all of their business to another charity. Such transfers may well invoke the TUPE provisions, which require employers to consult with any employees who are affected by the transfer. (See Chapter 26 for further details of the consultation requirements on a TUPE transfer.) Employers need to consider what is meant by consultation in this context; when the obligation will arise; and in relation to what areas there is a need for consultation.

15.7 WITH WHOM SHOULD CHARITIES CONSULT?

In both instances, where charities propose redundancies and/or a TUPE transfer, charities must consult with 'appropriate representatives'.

If a charity recognises a trade union for the purposes of staff consultation on collective bargaining, the union representatives will be the appropriate representatives. If the charity does not recognise a union for these purposes it must consult with elected representatives of the employees affected by the transfer. If such representatives have been elected for purposes other than TUPE, the charity must ensure that the representatives are able to deal with issues that might arise from the transfer. For example, a committee set up to deal with social functions is unlikely to have the implied authority to be consulted on the transfer. If necessary, a charity will have to set up elections of the representatives. DTI guidance suggests that this should be done by a secret ballot, and an employment tribunal has found that an employer putting in place less formal procedures for the election did not carry out the election with sufficiently high regard for its process.

If the employees fail to elect representatives, then the employer must supply all the affected employees with the required information and consult with them directly.

15.8 PRACTICAL GUIDANCE – HOW TO CONSULT

In order to avoid a claim being brought for failure to consult, a charity should do the following:

- ensure all information is disclosed formally, ie provided in writing to representatives;
- set up regular meetings with representatives and/or employees;
- keep accurate records of what is said at all meetings; and
- ensure that it responds to all representations made by employees or their representatives.

15.9 EUROPEAN WORKS COUNCILS

For those charities with employees in more than one country in Europe there may be an obligation to establish a European Works Council. The obligation arises when the following criteria are satisfied: the charity must employ at least 1,000 workers in the European Economic Area (EEA) (the EEA comprises the European Union plus Norway, Iceland and Liechtenstein), at least 150 workers must be employed in each of at least two member states; and the management of the charity must have received a written request from at least 100 employees or their representatives in two or more member states.

If a proper request is received, the charity should set up a special negotiating body (SNB) to represent the employees in setting up the Works Council. This should consist of employees from all the EEA states in which the charity operates. The SNB should then reach an agreement with the charity's management to establish a Works Council. The agreement must specify:

- which establishments of the charity are covered;
- the composition of the Works Council;
- the procedure for providing information and consultation;
- the venue, frequency and duration of meetings;
- the resources allocated to the Works Council; and
- the duration of the agreement and procedure for its renegotiation.

The Regulations that transposed the original European Directive into UK law do not state what areas of consultation must be included. However, they do set out a default position if the two parties are not able to come to an agreement regarding a Works Council. This states that the Works Council should be consulted with regard to, amongst other things:

- the structure, economic and financial situation of the business;
- the probable development of the business;
- the situation and probable trend of employment;
- introduction of new working methods;
- any transfers, mergers, cut-backs or closures of any establishments; and
- any collective redundancies.

Charities are obliged to allow members of SNBs or Works Councils reasonable time off to carry out their duties and it is unlawful to subject employees to any detriment due to their membership of, or attitude towards, an SNB or Works Council or the setting up of such a body.

15.10 INFORMATION AND CONSULTATION DIRECTIVE

In March 2002 the European Union passed a directive which will make it obligatory for all businesses, including charities, to consult their workforce on a range of matters.

15.10.1 New employee consultation law

The Information and Consultation Directive (ICD) increases the rights of employees to information and consultation in the event of a business reorganisation. The ICD defines information and consultation as including:

- information on recent and probable development of the undertaking's/establishment's activities or economic situation;
- information and consultation on the situation, structure and possible development of employment within the undertaking/establishment, and on any envisaged matters (for example, where there is a threat to employment);
- decisions likely to lead to substantial changes in work organisation or in contractual relations (for example, redundancy situations).

The draft regulations define an 'undertaking' as 'a public or private undertaking carrying out an economic activity, whether or not operating for gain'. The Government's view is that an undertaking is a legal entity such as a company, a co-operative or a partnership. Other types of organisations, such as charities, are not expressly included in the definition, but may well fall within it as the definition extends to non-profit-making organisations.

15.10.2 Negotiated agreements

Under the draft regulations, employees or their representatives may request information and consultation arrangements. To be valid, a request must be:

- made by 10% of employees in the undertaking/establishment, subject to a minimum of 15 and a maximum of 2,500 employees (in some cases the 10% threshold may not be achieved by a single request, but by combining two or more requests from different parts of the workforce);
- in writing and specify the date on which it was sent;
- sent directly to the employer, or anonymously to the Central Arbitration Committee (CAC) or a Qualified Independent Person, who will notify the employer that a request has been made.

Employers that are able to demonstrate that their existing arrangements have the support of employees (for example, through a formal arrangement with employee representatives or union officials) will be afforded special protection. Such companies will be entitled to hold a further ballot of the workforce (after the initial request from 10% of employees) in which 40% will have to vote in favour of a review.

15.10.3 Default model

The default provisions apply where the employer and negotiating representatives do not reach an agreement within 6 months (or such longer period as agreed). Under the model, the employer must provide the representatives with information on:

- the recent and probable developments of the undertaking's/establishment's activities and economic situation;
- the situation, structure and probable development of employment within the undertaking, in particular, where there is a threat to employment within the undertaking/establishment; and
- provisions likely to lead to substantial changes in work organisation or contractual relations, including redundancies.

The information must be given at such time, fashion, and with such content as is appropriate to enable the representatives to conduct an adequate study and prepare for consultation.

The new provisions will be enforced by a range of means, with a maximum fine of £75,000 depending on the size of the organisation.

Employee representatives will be entitled to paid time off work to fulfil their functions. Representatives are also protected against unfair dismissal, or suffering any other detriment, related to their performance as representatives.

15.10.4 Practical issues

The new obligations will be in addition to existing information and consultation procedures on collective redundancies and TUPE. There is, therefore, potentially an overlap between the new proposals and existing legislation.

It is important that all charities take steps to prepare for the introduction of the new law. The staggered implementation means that the laws will apply to:

- undertakings employing at least 150 employees from 23 March 2005;
- undertakings employing at least 100 employees from 23 March 2007;
- undertakings employing at least 50 employees from 23 March 2008.

If charities wish to avoid implementation of the default scheme they should agree their own arrangements or undertake action covered by the regulations before these dates.

15.11 COLLECTIVE BARGAINING RECOGNITION

'Collective bargaining' means negotiations relating to matters affecting the workplace: for example, terms and conditions of employment, allocation of work and work duties, discipline, pay and facilities for union officials. There is now a statutory recognition procedure, discussed in more detail below, which allows trade unions to apply for statutory recognition but only in relation to pay, hours of work and holidays.

Recognising a union for the purposes of collective bargaining is different from recognising a union for the purposes of consultation. When a charity recognises a union for collective bargaining it accepts that it will negotiate with the union with regard to any or some of the following: terms and conditions of employment, physical conditions of work, recruitment, dismissal and suspension, allocation of work, matters of discipline, union membership, facilities for union officials, and bargaining procedures.

Ideally, a recognition agreement should set out the purposes for which there is a collective agreement in place. Charities are free to recognise a union voluntarily and, if they do so, are free to agree with the union the basis of collective bargaining. They are also free to limit the areas which they wish the collective bargaining to cover; practically, this is a matter for negotiation.

15.11.1 Union right to request recognition

Unions now have the right to make a written request for formal recognition by an employer. If they are recognised, they will have the right to conduct collective bargaining on behalf of a particular group of workers.

Once a request has been made, the process of recognition moves along one of three different paths:

- the employer may either accept the request for recognition or inform the union that, although the request is rejected, it is prepared to negotiate. ACAS can be invited to assist in negotiations at any time;
- the employer can reject the request or fail to respond. If it does fail to respond, this will be deemed a rejection. The union can then apply to the CAC for statutory recognition;
- if negotiations fail, the union can apply to the CAC.

Role of the CAC

If the union applies to the CAC, the CAC must first decide what is an appropriate 'bargaining unit'. The bargaining unit is essentially a group of workers covered by a recognition agreement. It may cover the whole of the charity's undertaking or a particular site or sites where it has employees. If the CAC is satisfied that a union is likely to have the support of the majority of workers constituting the above unit, it will issue a declaration that the union is recognised for the purposes of collective bargaining. If it is not clear whether it will have the support of the majority of workers, the CAC can arrange for a secret ballet to be held. If the union is supported by a majority of those who vote and, further, this constitutes at least 40% of the bargaining unit, the CAC will issue a declaration that the union is recognised.

If a union is recognised, it has the right to enter into negotiations relating to pay, hours of work and holidays. The employer and the union may agree a recognition agreement setting out the method of collective bargaining but, if they fail to do so, there is a default agreement which sets out the method deemed to apply. Once a union is recognised, any application by another union for recognition will not succeed. As a result, the employer often decides that it is better to enter into a voluntary arrangement where it can have some control over the process and can agree what will be covered by the collective bargaining arrangement and how negotiations will operate.

The circumstances in which union applications to the CAC for compulsory recognition fail are rare. However, the CAC is unlikely to disrupt existing mechanisms for employee negotiation on pay, hours of work and holidays, and some charities have taken avoiding action by recognising staff councils and alternative employee representatives on these issues. This also addresses the needs of staff who wish for some organised staff representation, and anticipates the introduction of the Information and Consultation Directive.

15.11.2 Practical guidance

A charity's recognition agreement should include the following:

- a method of collective bargaining;
- facilities available to the union;
- areas to be covered by collective bargaining, eg hours of work, pay, holidays, etc;
- how the agreement can be terminated.

15.12 RIGHTS FOR TRADE UNION OFFICIALS AND MEMBERS

Trade union officials and members of recognised unions have the right to take time off to carry out their duties as officials or members. Officials of a trade union which is recognised by a charity are entitled to time off to undertake negotiations with the charity over areas covered by the recognition agreement. (There is no obligation to provide time off for officials of unrecognised unions.) They are also entitled to be consulted in relation to redundancies where it is proposed that 20 or more employees are to be made redundant and in relation to any transfers covered by TUPE.

Officials are entitled to reasonable time off for these duties. ACAS has issued a Code of Practice on Time Off for Trade Union Duties and Activities and this provides examples of when it would be appropriate to allow time. These include allowing time for the preparation of meetings to conduct collective bargaining, the meetings themselves, and also allowing time to meet employees covered by the recognition agreement to explain and discuss the outcome of the collective bargaining. The officials are entitled to be paid for any time off provided to carry out their duties.

Members of a recognised trade union are also entitled to take reasonable time off to take part in certain trade union activities during working hours. As with trade union officials, there are no obligations in relation to unrecognised unions. The ACAS Code of Practice lists examples of appropriate activities, which include attending workplace meetings to discuss outcomes of negotiations with their employer and meeting with full-time officials to discuss issues relevant to their workplace. Employees are expressly not entitled to reasonable time off to take part in industrial action. Employees are not entitled to be paid for any time off they are granted, although the charity may wish to consider paying their employees for attending workplace meetings to ensure that these meetings are fully attended.

A charity may wish to consider formalising its arrangements for time off either by introducing a policy to be used when requests are made to take time off or by reaching agreement with the recognised union. The agreement should specify the amount of time off permitted, when time off can be taken, if the time off will be paid and the procedure for requesting time off. The ACAS Code of Practice has further guidance on what should be included in an agreement and can be accessed at www.acas.gov.uk.

Charities should be aware that they cannot refuse any individual employment on the basis of his or her trade union membership and that any dismissal which is based on an employee's membership of a trade union or on his or her trade union activities will be automatically unfair. Employees are also entitled to complain to an employment tribunal if they suffer a detriment based on their membership of a trade union or their trade union activities. These conditions apply regardless of whether the charity recognises a trade union.

Chapter 16

THE WORK–LIFE BALANCE AND FAMILY FRIENDLY RIGHTS

16.1 INTRODUCTION

There is no legal obligation on employers to provide staff with a work–life balance. However, it is something that many employees aspire to. According to the DTI's Work–Life Balance Campaign (see www.dti.gov.uk/work-lifebalance) one in five employees want a better work–life balance, and would prefer working shorter hours to winning the lottery.

A survey of 508 employers by the DTI in 2002 shows a steep rise in the number of workers putting in long hours, with more working over 60 hours a week. The study also highlights concerns about long hours and illness. Almost 72% of highly stressed workers have no access to any formal flexible working practices, and 25% of workers are reported as wanting a better balance but think their career would suffer as a result.

For these reasons, a work–life balance is perceived as being in the public interest, and the Government has developed a number of initiatives to help working parents balance work and family life. The Secretary of State for Trade and Industry (Patricia Hewitt) has said that she 'is determined to get the merits of flexible working onto the business agenda – especially for the parents of young children'. The starting point is the family friendly provisions set out in the Employment Act 2002 (EA 2002) (which provisions came into force on 6 April 2003).

This emphasis on family friendly rights and giving a work–life balance to families is as far as the law intends to go at present; the law does not advocate a work–life balance for those without children. However, while there is no such legal right, there is law which seeks to protect staff who do not have the same benefits as full-time typical workers, and which addresses an employer's obligation to look after the health and safety of its employees.

Over the last 4 years the law has developed to give employment rights to employees who do not fall into the category of permanent '9 to 5' staff: in 1998, the Working Time Regulations were introduced, limiting the working week to 48 hours, giving holiday to all workers and providing for regular breaks. In 2000, the Part-time Workers (Prevention of Less

Favourable Treatment) Regulations were introduced, outlawing discrimination against part-time workers. In 2002, the Fixed-term Employees (Prevention of Less Favourable Treatment) Regulations took effect. These introduced new legislation for employees working on fixed-term contracts and outlined their rights against discrimination (see Chapter 7 for a full outline of these new regulations).

The theme running through this recent law is that women are the main beneficiaries; this is because it is accepted that women are those most likely not to work a regular '9 to 5' work pattern. The Labour Force Survey for 2002 records that 53% of the workforce now works part time, of which the greater part is women workers (44% of the workforce). The legislation is EU inspired, but supports the Government's commitment to a work–life balance by giving rights to women, who it is acknowledged undertake the majority of childcare. There is also existing law, which has been used by individual employees to support legislation for a work–life balance.

16.2 SEX DISCRIMINATION

The Sex Discrimination Act 1975 (as amended) (SDA 1975) outlaws direct or indirect discrimination between men and women in relation to employment, including engagement, promotion, transfer, training or dismissal (see Chapter 7). Examples of indirect discrimination have included discrimination against part-time workers (the majority of whom are women), age restrictions (for example, requiring that an applicant for a job involving travel must be aged between 17 and 30 is considered to be indirectly discriminatory against women because of family commitments) and the inclusion of a mobility clause in the employment contract, which allows an employer to relocate an individual at will (again, found to be indirectly discriminatory due to women's family commitments).

A part-time employee can bring a case under the SDA 1975 claiming that a requirement to work full time constitutes indirect sex discrimination. This has led to a revolution in the way that the courts view women returning from maternity leave to part-time work and women who wish to work flexibly.

The law states that, in bringing a claim for indirect sex discrimination, an employee will have to show:

- a neutral provision, criterion or practice imposed by the employer to provide full-time work;
- that such a provision, criterion or practice has a disparate effect on one sex (ie that a considerably larger proportion of people sharing the same sex or marital status as the employee cannot comply with the employer's requirement);

- that such a requirement is to the employee's detriment, and
- that the employer's requirement is unjustified.

In recent years it has become easier for staff who wish to return to work part time after maternity leave to show that an employer's requirement that they return full time or not at all will cause them detriment and does affect more women then men (as women carry out more childcare than men). An employer can therefore defend its position only by justifying the need to require the member of staff to work full time, which is difficult to do. Increasingly, it can only do so by showing one of the reasons set out at **16.8**.

16.3 EQUAL OPPORTUNITIES CODE OF PRACTICE

Employers should note that the Equal Opportunities Commission (EOC) Code recommends that employers should consider whether certain jobs can be carried out on a part-time or flexi-time basis (see para 43 of the Code).

16.4 WORKING PARENTS

Working parents are perhaps the most likely of all employees who wish to establish an equal balance between their work and home life. This is certainly the focus of the Government's drive to improve the work–life balance of employees.

16.4.1 Right to time off for ante-natal care

An employee is entitled not to have her request for paid time off to attend ante-natal care unreasonably refused. This can be a right that some charities perceive to be abused; it is difficult to judge how much time is reasonable for ante-natal care. The employee must provide the employer (if requested) with an appointment card for the ante-natal care, and proof of her pregnancy.

Managing such a request, therefore, is a matter of negotiation with the employee, considering the effects on the employer and the opportunities for the employee to attend alternative appointments.

From 6 April 2003, employees have enhanced rights, introduced to improve the work–life balance for parents.

16.4.2 Maternity leave and pay

The EA 2002 contains a number of improvements to the current arrangements for statutory maternity leave and pay, which took effect from 6 April 2003. In particular, the Act:

- gives Ordinary Maternity Leave (OML) of 26 weeks, and Additional Maternity Leave (AML) of 26 weeks, giving mothers up to one year's maternity leave (previously, women could take up to 40 weeks, of which 18 weeks were paid);
- extends the period during which Statutory Maternity Pay (SMP) is payable from 18 to 26 weeks;
- increases the standard rate of SMP to £100 per week, or 90% of weekly earnings if this is less than £100. In addition, a woman will also receive 90% of her average weekly earnings for the first 6 weeks for which SMP is payable (as now);
- increases the minimum period of notice that must be given to employers for maternity leave and SMP from 21 days to 28 days;
- allows an employer to offset its SMP payments against any payments due to be made to the Inland Revenue as may be prescribed in regulations issued by the Inland Revenue. Regulations may also provide for employers to apply for advance funding if the amount they are due to pay in SMP will exceed the tax, national insurance and other allowable payments due to be made to the Inland Revenue.

Most employers will be able to recover some of the amount paid by way of SMP, and small employers will be able to recover all SMP paid, plus an additional amount in compensation for the employer's share of national insurance contributions paid on SMP. As now, the meaning of 'small employer' will be defined in regulations by reference to the amount of contribution payments made by an employer.

During OML (the first 26 weeks) the position of the employee is protected so that the woman has a right to return to work to the same job and on the same salary as beforehand. At the end of AML, the woman will have a right to return on no less favourable terms.

The new law introduces a benchmark of minimum standards for maternity leave and pay. Many charities operate enhanced benefits in addition. It is important that this is reflected in relevant policies and procedures.

16.4.3 Protected rights

An employee who is pregnant or exercises her maternity rights is protected from dismissal or detriment. She will be deemed to have been automatically unfairly dismissed if her dismissal is connected to her pregnancy or maternity rights.

16.5 HEALTH AND SAFETY RIGHTS

A charity owes particular health and safety obligations to pregnant women. Ultimately, in some circumstances, it is within the law to suspend an employee from work for health and safety reasons when she is pregnant.

16.6 PATERNITY LEAVE AND PAY

From 6 April 2003, employees have had the right to take 2 weeks' paid paternity leave. The leave may be taken in respect of natural children and adopted children.

Regulations provide for paternity leave to be taken in a single block of one week or 2 weeks at the choice of the parent. The leave must be taken within a period of 56 days beginning on the date the child is born or placed for adoption.

A number of preconditions will have to be satisfied by parents who want to take paternity leave. Paternity leave is available only to an employee:

- who has, or expects to have, responsibility for the upbringing of a child, and who must either be the biological father of the child, or married to, or the partner of, the child's mother. 'Partner' is defined as a person, whether of a different sex or the same sex, who lives with the mother (or adopter) in an enduring family relationship but who is not a blood relative;
- for the specific purpose of caring for a newborn child and supporting the mother or for the purpose of caring for a child newly placed for adoption and supporting the adoptive parents;
- who gives to his or her employer a self-certificate of entitlement to leave; and
- who has continuous service with the same employer for at least 26 weeks by the 15th week before the child is expected to be born, or by the week in which an approved match with the child is made (a match occurs when an approved adoption agency matches an adopter with a child).

Employees taking paternity leave have important employment protection rights, similar to those of women taking maternity leave. Employees will have the right to return to work following a period of paternity leave and protection from detriment and unfair dismissal in connection with paternity leave.

The rate of statutory paternity pay is the lesser of £100 or 90% of the employee's average weekly earnings.

16.7 ADOPTION LEAVE AND PAY

The EA 2002 gives employees a new statutory right to 26 weeks' paid adoption leave, to be taken around the time of the adoption. In addition, an adopting parent will be entitled to take an additional 26 weeks' unpaid adoption leave, giving a total of up to one year's leave.

For the first time, this means that adopting parents can take the same leave as other parents: the principal carer can take adoption leave and his or her partner paternity leave.

Adoption pay will be paid at the same rates and administered in the same way as maternity pay.

16.8 STATUTORY RIGHT TO REQUEST FLEXIBLE WORKING

This is the biggest show of commitment from the Government to the work–life balance. From 6 April 2003, there is a new obligation on employers to consider a request by working parents with children aged up to 6 (or 18 if disabled) for flexibility in both the hours they work and their required place of work.

The law provides that the employee and employer follow a set procedure in considering the request to work part time, including a meeting on how to make the request. Failure to keep to the procedure gives rise to an employee's right to bring a claim for damages of up to 8 weeks' pay. The procedure is as follows:

(a) the charity receives an application for flexible working;
(b) within 28 days the charity must meet the employee to discuss the application;
(c) the charity must notify the employee of the decision within 14 days of the meeting;
(d) if rejected, the employee has 14 days to appeal in writing, setting out the grounds of appeal;
(e) within 14 days of receipt of the appeal, the charity must hold a meeting with the employee;
(f) the charity must notify the employee of the decision of the appeal in 14 days.

An employer can refuse the request for one of the following reasons:

- the burden of additional costs;
- detrimental effect on ability to meet customer demands, quality and/or performance;
- inability to reorganise work amongst existing staff;
- inability to recruit additional staff; and
- planned structural changes.

It is automatically unfair for an employer to dismiss an employee who has made a request to work flexibly for that reason.

It will be interesting to see how the law changes to reflect the apparent needs of society to work more flexibly. Courts have previously considered justifications given by employers refusing to allow employees to work part time under case law for sex discrimination and have generally found in favour of the employees – if those decisions are followed here, the reasons for refusing requests to work part time will be considered very restrictively by the courts. Tribunals have also considered the reasons for refusal when looking at justification for indirect discrimination.

16.9 PARENTAL LEAVE

Parents also have a right to unpaid leave to maintain a work–life balance. Every parent with one year's service is entitled to a total of 13 weeks' unpaid parental leave for each child under the age of 5. An employee is entitled to take time off to care for his or her child if:

- she or he has or expects to have responsibility for a child;
- the leave is for the purpose of caring for that child;
- she or he is the parent of a child born on or after 15 December 1999, who is under 5 years old; or she or he is an adoptive parent, who, on or after 15 December 1999 has had a child placed with him or her for adoption, or she or he is the parent of a child entitled to a disability living allowance who is under 18; or
- she or he is the parent of a child born between 15 December 1994 (or 15 December 1981 if the child is disabled) and 14 December 1999, as long as the leave is taken before 31 March 2005.

A person has responsibility for a child if either she or he has parental responsibility under the Children Act 1989 (ie the mother and father if the father is married to the mother, or the father is not married to the mother but is registered on the birth certificate).

The leave can be taken in tranches of 4 weeks at a time; as a result of this, and the leave being unpaid, very few employees take the benefit. It is usually taken by the mother after the end of maternity leave.

16.10 TIME OFF FOR DEPENDANTS

An employee can also take time off to care for or to make arrangements for the care of a dependant where the dependant is ill, gives birth or dies, or where there is an unexpected incident involving a child at school.

A dependant is a spouse, child, parent, person living in the same household as the employee (other than as an employee, tenant or lodger). The time off is unpaid although many charities will pay a few days as a benefit each year. The employee is allowed a reasonable amount of time off and the employee who takes time off is protected against dismissal and detriment. It may be reasonable to refuse time off if the employee's spouse or partner is not working and is available to take care of the child, although this depends on the individual circumstances of the employee (rather than the charity).

Similarly, recent case law has stressed that the time off is to make arrangements for the care of a dependant, not to undertake the care.

CASE STUDY

Guidance to an employer of a new parent

Zed charity employs Anna and Ben as support workers; they are long-term employees. They are partners and Anna is pregnant with their first child. The baby is due on 1 September 2003. The couple want to share the responsibility of looking after the baby and maximise their rights to time off work. They ask for advice on what their rights are.

Anna will be entitled to one year's maternity leave. The first 6 weeks are paid at 90% of her gross weekly pay, and the next 20 at £100 per week. She is also entitled to 20 days' holiday per year paid at her normal salary, so she decides to take the first 4 weeks of her absence as holiday, from 1 August 2003. The baby, Charlie, is born on 1 September 2003.

Ben is entitled to 2 weeks' paternity leave at £100 per week, which he must take by 25 October 2003. He can take it in two tranches of one week each, and does so, taking one week when the baby is newborn, and the second on 21 October 2003.

Anna is on maternity leave until 31 August 2004. Under her contract she has paid holiday during her maternity leave. She therefore decides to take the holiday she has accrued to date in 2004 during September, and so has a period of 3 weeks' fully paid holiday to take from 1–21 September 2004.

She then decides that, despite giving notice of her return to work, she would rather stay at home with Charlie for some more time. She therefore takes her parental leave of one month's unpaid leave from 21 September 2004 to 21 October 2004. Ben is keen to take his parental leave at the same time, but they cannot afford to have both parents at home at the same time. So, instead, Ben takes annual leave from 24 October 2004 until 14 November 2003.

During the autumn, Charlie develops a series of colds and coughs, and Anna and Ben do not feel they can leave him at the nursery as planned. Therefore, Ben applies for his parental leave of one month's unpaid leave from 15 November to 14 December 2004.

Anna then re-evaluates her priorities and decides they have managed on a lower income for the last year and that she would rather be at home with Charlie some of the time. She therefore applies to work part time, 3 days a week. Her request for a change to her hours is a request under the Employment Act 2002 to work flexibly, which the charity must take seriously and consider. In the event, it feels able to grant her request for a jobshare and advertise for another person to work with her in a sharing role, 2 days a week. The charity is able to recruit someone on that basis, and Anna commences working 3 days a week from 1 January 2005.

Chapter 17

TIME OFF FOR PUBLIC DUTIES

17.1 INTRODUCTION

Employers increasingly face pressure to encourage flexibility in the workplace. This inevitably means a relaxation of old-fashioned time keeping. As such flexibility increases, managing employees' out-of-work activities becomes more important. Without looking at the move to work flexibly as part of a work–life balance (which is covered in Chapter 16), there are many other sorts of out-of-work activities, giving employees varied rights to time off to pursue them.

This chapter considers:

- rights of employees to take time off to carry out specific activities;
- instances where employees' out-of-work activities conflict with their role in the workplace.

17.2 EMPLOYEES' RIGHTS TO TAKE TIME OFF WORK

17.2.1 Public duties

Certain classes of employees may take time off work in order to pursue the following public duties:

- acting as a Justice of the Peace;
- acting as a member of:
  - a local authority;
  - a statutory tribunal;
  - a police authority;
  - a board of prison visitors or a prison visiting committee;
  - a relevant health body;
  - a relevant education body; or
  - the Environment Agency or the Scottish Environment Protection Agency.

Certain classes of employment are excluded from the right to time off for public duties. These are as follows:

- the armed forces;

- overseas employment (other than certain employment in territorial waters or on the continental shelf);
- share fishermen;
- merchant seamen;
- police service.

The right is to take time off to carry out specific duties. It is not a right to take paid time off work, although many employers do choose to pay their employees for carrying out public duties.

Specific purposes

A Justice of the Peace is to be allowed time off 'for the purpose of performing any of the duties of his office', including:

- sitting in court session;
- making visits to penal institutes;
- attendance at training sessions;
- extra commitments such as membership of a Probation Committee or a Juvenile Court panel.

People carrying out the other public duties listed above can do so:

- to attend a meeting of the body or any of its committees or sub-committees;
- to carry out activities approved by the body for the purpose of discharging the function of the body to which they belong or of any of its committees or sub-committees.

'Approved' activities means that the public body has the power to decide for itself which of its activities it would classify as duties. The only way in which an employer can challenge a decision made by such a public body will be if the body has acted beyond the powers which have been given to it.

Example of public duties

An employee who was leader of the opposition on a council was involved in planning the arrangements for a royal visit and other similar civic occasions. An employment tribunal found that these activities fell within the definition of public duties.

17.2.2 How much time off is allowed?

The law is unhelpful in saying that the amount of time off, the occasions on which it is to be permitted and the conditions under which the time off may be taken are defined as 'those that are reasonable in all the circumstances'.

In analysing this the employer must take the following factors into account:

- how much time off is required for the performance of the duties of the office or as a member of the body in question, together with how much time off is required for the performance of the particular duty. The Justices of the Peace Act 1997 provides that a Justice of the Peace has to be provided with training courses. Thus, although there is no specific right to time off for training, a Justice of the Peace shall be treated as acting in the performance of his or her duties;
- the circumstances of the employer's business and the effect of the employee's absence on the running of that business.

Where the employer only allows the employee to rearrange his or her duties in such a way as to allow lost time to be made up, the employer is not allowing the employee the right to time off work.

Examples

- An employee argued unsuccessfully that 104 days' absence each year in addition to a week for conferences was not adequate to cover his duties on four separate local authorities.
- In another case, an employee claimed 124 days off a year as he wanted to take on extra duties for a local council and a planning board. This would constitute more than half his working hours. The tribunal found that, taking into account his role in his employer's business, it was unreasonable to expect the employer to allow any more than 45 days' absence.
- It is possible that personal reasons may make extra time off reasonable.
  - A councillor who worked some distance from the council offices had to rely on public transport for which, the tribunal held, a reasonable time allowance should be made.
  - An employer could not reasonably refuse to increase an employee's yearly allowance of 18 days' time off as the employee had become the leader of the opposition on a council.
- The tribunal will also consider the amount of time the employee has taken off already in order to determine the reasonableness of the request. It is possible that the tribunal might find that an employee requiring a large amount of absence will be expected to minimise the number of days taken off work by using some of his or her holiday entitlement.
- An employee, a qualified shift supervisor without whom no productions could take place, was also a magistrate. In addition, the company was in a bad financial position. The tribunal rejected the employee's claim for 7 days off work a year but thought that 5 days a year should be allowed, as this would allow the employee to perform the minimum level of duties required of any magistrate.

- Where an action by the teaching unions was causing a shortage of supply teachers to provide cover, an employee claimed that he had been unreasonably refused time off to attend his duties as a local councillor, but this claim was rejected by the tribunal. It was held that, given the circumstances, the amount of time off that was reasonable was necessarily determined by the availability of cover and the adequacy of the advance warning so that the cover could be arranged.

17.3 DISMISSAL FOR TAKING TIME OFF

An employer has the right to discipline an employee who abuses his or her right to time off, eg by taking time off without permission. If the employee's behaviour persists then he or she may end up being fairly dismissed.

The Local Government and Housing Act 1989 gives guidance on what might be reasonable for local authority employees, and provides that local authority employees cannot be granted more than 208 hours' paid time off per annum for the performance of duties as elected councillors.

17.4 REMEDIES AVAILABLE TO THE EMPLOYEE

If an employer denies an employee the right to take time off for public duties, the employee is entitled to present a complaint to an employment tribunal.

The complaint must be presented:

- within 3 months of the date on which the failure complained of occurred; or
- within such further period as the tribunal considers reasonable where it is satisfied that it was not reasonably practicable for the complaint to be presented before the end of the period of 3 months.

17.4.1 Compensation

The tribunal may make an award of compensation to be paid by the employer to the employee if it finds the employee's complaint well founded.

The right is a right to take time off for public duties and not a right to paid time off.

The sum payable will be an amount which the tribunal considers just and equitable. The tribunal will have regard to the employer's default in failing to permit time off and the loss sustained by the employee which is attributable to the matters to which the complaint relates.

In practice there should be a correlation between the amount of compensation awarded and the amount which the employee might have been expected to receive for the period for which time off is found to have been wrongly refused.

17.5 JURY SERVICE

All persons between the ages of 18 and 70 can be called up for jury service, except specific persons including the judiciary, barristers, solicitors, the clergy, persons with a mental disorder and those with serious criminal convictions. Any person who has in the last 10 years served any part of a sentence of imprisonment, youth custody or detention, been detained in a young offenders' institution, had a suspended sentence of imprisonment, or been the subject of an order for detention or a community service order cannot be called as a juror. The same is true of any person who at any time in the last 5 years has been placed on probation.

If employees are otherwise able to show 'good reason' why they cannot attend, they can apply to the Jury Summoning Officer to have their jury service deferred or be excused.

An employer is not under any legal obligation to pay an employee for time spent away from work on jury service, although it is common for most employers to do so. The Jurors' Allowances Regulations 1978 entitle jurors to receive some compensation from the court.

A 'good reason' to defer jury service may be the needs of the employer. If a 'good reason' cannot be found, the employer is under a duty to release the employee to carry out jury service. To dismiss or threaten to dismiss an employee because he or she has been summoned to carry out jury service is a contempt of court.

17.6 OTHER COURT ATTENDANCE

There are other occasions when an employee may be asked to attend the court, eg in the capacity of a witness. There is no legal obligation on the employer to release the employee for this purpose, although a witness summons may be issued requiring the employee's presence. An employer refusing to acknowledge the witness summons is in danger of being held in contempt of court.

17.7 PENSION FUNDS TRUSTEES

An employee who is a trustee of a relevant occupational pension scheme or an employee who is director of a company which is a trustee of the relevant occupational pension scheme has the right to paid time off during working hours.

The right to time off can be taken for the purpose of:

- performing any of the employee's duties as trustee, or
- undergoing training relevant to the performance of those duties.

The only employees for whom this right is not available are members of the armed forces, and House of Lords and House of Commons staff.

The amount of time off which an employee is to be permitted to take, the purposes for which this can be taken, the occasions on which it may be taken and any conditions subject to which time off may be taken, are those that are 'reasonable in all the circumstances'.

In determining the reasonableness of the time taken, the following factors should be considered:

- how much time off is required for the performance of the duties of a trustee of the scheme and the relevant training, and how much time off is required for performing the particular duty or undergoing the particular training; and
- the circumstances of the employer's business and the effect of the employee's absence on the running of that business.

17.7.1 Payment for time off

The employee has the right to receive payment for the time taken off. This right to payment is as follows:

- where the employee's remuneration does not vary according to the amount of work done, the right to receive the amount which would have been paid had the employee worked for the whole of the time taken off;
- where the employee's remuneration does vary according to the amount of work done, the employee will receive an amount which is calculated by reference to the average hourly earnings for that work;
- where the employee's average hourly earnings cannot be calculated or fairly estimated, the average of the employees in comparable employment with the same employer can be used;
- if there are no such employees, a figure of average hourly earnings which is reasonable in all the circumstances will be used.

The employee can present a complaint to the employment tribunal for a finding that the employer has behaved unreasonably and/or for an award of compensation. A complaint must be presented within 3 months from the date on which the failure occurred, or within such further period as the tribunal considers reasonable once it has satisfied itself that it was not reasonably practicable for the employee to present the complaint within the time-limit.

17.8 TRADE UNION OFFICIALS

A union official (an employee who is a representative of union members in the workplace) may claim time off either to carry out certain official duties or to undergo certain training:

- negotiations with the employer related to or connected with collective bargaining for which the trade union is recognised by the employer;
- the employee's performance of any function related to or connected with any matters which the employer has agreed may be performed by the trade union.

The training an official is allowed to undertake must be training in aspects of industrial relations which are relevant to the carrying out of duties and approved by the Trade Union Congress or by the independent trade union of which he or she is an official.

Where an official wants to attend a training course, management should be given as much notice as possible (at least a few weeks) of the time, purpose, place and duration, and the employer should be supplied with a syllabus or prospectus indicating the contents of the course.

The time off must be reasonable in all the circumstances. The employee is entitled to be paid for time off work. If the employee is paid on a time rate, he or she will get the full pay that would have been earned if he or she had worked the hours in question. If the employee is on a payment by results contract, the employee's average pay packet for the relevant hours should be paid. In a case where there are no comparators, the average will be a fair estimate.

An employee can present a claim to a tribunal for a declaration that his or her employer has failed to allow the employee time off and/or compensation. The complaint must be brought within 3 months, ending with the date on which the failure occurred. The tribunal has a discretion to extend this time-limit if it wishes.

17.9 TRADE UNION MEMBERS

A union member has a right to claim time off work to participate in union activities. There is one exception to this: an employee is not entitled to claim time off work to participate in a strike or other industrial action. There is, therefore, no right to claim time off for union activities which consist of industrial action. This will include activities in contemplation of or furtherance of a trade dispute.

Activities include the following:

- attending workplace meetings;
- consulting union officials;

- voting in union ballots;
- voting in union elections.

This right is available to a member of an independent trade union which is recognised by the employer.

An employee is allowed such time off as is reasonable but there is no statutory right to be paid for the time off work. There may, however, be a contractual right to be paid for it. The ACAS Code recommends that an employer should consider paying 'in certain circumstances, for example to ensure that workplace meetings are fully representative'.

An employee can present a claim to a tribunal that his or her employer has not permitted the requested time off. The tribunal can make a declaration that the employer has failed to allow the employee time off to which he or she was entitled and/or compensation. The complaint must be brought within 3 months, ending with the date on which the failure occurred. The tribunal has a discretion to extend this time-limit if it wishes.

17.10 UNION LEARNING REPRESENTATIVES

As part of the Government's commitment to education there is a new right for employees who are the Union Learning Representatives (ULRs) in the workplace.

A union gives the employer notice of this appointment and the training condition being met, and the ULR is entitled to paid time off work for:

- analysing learning or training needs;
- providing information and advice about learning or training matters;
- arranging learning or training;
- promoting the value of learning or training;
- consulting the employer about carrying on such activities;
- preparation of any of the above activities;
- undergoing relevant training to carry out the above tasks.

17.11 EMPLOYEE REPRESENTATIVES ON REDUNDANCY AND TUPE

An employer who is proposing collective redundancies or to transfer staff under TUPE must in both cases provide information to and consult with 'appropriate representatives', which can be either:

- union representatives; or
- employee representatives; or
- employees.

An employee representative is an employee of the employer who has been elected by his or her fellow workers either for general purposes or for specific purposes such as being consulted about redundancies or being informed or consulted about a transfer of undertakings.

An employee is entitled to whatever time off is reasonable in the circumstances. The starting point for determining how much time off is reasonable is to assess the needs of the job as representative or candidate and then how much time off the employee needs to discharge properly his or her functions. In addition, the employee can only take time off that is reasonable for his or her employer to allow.

An employee who is an employee representative, or is a candidate for election as an employee representative, is entitled to paid time off in order to carry out his or her duties. This time will be paid time only if it falls within the hours that the employee is required by contract to be at work. There is no contractual right for an employee to claim pay for any duties which have been performed during his or her free time. The employee has the right to be paid at the appropriate hourly rate. This is calculated by using the employee's week's pay and his or her normal working hours. These are calculated as follows.

- The calculation date for a week's pay is the day on which the time off was taken.
- The appropriate hourly rate for an employee whose normal working hours are regular is the amount of the week's pay divided by the number of hours worked.
- The appropriate hourly rate for an employee whose normal working hours vary is the average number of normal working hours taken over a 12-week period. If the employee has not been employed for a 12-week period, the average will be the employee's expected average, or the average of employees in comparable employment.

An employee can present a complaint to the tribunal that his or her employer has unreasonably refused time off. The tribunal can award payment which is reasonable in the circumstances, which can be in addition to pay received, effectively doubling pay.

The complaint must be made within 3 months beginning with the day on which it is alleged that time off should have been allowed or was taken. The tribunal has a discretion to extend this time-limit.

17.12 STUDY/TRAINING TIME FOR YOUNG PEOPLE

Employees can take time off work for study and training where they are:

- aged 16 or 17;
- are not receiving full-time secondary or further education,

and have not attained the standard of achievement which has been prescribed by regulations made by the Secretary of State, which is at the time of writing:

- grades A to C in five subjects in GCSE examinations;
- SQA Standard Grades at grades 1 to 3 in five subjects;
- one Intermediate level GNVQ or one GSVQ at level 2;
- one NVQ or SVQ at level 2;
- one BTEC First Certificate awarded by the Edexcel Foundation;
- one BTEC First Diploma awarded by the Edexcel Foundation;
- the City and Guilds of London Institute Diploma of Vocational Education at Intermediate level; or
- 16 SQA unit or assessment credits, at least 8 of which are at Intermediate 2 or above and the remainder at Intermediate 1.

The right to time off work is also available to 18-year-olds who are undertaking study or training leading to relevant qualification and who began the study or training before the age of 18. Members of the armed forces are excluded from this right.

The employee has a right to take time off during his or her working hours (with the employer's permission) in order to undertake study or training leading to an external qualification which would contribute to the attainment of the standard prescribed above and would be likely to enhance the employee's employment prospects. An employer must ensure that the amount of time off, the occasions on which the employee is allowed to take time off, and any conditions that may be imposed are such as are reasonable in the circumstances.

The employee has the right to be paid whilst undertaking study or training and will be entitled to be paid at the appropriate hourly rate for the time taken off. This rate is calculated at one week's pay divided by the number of normal working hours in a week for that employee when employed under the contract of employment in force on the day when the time off is taken.

An employee can complain to a tribunal for a declaration that the employer has unreasonably refused to permit time off and/or compensation equivalent to the pay the employee would have received for the time off which was not permitted. An employee can also complain that the employer has failed to pay the whole or part of the remuneration which the employee is entitled to. In this situation the tribunal will award compensation equivalent to the amount to which the employee is entitled.

Any complaint must be brought within 3 months from the date upon which time was taken off or should have been permitted. The tribunal has a discretion to extend this time-limit.

17.13 MEMBERS OF EUROPEAN WORKS COUNCILS

There is a right to time off work for participation in a European Works Council and related activities. Employees who have entered into or worked under a contract of employment are eligible. Employees in Crown employment, the armed forces and the police service are excluded.

An employee will be entitled to take time off during working hours in order to perform functions as one of the following:

- a member of a special negotiating body (established for the purposes of negotiating with central management an agreement for a European Works Council or an information and consultation procedure);
- a member of a European Works Council;
- an information and consultation representative; or
- a candidate in an election in which any person elected will, on being elected, be such a member or representative.

The right to take time off is limited to reasonable time. An employee who is permitted to take time off is entitled to be paid remuneration by his or her employer for the time taken off at the appropriate hourly rate.

An employee may complain that the employer has not allowed him or her to take time off and/or claim compensation. The complaint must be brought within 3 months of the date upon which the time off was taken or should have been permitted. The tribunal has a discretion to extend this time-limit.

17.14 TERRITORIAL ARMY RESERVE FORCES

An employee may wish to take time off work in order to participate in territorial army duties. There are no minimum statutory provisions for time off work to participate in territorial army duties. Rights to time off will depend on the terms of the contract of employment. There is no obligation on an employer to allow an employee to take time off work during working hours for territorial army duties. However, as a matter of good industrial relations practice, a charity should, where practicable, be flexible in terms of permitting annual leave between employer and employee so that territorial army duties or training courses can be attended.

There is also no statutory right to be paid for time taken off work to participate in territorial army duties.

In a case where reservists are formally called up to serve in the armed forces they gain protection from the Reserve Forces (Safeguard of Employment) Act 1985 (RF(SE)A 1985). The Act provides that an employer must re-employ an employee if he or she applies for reinstatement after the military service has ended.

The re-employment must be in the occupation in which the employee was last employed before the full-time service and on terms and conditions not less favourable than those which would have been applicable had the employee not undertaken full-time service.

If reinstatement is not reasonable and practicable, the employee must be offered the most favourable occupation, on the most favourable terms and conditions as are reasonable and practicable in the particular case. This right is not available to volunteers, but rather only to those who are formally called up as reservists.

Example

In the case of *The Meteorological Office v Mr HR James* (unreported) 23 February 2001, EAT, the applicant was offered a casual appointment at the Meteorological Office and was then commissioned in the Operations Support Flight Operations branch of the RAF Reserve in the rank of Flight Lieutenant. He was called out for short intervals, authorised under the Reserved Forces Act 1996. The applicant's employment with the Meteorological Office was due to terminate in September 1999. The applicant hoped that his employment would continue beyond this date but was unsuccessful at interview and was told that his employment would cease. He applied under s 8 of the RF(SE)A 1985, which provides for an employee to claim against the denial of rights by an employer. The applicant's case failed as he was claiming a right to reinstatement which arises under RF(SE)A 1985 only, and his application did not comply with the machinery of the Act.

The application for reinstatement must be:

- made in writing;
- made by the applicant or some person acting with his or her authority;
- made during the period beginning with the end of the applicant's whole-time service and ending with the third Monday after the end of the applicant's whole-time service.

Section 8 of the RF(SE)A 1985 provides that a person who has:

- entered on a period of whole-time service; and
- claimed that he or she has rights under the sections of the Act which have been denied,

may, within the time-limits set, apply to a Reinstatement Committee for the determination of any question relating to his or her rights.

Section 9 of the RF(SE)A 1985 provides for an appeal mechanism.

17.15 PRACTICAL GUIDANCE

A reasonable charity will be mindful of its obligations to participate in civic life but must be aware of the issues that will arise to where these duties conflict with working practices. How does a charity manage that conflict?

The first step is for a charity to know its obligations to staff. An employee can, in every case, enforce his or her rights to time off. An employer should always consider a request before refusing time off.

Each request should be considered individually. Case law shows that an employee's request for time off must be considered in the light of its own circumstances. However, by considering a request on a case-by-case basis, a charity employer risks treating individuals inconsistently and potentially unfairly. In some circumstances it may be appropriate for the charity employer to consider a blanket policy treating employees, for instance, over a certain grade, or at specific times of the year, in the same way. However, this may not be acceptable in some circumstances: for instance, on an application for exemption from jury service. It is therefore sensible for the charity to put in place a policy setting out the process by which each request is considered.

The requests should be considered by the same person, such as the HR officer, to ensure consistency.

The application must set out the need and circumstances involved.

Consideration should be given to offering staff paid time off, even where there is no statutory right to pay.

17.16 TIME OFF FOR POLITICAL AND RELIGIOUS AFFILIATIONS

The law governing this area is the Human Rights Act 1998 (HRA 1998) which gives statutory effect to the European Convention on Human Rights, the relevant Articles of which are, in particular, Art 10 which provides for freedom of expression, and Art 9 which provides for freedom of thought, conscience and religion. The HRA 1998 directly applies to 'public authorities' which will not necessarily include charities. Employees of charities can, however, rely on the HRA 1998, when making other claims, as the courts must interpret all claims in light of the HRA 1998.

Workers will also have rights, from late 2003, not to be discriminated against on the grounds of religion or belief (see Chapter 7). Charities must therefore treat staff equally in allowing them time off for religious observance.

Example

The balancing act required by virtue of the HRA 1998 has previously been considered with reference to the European Convention on Human Rights. The relevant case was *Van der Heijden v the Netherlands* [1986] 8 EHRR CD 279.

The applicant was employed by an immigration foundation in Holland. The applicant was dismissed on the grounds of his membership of a political party which had a policy of hostility toward the presence of immigrant workers in the Netherlands. The Commission held that the employer's interference with the applicant's freedom of expression was justified as it was reasonable for it to have a discretion regarding the composition of its staff. In addition, the duties which the applicant had to carry out meant that it was reasonable for the employer to take into account the potential adverse effects which his political activities might have on the employer's reputation. This was an issue, particularly given the client group for which the employer catered.

Chapter 18

HEALTH AND SAFETY

18.1 INTRODUCTION

The law places onerous obligations upon all employers (including charities), persons in control of workplaces, employees and other categories of obligation holders to ensure that other persons are not exposed to a risk of illness or injury as a result of work practices.

It is important for a charity to understand how its health and safety obligations arise and what can be done to fulfil these obligations and keep workers safe.

18.2 SOURCES OF SAFETY OBLIGATIONS

There are three main sources of health and safety obligations:

- the duty of care owed by employers to their employees;
- contractual obligations, such as contracts of employment with individual employees and agreements with sub-contractors which include health and safety obligations; and
- the Health and Safety at Work Act 1974 (HSWA 1974) and the regulations made under it ('the Regulations').

The HSWA 1974 and the Regulations are the most important source of health and safety obligations.

18.3 DUTY OF CARE

Every member of society (including a charity employer) is under a general duty to take reasonable care in doing or not doing something, where it is reasonably foreseeable that injury may be caused to another person or category of persons. Charities owe a duty of care to employees, workers, contractors, visitors and service users. This will include volunteers and self-employed consultants.

An employer's duty of care to employees includes the duty to provide:

- safe premises;
- a safe system of work;
- safe plant and equipment; and

- competent and safe fellow workers.

If a charity breaches its duty of care obligations, it can be sued and ordered to compensate any person who suffers illness, injury or loss as a result of the breach.

18.4 CONTRACTUAL OBLIGATIONS

There is an implied term in every employment contract that the employer should take reasonable care for the health and safety of its employees. Contracts of employment may also provide that employees need to comply with certain health and safety practices, such as wearing safety goggles or following kitchen safety guidance.

Other types of contracts, such as those used when engaging contractors and sub-contractors, often include health and safety obligations.

If contractual health and safety obligations are breached, a person can be sued and ordered to compensate the other party to the contract, if that party suffers illness, injury or financial loss as a result of the breach.

18.5 HEALTH AND SAFETY AT WORK ACT 1974

18.5.1 General obligations

The HSWA 1974 places broad general obligations upon employers, employees and persons in control of a workplace to ensure health and safety. These obligations are similar in some respects to the duty to take reasonable care.

Breaching these obligations is a criminal offence. The onus lies upon the prosecution (being the Health and Safety Executive (HSE) or relevant local authority) to prove that the obligation holder has failed to ensure health and safety. Often this will not be difficult, particularly where there is a visible injury as a result of a work accident. However, the prosecution need only show that the obligation holder created a *risk* of injury for a prosecution to be successful.

The key general obligations for charities are set out below.

Employers

Under the HSWA 1974, employers must:

- ensure the health, safety and welfare of employees at work, insofar as this is reasonably practicable;
- conduct the business in such a way as to ensure that persons other than employees are not exposed to risk, insofar as this is reasonably practicable.

The employer's general duty is broad enough to cover the health and safety of employees, contractors, workers, service users, visitors to employer's premises and members of the general public.

The HSWA 1974 also specifically requires employers to:

- maintain a safe place of work, safe plant and equipment, and safe systems of work;
- make adequate arrangements for the safe use, handling, storage and transport of articles and substances;
- provide employees with sufficient information, instructions, training and supervision to be able to work safely;
- maintain in a safe condition the place of work and access to and from it; and
- provide and maintain a working environment that is safe and without health risks.

An employer cannot avoid responsibility for its obligations by delegating them to an appointed safety officer or any other person.

Persons in control of workplaces

Employers are not the only people who are responsible for health and safety in workplaces. It is the duty of each person who has, to any extent, control of premises or means of access or egress from premises or control of any plant or substance in such premises, to take responsibility for the health and safety associated with these premises, including the safety of those who are not their employees. This duty in relation to control of premises extends to a person who by virtue of a contract or tenancy has an obligation to maintain premises or maintain access to the premises. The control must be in relation to the carrying out of the trade, business or other undertaking (whether for profit or not).

Charities must also comply with the Occupiers' Liability Act 1957 which requires occupiers to take reasonable care to see that a visitor will be reasonably safe in using the premises for the purposes for which the visitor is permitted to be there.

Employees

The general duty of employees is to take reasonable care of their own health and safety and the health and safety of others who may be affected by what the employee does or fails to do at work. This duty is broad enough to cover the health and safety of other employees, employees of other employers, contractors working alongside employees, visitors to the workplace and members of the general public.

Other obligation holders

The other categories of obligation holder under the HSWA 1974 with general duties are manufacturers, importers, suppliers and the installers of plant and substances.

18.5.2 Discharging the general obligations

The defence to any claim for a breach of the general health and safety obligations is essentially one of acting reasonably. This means that the degree of risk in a particular job or workplace needs to be balanced against the time, trouble, cost and physical difficulty of taking steps to avoid or reduce the risk. The onus is upon the obligation holder to prove the defence, and it is often difficult to prove. The courts have tended to have a very high expectation of what needs to be done by those with health and safety obligations.

18.6 OTHER SOURCES OF OBLIGATIONS

18.6.1 HSWA 1974 Regulations

Numerous Regulations are made under the HSWA 1974. The Regulations underpin the general obligations placed upon the duty holders to ensure the health and safety of other persons by prescribing more specific ways of managing health and safety, often in specific situations. For example, there are specific Regulations in respect of dealing with hazardous substances, electricity, and manual handling. While failure to comply with a regulation will be evidence of a failure to discharge a general duty contained within the HSWA 1974, obligation holders can also be separately prosecuted for a breach of the particular regulation itself.

For charities, important Regulations include:

- the Management of Health and Safety at Work Regulations 1999: these regulations establish a general requirement for a risk management approach to health and safety at work;
- the Manual Handling Operations Regulations 1992: these regulations apply wherever things are moved by hand or bodily force, such as moving boxes;
- the Health and Safety (Display Screen Equipment) Regulations 1992: these regulations provide, for example, the maximum amount of time that workers are allowed to spend in front of a computer screen;
- the Health and Safety (First Aid) Regulations 1981: these regulations cover requirements for first aid;
- the Employers' Liability (Compulsory Insurance) Regulations 1998: these regulations require employers to take out insurance against accidents and ill health of their employees and prohibit certain conditions in insurance policies which would prevent claims arising against the insurers under the insurance policies; and
- the Reporting of Injuries, Diseases and Dangerous Occurrences Regulations 1995 (RIDDOR 1995): these regulations require

employers to notify certain occupational injuries, diseases and dangerous events.

18.6.2 Approved Codes of Practice

Approved Codes of Practice (ACOPs) are published by the HSE and are intended to provide practical guidance as to how the obligations under the HSWA 1974 and the Regulations can be complied with. For example, an ACOP might provide guidance about what is a reasonably practicable measure to take to manage a particular safety risk. ACOPs are not mandatory, but if a charity does not follow an ACOP, it will be necessary for it to show that it has complied with its health and safety obligations in some other way.

In addition, the HSE publishes various other guidance materials, which summarise the law and are intended to assist obligation holders to comply with the HSWA 1974 and the Regulations by providing practical guidance. (Copies of these publications are available from HSE Books, PO Box 1999, Sudbury, Suffolk CO10 6FS.)

18.7 RISK MANAGEMENT AND ASSESSMENT

In many instances, the HSWA 1974 and the Regulations tell obligation holders exactly what they need to do to manage certain health and safety risks. However, the general obligations placed upon the obligation holders are broad, and exist on the basis that it is not possible to prescribe ways of acting safely to cover all possible scenarios.

It is in these cases that a risk management approach is vital. If a way for managing a particular health and safety risk is not prescribed, the charity must follow risk management procedures to eliminate or minimise the risk. The Regulations which imposed the general obligation for employers and others to adopt a risk management approach in these circumstances are the Management of Health and Safety at Work Regulations 1999. The risk management approach is also consistently endorsed and referred to in other Regulations.

The HSE has published guidance to assist obligation holders to comply with the Management of Health and Safety at Work Regulations 1999, namely by adhering to the following five steps:

- Identify any hazards. A hazard is anything that can cause harm – for example, chemicals, electricity, heavy boxes.
- Assess the risks. Decide who might be harmed and how, and how likely it is that the hazard will in fact cause harm.
- Take appropriate action and implement any appropriate controls either to eliminate the risks or to reduce them as far as possible. Weigh up the risks and decide whether any existing precautions are sufficient or whether anything more should be done.

- Record the findings. Charities with five or more employees need to record the significant findings of the risk assessment.
- Re-check the risks from time to time and take further steps if needed.

18.8 SPECIFIC OBLIGATIONS UPON EMPLOYERS

Employers also have a number of specific obligations under the Regulations. Importantly, under the HSWA 1974, an employer will need a written health and safety policy statement. The document must include the health and safety policy and details of the arrangements in force for carrying out the policy. The policy should also identify who in the organisation has particular health and safety responsibilities and what those responsibilities are.

Employees are required to appoint one or more competent persons to assist in implementing and undertaking the health and safety measures required (often called a 'safety officer'). This person must have adequate training or experience to be able to fulfil this role. The person might also be responsible for procedures dealing with serious and imminent danger, such as fire evacuation.

Every employer shall ensure that employees are provided with such health surveillance as is appropriate having regard to the risks to their health and safety which are identified by the risk assessment.

Every employer must establish and give effect to appropriate procedures to be followed in the event of serious and imminent danger to persons at work in their business.

18.9 HEALTH AND SAFETY ISSUES FOR CHARITIES

Historically, health and safety at work was associated more with heavy industry such as factories, mining and construction. However, in modern times, health and safety law has been important for all workplaces and has been focused on preventing the risk of psychological as well as physical illness and injury. Some important issues for charities are outlined below.

18.9.1 Working from home

Charities may employ people who work from home. The HSWA 1974 and many of the Regulations also apply to home-workers. Accordingly, charities are required to do a risk assessment of the work activities carried out by home-workers or, where reasonable, require the home-worker to undertake the risk assessment. The normal five steps of risk assessment need to be followed. Home-workers must help their employers to identify and manage hazards. The HSE has recently published guidance entitled 'Homeworking: Guidance for employers and employees on health and safety'.

18.9.2 Stress

Claims for stress-related illness are becoming more prevalent. Given that many charities deal with issues relating to violence and deprivation, their staff may be more prone to stress-related illness than other organisations. It is part of an employer's duty to make sure that employees do not become ill as a result of their work. Stress can make employees ill, by leading to either a mental illness or physical ill health (see Chapter 12).

Stress can be caused or made worse by work, and thus an employer must assess the risk of harm. A risk assessment for stress involves looking for pressure at work that could cause high and long-lasting levels of stress, deciding who might be harmed by these, and deciding whether enough is being done to prevent that harm. Stressful areas of a charity might be identified by considering staff turnover, increase in sickness absence, reduced work performance, poor time-keeping and customer or client complaints. One way in which many organisations cope with stress-related illness or avoiding stress in the first place is to provide a free counselling service or free telephone care line so that employees can discuss their concerns before the stress turns into an illness. It is important, however, that employees can approach their employer to discuss situations which are making them stressed. The duty is on the employer to create an environment which is stress-free. The HSE has published guidance entitled 'Work-related stress: a short guide' and 'Tackling work-related stress – A guide for employees'.

18.9.3 Bullying

Related to claims of stress are claims of bullying (see Chapter 20). An employee may make a claim for personal injury as a result of any illness caused by bullying by another employee. This is because an employer is vicariously liable for any negligent acts carried out by employees in the course of their employment. The best way to deal with this is to have a policy in place which covers bullying, such as a grievance policy or bullying and harassment policy. It is also important that employees feel that they can approach their employer with any grievances in relation to bullying.

18.9.4 Pregnancy

The HSE has recently published guidance to ensure that pregnant women have a safe and healthy experience at work – 'New and expectant mothers at work, a guide for employers'. This sets out, amongst other things, that new and expectant mothers should avoid:

- lifting heavy loads;
- working in confined spaces;

- working at unsuitable work stations;
- working in stressful environments; and
- working with lead.

18.9.5 Working alone

Some charity workers are at risk of assault or injury from working alone. Charities must look after the health and safety of such persons. The HSE has published guidance entitled 'Working alone in safety: controlling the risks of solitary work' which offers advice about how to comply with duties towards home-workers.

18.10 ROLE OF THE HEALTH AND SAFETY COMMITTEE AND HEALTH AND SAFETY EXECUTIVE

The Health and Safety Committee (the HSC) aims to protect the health, safety and welfare of employees and others, principally the public, and to ensure that risks to people's health and safety from work activities are properly controlled. It has overall responsibility for drawing up proposals and policies on health and safety at work.

The HSE is the operational arm of the HSC. It also provides guidance to obligation holders. Its main function is to enforce health and safety legislation, to carry out research and to conduct special investigations for the HSC on health and safety matters, including developments in science and technology.

18.10.1 Health and safety inspectors

The HSE has inspectors who help to enforce the health and safety legislation. The role of the inspectorate is to carry out routine inspections of premises, investigate workplace accidents, dangerous occurrences or cases of ill health, and provide advice to companies and individuals on the legal requirements under the health and safety legislation.

A health and safety inspector may visit a workplace either to investigate an accident or dangerous incident which has been reported, or simply to conduct a routine inspection. Inspectors have broad powers as part of their duty to ensure compliance with the HSWA 1974 and the Regulations and in recognition that health and safety is a serious matter. These include the power to enter and search premises; the power to direct that a premises or part of it be left undisturbed; the power to require production of documents and to take copies; the power to question persons and require answers to those questions; the power to require a person to provide the inspector with reasonable assistance to enable the inspector to fulfil his or her duties; and the power to issue improvement or prohibition notices.

An improvement notice is a notice requiring the obligation holder to do something in particular to improve health and safety within 21 days or more. For example, an inspector might require an employer to give certain training to its employees within 21 days. A prohibition notice is a notice requiring the obligation holder to stop doing something and is usually effective immediately. For example, an inspector might prohibit the use of a particular piece of machinery until the appropriate guard is fixed. Prohibition notices can be issued only where an inspector believes that the activities involve or will involve a risk of serious injury.

A number of offences have been created to ensure that inspectors can properly discharge their duties and powers. It is an offence:

- to contravene a requirement imposed by an inspector (for example, if an inspector requires the production of a document or the answer to a question);
- to prevent or attempt to prevent a person from appearing before an inspector or from answering his or her questions; and
- intentionally to obstruct an inspector in the exercise of his or her powers.

18.11 BREACH OF THE HSWA 1974 AND REGULATIONS

If there is evidence that a breach of the HSWA 1974 or the Regulations has or may have occurred, the inspector must decide if any action should be taken. Sometimes, issuing an informal warning is enough; on other occasions an improvement or prohibition notice might suffice. However, the inspector can also prosecute for a breach of the general obligations under the Act and/or the specific obligations under the Regulations. It is quite common for an improvement or prohibition notice to be issued and for a prosecution to be commenced at the same time in respect of the same risk. They are aimed at achieving different ends: improvement and prohibition notices are aimed at fixing the problem, and the prosecution is designed to punish and deter.

18.11.1 Sanctions

Fines

Persons (including charities) can be prosecuted either in the magistrates' courts for less serious cases or in the Crown Court for more serious cases. Initially, the inspector decides which court to proceed in; and ultimately the court has the power to decide. The maximum fines for breach of health and safety obligations are as follows:

- prosecutions commenced in the magistrates' court – a maximum fine of £20,000 for a breach of the general obligations and £5,000 for a

breach of a Regulation (although this may soon be increased to £20,000); and
- prosecutions commenced in the Crown Court – there is no limit on the fine which may be imposed.

Imprisonment

Persons, including officers of charities, may imprisoned for up to 2 years for:

- breaches of improvement or prohibition orders; and
- breaches of court orders to remedy whatever has caused an obligation holder to commit an offence.

Other criminal offences

In the very worst cases, corporations and individuals can be prosecuted for criminal offences such as manslaughter, although there can be difficulties in successfully prosecuting corporations for such offences.

Directors and officers

Where an offence is committed by a body corporate, including a charity, directors and senior management of the body corporate may also be prosecuted if the offence has been committed with the consent or connivance or is attributable to the neglect of those persons.

18.11.2 Civil actions

Following a successful health and safety prosecution, the guilty obligation holder can find itself in the civil courts attempting to defend a claim that it was negligent or in breach of contract and that this caused a person to suffer personal injury or death. A conviction under the HSWA 1974 does not make the obligation holder automatically liable for negligence but can be cogent evidence of negligence.

18.12 EMPLOYMENT PROTECTION

18.12.1 Right not to suffer a detriment in health and safety cases

Employees have the right not to be subjected to a detriment by their employer for acting or failing to act in certain circumstances related to health and safety. For example, if an employee evacuated the workplace on the reasonable belief that there was a fire, and it later turned out that there was no fire, the employee could not be subjected to a detriment, such as disciplinary action. If the employee does suffer a detriment, he or she can make a complaint to an employment tribunal. The employee may receive compensation if the complaint is upheld.

18.12.2 Public interest disclosure

Workers are protected when making qualifying disclosures under the Public Interest Disclosure Act 1998 (see Chapter 20) against dismissal or detriment due to the disclosure. The worker must have a reasonable belief of the danger and make the disclosure in good faith. The dismissal or detriment will be held to be unlawful if the disclosure is protected under the Act.

18.12.3 Automatic unfair dismissal

Dismissal for the reason or principal reason of acting or failing to act in certain circumstances related to health and safety is also automatically unfair. There is also no limit to the compensation available to such workers, and there is no qualifying employment period.

Chapter 19

MANAGING ADVERSE INCIDENTS

19.1 INTRODUCTION

It is a truism that for every action there is a reaction. This is particularly so, however, when things go wrong in a charity: it might be a breach confidentiality, a fraud or an accident resulting in injury. Employees may directly or indirectly be the victims of an accident, potentially liable for causing it or witnesses to the event. It is often unclear what the response to such an incident should be, particularly where there is some personal involvement or responsibility. This chapter considers the implications of such adverse incidents and how a co-ordinated and informed response can help to reduce the adverse consequences for charities and their employees.

19.2 FIRST RESPONSE

Initial responses are likely to be covered by existing fire or health and safety guidance, and will usually ensure that the appropriate emergency services are called without delay and, where possible, fire wardens and first-aiders provide assistance. The first response to the incident can affect the final outcome and may, in itself, be the subject of scrutiny.

At this stage, a nominated project manager or co-ordinator or others can usefully co-ordinate action, ensure that proper records are kept and operate as a first point of reference for any employees or others affected. Access to counselling services or simply some time off for affected staff should be considered, particularly where there has been a death or serious injury. Supporting key employees enables the employer to minimise the effect of being witnesses to the incident and then participating in the subsequent inquiry process. Keeping open a dialogue will enable the employer to assess the needs of employees and prevent them from becoming alienated from the employer.

19.2.1 Reporting obligations

An adverse incident can trigger a legal duty to notify others. Such obligations may be statutory, contractual or part of the reasonable expectation arising from the duty of care.

In particular, the reader should note the Reporting of Injuries, Diseases and Dangerous Occurrences Regulations 1995 (RIDDOR 1995), which require the following to be reported:

- deaths;
- accidents resulting in over 3 days off work;
- diseases;
- dangerous occurrences.

All accidents, diseases and dangerous occurrences may be reported to the Incident Contact Centre, which will forward details of the incident to the relevant enforcing authority – this may be the Health and Safety Executive (HSE) or the local authority. (Further information on RIDDOR 1995 can be obtained from: *A Guide to the Reporting of Injuries, Diseases and Dangerous Occurrences Regulations 1995* (L73), ISBN 0-7176-1012-8, available from HSE Books, PO Box 1999, Sudbury, Suffolk CO10 6FS.)

19.2.2 Record keeping

The Health and Safety at Work Act 1974 (HSWA 1974) requires that a record be kept of any reportable injury, disease or dangerous occurrence. This must include the date and method of reporting, together with the date, time and place of the event, personal details of those involved and a brief description of the nature of the event or disease.

Best practice requires that legible and informative factual records are kept. Opinion, speculation and third party reports should be treated with particular care.

19.2.3 Insurance

If an employee or a third party has been injured, insurance policies are likely to contain a contractual provision requiring early notification. To protect the validity of the insurance policy, insurers should be informed at the earliest opportunity.

19.2.4 Dealing with the press

It is sometimes appropriate to prepare a short factual statement for release to the press. Where the cause of the accident remains unknown or uncertain, speculation is best avoided. A balance must be struck between advantages of being open and providing information and the risk of providing information or comment which subsequently proves to be inaccurate or misleading.

19.2.5 Legal advice

Early legal advice may be appropriate, particularly if disciplinary action against an employee is being considered. Depending on the terms of the insurance policy, cover for legal advice and representation by the employer's solicitors or the insurance panel solicitors may be available.

19.2.6 Supporting staff

Even where employees have not suffered a physical injury, there is an increased risk of psychological stress either as a result of the incident itself or the involvement in the necessary inquiries. Stressed employees make poor witnesses and may also be potential claimants in a claim against their employer. (See **19.8** for a more detailed commentary on claims concerning stress at work.) In the recent Court of Appeal guidance on stress in the workplace, it was emphasised that the availability of confidential help for employees not only helped the parties to deal with the issues but also meant that the employer was unlikely to be found in breach of its duty of care towards employees.

19.3 THE INQUIRY TRAIL

After these early steps have been taken, a number of inquiries may be necessary which will review the facts surrounding the incident and determine the extent of any legal liability. Each of these will have different terms of reference but all are likely to involve examination of the same documents and witnesses. The most likely inquiries are the following.

19.3.1 Non-judicial inquiries

Non-judicial inquiries are common practice following an adverse incident. The terms of reference of the inquiry will, however, vary. An internal inquiry will define its own terms of reference and often will operate as a preliminary to other processes. It offers the employer an opportunity to investigate and obtain an objective view of the facts and areas of risk. If this inquiry can be carried out before other agencies are involved, the position of the charity is greatly strengthened vis-à-vis the other agencies.

Other statutory inquiries may be convened as a result of a statutory provision or by the designation of the Lord Chancellor and the Secretary of State. Public inquiries are detailed and extensive and usually arise where there is an issue of public importance: for example, a murder by a patient of an NHS Trust. They can attract a great deal of publicity. The person appointed to hold the inquiry may have extensive powers to summons employees to give evidence or to produce documents.

19.3.2 Complaints procedures

Whether the charity has a formal complaints procedure in place or not, the receipt of an oral or written complaint in respect of the circumstances surrounding the incident may be a first indication that the victim or the victim's family intends to take legal action. This will require an investigation of the events surrounding the incident by reference to the terms of the complaint. There is significant overlap between initial internal inquiries and complaints.

19.4 DISCIPLINARY AND TRIBUNAL PROCEEDINGS

The conduct of disciplinary and tribunal proceedings is covered elsewhere in this book. The conduct of an internal inquiry may trigger disciplinary action or consideration of disciplinary action may be the reason for the inquiry. Disciplinary action clearly affects the employer–employee relationship. It may also, however, affect the position of the organisation during the course of one of the other inquiries arising from the incident.

It may therefore be prudent to consider whether disciplinary proceedings are best taken at an early stage or postponed until after the relevant inquiries have reported. If the issues are unclear, early action against an employee could result in adverse conclusions being drawn in other inquiries. In other cases, it may not be possible to carry out the investigation whilst a criminal investigation is pending as it would frustrate the police inquiry. The risk then is that an employee may remain suspended for a considerable period of time until the issue is capable of resolution.

19.5 CORONER'S INQUESTS

Where a coroner is informed that the body of a person is lying within his or her district and there is reasonable cause to suspect that the deceased:

- has died a violent or unnatural death; or
- has died a sudden death of which the cause is unknown; or
- has died in prison or in such a place or in such circumstances as to require an inquest under any other Act,

then the coroner must, as soon as practicable, hold an inquest into the death of the deceased.

An inquest is an inquisitorial process carried out by a coroner. Preliminary investigations on behalf of a coroner are carried out by the coroner's officer. The coroner's officer will usually be a nurse, social worker or a retired police officer. Employees can be interviewed by the coroner's officer and requested to attend the inquest to provide evidence. An inquest can be highly charged emotionally; it is often the first public opportunity that a family has had to establish the cause of death and an inquest can be extremely stressful for staff who are called to give evidence.

The terms of reference in an inquest are in fact very narrow. The proceedings and evidence must be directed solely to ascertaining the following matters:

(a) who the deceased was;
(b) how, when and where the deceased came by his or her death;
(c) the particulars of the time required by the Births and Deaths Registration Act 1953 to be registered concerning the death.

Inquests are often the subject of an alternative agenda by a family considering further action over the death, but neither the coroner nor the jury can express an opinion on any other matters, and a verdict cannot be framed in such a way as to appear to determine any questions of criminal or civil liability.

The coroner has the discretion to decide which witnesses to call to give evidence and which witnesses will be examined on oath at the hearing. The coroner will carry out the primary examination but other people are entitled to examine witnesses. These include a parent, child, spouse, any personal representative of the deceased, or any person whose act or omission or that of his agent or servant may, in the opinion of the coroner, have caused or contributed to the death of the deceased, or any other person who, in the opinion of the coroner, is a properly interested person.

The questions should be directed solely to answering how, when and where the deceased came by his or her death; in reality, the examination of the relevant facts may call the conduct of an employee into question. An employer might, therefore, consider providing support and legal representation to an employee who may be called as a witness. This will not only support the employee, but will also enable the charity to protect its position and reputation at the inquest. If there is a conflict of interest between employer and employee, particularly if disciplinary proceedings are pending, it is appropriate to advise the employee to seek independent representation.

19.6 CRIMINAL PROCEEDINGS

An accident may result in a criminal investigation by the police. If satisfied that there is sufficient evidence to bring a prosecution and it is in the public interest to do so, the Crown Prosecution Service (CPS) may bring criminal proceedings. The proceedings may be brought against the employer or an individual, depending on the nature of the alleged offence. Employees at all levels may be required to answer the charge or, alternatively, provide evidence for the defence or the prosecution.

Where there has been a breach of health and safety legislation or the Care Standards Act 2000, regulatory proceedings may be brought by the HSE, the local authority or the National Care Standards Commission (NCSC).

Both criminal and regulatory proceedings will proceed in the magistrates' court or the Crown Court, which may result in fines, imprisonment or cancellation of registration.

19.7 CIVIL PROCEEDINGS

Where an incident has occurred which has resulted in personal injury or loss or damage, civil proceedings in the county court or the High Court may be brought by those affected. The majority of claims will be brought on the basis of negligence. The law requires everyone to take reasonable care to avoid acts or omissions which can reasonably be foreseen to be likely to injure someone to whom a duty of care is owed.

Employers owe a duty of care to their employees in the same way that a duty of care is owed to visitors to premises, service users or people who are reasonably affected by their actions. If the breach of the duty of care causes injury or harm the victim will be entitled to financial compensation which is intended to put them in the position they would have been in had the injury not occurred.

The cost of accidents is of great concern to the NHS, and in September 2002 the Department of Health published a consultation document under which the Government is seeking to recover the costs of hospital treatment from employers that have been held responsible for causing accidents or injury to their staff. It is the view of the Department of Health that wrongdoers should meet the cost of their actions and this will include the cost of hospital treatment and associated ambulance costs. It will not include primary care costs, such as GP follow-ups. If made law, this may well affect insurance premiums and it would be advisable to check that policy cover extends to these fees.

Where there is damage to property or financial loss, a range of other civil proceedings arising from breach of contract, conversion or negligence could follow an incident. All will seek financial compensation and, if there is fraud or financial misconduct, emergency injunctions may be obtained to freeze assets or assist in an asset-tracing exercise.

Detailed discussion of the implications of these types of proceedings is outside the scope of this chapter but the implications for employers managing employees who are party to or witnesses in these proceedings are significant, both in terms of the time spent and the damage that may be caused to the individuals and the reputation of the organisation.

19.8 MANAGING EMPLOYEE STRESS

Being the subject of an inquiry and appearing in court are events which may be difficult for an employee to cope with and there is a risk of these events triggering illness. To what extent might an employer then acquire another liability? Liability for work-related physical or psychiatric illness is a developing area of personal injury law. There is also a growing awareness of the impact of stress in the workplace. This has been considered recently by, amongst others, the Department of Health and the Education Service Advisory Committee. The HSE has also issued a general booklet of guidance on stress at work (see **18.9.2**). All these bodies recognise that every job has some pressure and that some pressure can be a good thing. However, excessive workplace pressure and the stress to which it can lead can be harmful and can result in injury. Clearly there are sound operational reasons for ensuring that stress is properly managed, but when might it become the subject of legal proceedings?

The issue of legal liability for workplace stress has recently been addressed by the Court of Appeal in *Sutherland v Hatton* [2002] 2 All ER 1. In order to prove that a charity has been negligent, it is necessary to establish that it acted in breach of its duty of care by failing to protect an employee from a reasonably foreseeable risk of harm. The assessment of whether the risk of psychological damage due to stress was foreseeable can be very difficult as different people will react in different ways and psychiatric illness is not always apparent. Indeed, an employee may wish to conceal the true state of affairs from his or her employer through fear of being thought 'unable to cope'. As the Court of Appeal said: 'The issue will be whether the employer failed to take steps to safeguard the employee from harm; his sins are those of omission rather than commission'; and yet the employer's opportunities for acting may be very limited.

The Court of Appeal, recognising the balancing act required in order to achieve fairness, laid down some key principles which will do much to limit speculative claims and can be summarised as follows.

- An employee can claim damages for stress only if it can be established that he or she is suffering from a recognised psychiatric illness. The recognised disorders include psychoses, neuroses, clinical depressions and anxiety disorders.
- The employee must establish that the damage was foreseeable, ie that the employer knew or should reasonably have known that damage would be caused. Triggers for damage might be uncertainty over work or career prospects or where work schedules are inflexible or over-demanding.
- The individual's characteristics must be considered but there is a presumption that, unless it knows of any particular vulnerability, an employer can assume that an employee is able to cope with the ordinary pressures of a job.

Whilst the guidance is generally reassuring to charity employers and relieves them from an obligation to make what might be extensive and intrusive inquiries about an employee's mental health, the position may not be as clear-cut in the aftermath of a serious incident. Expecting an employee to carry out his or her normal workload, without any support or inquiry as to general wellbeing, together with attendance at inquiry hearings and interviews, could lead to a charity's liability.

In addition, it is worth remembering that stress is often an indicator of or exacerbates physical illness such as heart disease.

19.9 MANAGING INFORMATION

During the course of any investigation, an employer may be asked to give disclosure of information concerning the incident to a number of people. If requests are made by third parties direct to employees they should be referred to the appointed project manager for a response.

All disclosure should be considered first in the light of the Data Protection Act 1998 (DPA 1998). This will require consideration of whether the subject has given consent to the disclosure or whether there is other legal authority for it by means of statutory authority or an order of the court.

In a pre-litigation situation, there may be considerable pressure to disclose information. Care needs to be taken to ensure that disclosures are limited to what is relevant and authorised under the DPA 1998 or other legislation to avoid a breach of privacy. Often assurances of confidentiality are given to employees during the course of an investigation. An employer cannot, however, guarantee confidentiality in subsequent proceedings, particularly where an order is obtained from the court.

There are, however, two relevant 'privileges' against disclosure which it is worth being aware of.

The first is the privilege against self-incrimination. In civil proceedings a person has a right to refuse to answer questions or produce documents where to do so would tend to expose that person to proceedings for an offence or recovery of a penalty. There are exceptions to this privilege but an employee (or indeed the employer) should not be induced to do so or compromised so as to negate the value of this privilege. Where there is a prospect of criminal proceedings against an individual, he or she should be advised to seek independent legal advice at an early stage.

The second is that of legal professional privilege. Communications between a solicitor and his or her client are protected from disclosure. Communications which are made or come into existence where litigation is contemplated or pending are similarly protected. It is therefore good practice to seek legal advice from a solicitor at an early stage as it may be that the solicitor's review of the potential for proceedings arising from the incident will enable the client to plead privilege from disclosure of damaging statements or other evidence obtained as part of an internal inquiry. This also has the benefit of encouraging openness in the conduct of the inquiry. Unless such an inquiry is privileged, it is likely that any documents which are created will be open to an application for disclosure in other proceedings.

19.10 PRACTICAL GUIDANCE

It can be seen that a number of inquiries may follow from one incident. Each has a different purpose but all will relate to the same set of facts. An early internal inquiry by the charity should be capable of uncovering the key issues. In terms of managing the subsequent inquiries, it is in the employer's and the employee's interests to keep close control over the process, keeping in mind the following main objectives.

(i) Know your case

If an internal inquiry has been conducted, the charity will usually be aware of areas of risk. If there is a problem, an early admission of liability that may prevent more serious action being taken at a later stage and avoid negative publicity. If not, the charity can assert its case with confidence and possibly ward off any further proceedings.

(ii) Know your employees

Individuals will react differently to being a witness or subject to disciplinary proceedings. If, for example, an employee is a key witness to an event but is unlikely to be a robust performer in court, steps should be taken to minimise the stress of these inquiries; ensure that he or she understands the process, is properly prepared and supported at the hearing. If an employee is a hostile witness, he or she may also become a claimant and this should be discussed with legal advisers. It may not be possible to avoid an employee giving evidence but if the issues he or she is concerned about are addressed in a proactive way it may be possible to mitigate the effect of his or her evidence in court.

(iii) Know your evidence

Whatever the merits of the conduct in question, the best outcome is usually achieved where there is clear, relevant, detailed and consistent evidence. This objective is easily undermined where record keeping is poor or the records are unavailable and/or employees are required to give several interviews with different people. It may be possible to reduce the number of interviews given and for statements to be produced by working with legal advisers who can prepare and offer documentation and witness evidence to the relevant authorities as well as representing the organisation in court.

Employees, as witnesses, need time to reflect and record their actual version of events at an early stage. Whilst refinements of their evidence will be inevitable through the process, active management may reduce the stress on the employee and the risk of an adverse finding. With contentious issues relating to performance it is easy for the employer–employee relationship to

be damaged. Whilst disciplinary action or dismissal may be necessary in some circumstances, in the majority of cases the parties' interests run concurrently and support for the employee is a way of meeting the charity's duty of care to the employee.

19.11 THE EMPLOYEE'S DUTY

An employee is subject to a duty to carry out an employer's reasonable instructions. To what extent, however, does involvement with the inquiries and proceedings that have been identified fall within that obligation? The position is not entirely clear-cut but it is likely to be reasonable for an employee to be asked to attend an internal inquiry which examines factual or performance issues with which he or she is involved. For examples, if there has been an outbreak of food poisoning on the premises it would be reasonable for all catering staff to be interviewed.

If an employee refuses to co-operate with the inquiry, however, a charity has no legal power to require him or her to do so and it is unlikely to justify summary dismissal. Where there is the possibility, either actual or perceived, of disciplinary proceedings, an employee may quite reasonably not wish to discuss his or her conduct without first seeking advice from a union or staff representative or his or her own legal adviser. An unwilling witness is likely to be unhelpful if pressed but it clearly puts the employer in difficulty in terms of managing external proceedings and inquiries if it cannot access vital evidence.

As identified above, employees can be called as witnesses in all external proceedings and, if they do not co-operate, most courts of inquiry will have powers to issue witness summons requiring attendance. Failure to attend on receipt of a summons is a contempt of court and punishable by a fine or imprisonment. The duty of the employee is, at that stage, to the court of inquiry and not to the employer. Whilst most employees will remain supportive of their employers, when giving evidence the primary obligation is to the court. If, however, the witness is prepared and understands the process and the issues, it is less likely that irrelevant and prejudicial material will be made public or that private grievances will be aired.

CASE STUDY

A is a carer employed by Charity B which operates a registered care home. Her duties include the bathing of elderly residents. C is 86 years old and, following a stroke, has limited movement and sensation in her legs and suffers from bouts of severe confusion. Her care plan provides that she should be bathed by her carer, who should not leave her alone at any time. One day, having taken C into the bathroom and started to run the water for a bath, A remembers that she has forgotten C's dressing gown and she goes out along the corridor to C's bedroom to retrieve it.

On her return, she finds that C has fallen into the bath and suffered scalding to her back and legs. It is subsequently discovered that, contrary to the HSE Guidance, automatic thermostatic valves had not been fitted to the baths in each room, and the hot tap had discharged a burst of hot water above the recommended level. The wounds do not heal and septicaemia follows. C dies 10 days later.

On discovering C, A runs to fetch her manager, D, and then continues with other duties before going home at the end of her shift. She does not write any notes. She calls in 'sick' the following day and is away from work for 3 weeks with 'stress'. During that time she is interviewed by the coroner's officer and the HSE under caution, during which interviews she criticises her manager and other staff. She also attends an interview with the police and discloses copies of the care plan to the press. She refuses to co-operate with her manager and fails to attend a meeting to discuss the incident. She gives evidence at the inquest and breaks down in the witness box.

What inquiries might follow from this incident?

- internal inquiry;
- inquest;
- HSE investigation and prosecution;
- criminal investigation by the police;
- civil proceedings by C's husband for personal injury and death;
- disciplinary proceedings and dismissal for A;
- claim by A for unfair dismissal and personal injury arising out of stress at work.

What would be the appropriate first response?

The emergency services should be called by A's manager and first aid administered by a first-aider if possible. The area should be isolated and C's family and the appropriate people in the organisation notified. Other residents (unless there are reasons not to) and staff should be advised in brief factual terms of the incident.

A project manager should be appointed to act and staff notified that all documents and communications should be referred through him or her in the first instance.

A report under RIDDOR 1995 and to the NCSC should be completed, as soon as sufficient information is available, either by D or B's health and safety officer. If completed by B, the report should be agreed by D and a copy provided to her.

What steps would the project manager take then?

Being aware of the potential for legal proceedings, the manager notifies the insurers and seeks legal advice. Her legal adviser confirms the risk of legal proceedings and advises D to conduct an inquiry. D sees A and asks her what happened. She notes down the factual details that A provides and gives her a copy. A is requested to complete a full factual report as soon as possible and to return it to the manager. She is invited to discuss the incident with D again on her return. She is advised to refer all communications about the incident to D and in particular to notify her of any approaches by the police or the press. A is reminded of her duty of confidentiality to the resident. D then interviews all relevant staff members, keeping note of what is said and asking each to sign and confirm the contents of the notes taken. She also reviews the care plan and all other relevant documents.

As an alternative, D's legal adviser may be asked to take statements from all the relevant witnesses, with a view to maintaining a central bank of evidence. If appropriate these statements could be offered to the other investigating agencies at the appropriate time.

D also commissions a report on the maintenance of the water system. She notifies and seeks advice from B's appointed health and safety officer and takes remedial action in respect of the water heater.

How could the organisation ensure that its duty of care to A is met?

Immediately following the incident, D makes an assessment of A's ability to continue at work. Having conducted a short interview she then sends A home. D advises A of the charity's subscription to a confidential counselling service.

On receiving notice from A that the coroner's officer wishes to interview her, D arranges for the charity's legal adviser to see A, explain the process and take a statement from her using the initial manager's statement as a reference point. The interview is short and is attended by A with either the legal adviser or D present. Similarly, the police interview and HSE interview proceed in the same way with substantially the same evidence being offered.

Before the inquest, A is given time to review her statement and is represented by the legal adviser. D attends the inquest with her and takes a note of the findings of the coroner. A is advised of the possible further action that may be taken and in particular whether action is contemplated against her.

What steps might follow receipt of a letter of complaint and a request for a copy of C's file from her husband?

Having investigated the claim, D and/or her legal adviser will have a clear idea as to the merits of a claim by the family against B. A prompt and full response can therefore be prepared. An early decision can be made on the merits of the claim, possibly with an apology and appropriate offer of compensation being made prior to any proceedings being issued or evidence exchanged. Neither A's written note nor the manager's preliminary report are disclosed. These reports are, however, reviewed by the health and safety officer and any risk management officer or committee in order to avoid a similar incident occurring again.

Chapter 20

DEALING WITH EMPLOYEES' COMPLAINTS, GRIEVANCE PROCEDURES AND THE PUBLIC INTEREST DISCLOSURE ACT 1998

20.1 INTRODUCTION

Employers nowadays must be better prepared and more proactive than ever before when dealing with employee dissatisfaction. Failure to act appropriately can lead to anything from simple employee malcontent to expensive and time-consuming litigation. The overwhelming theme promoted by Parliament and the courts is one of ensuring that systems and procedures are in place to maximise the potential to settle matters swiftly, fairly and amicably rather than marching on to litigation.

20.2 GRIEVANCE PROCEDURE

> 'Good practice is not just a matter of fairness towards employees. It also makes it more likely that disputes will be resolved at the workplace and not by employment tribunals, where they can be lost because of procedural failings by the employer in handling the dispute.'
>
> (Alan Johnson, Minister for Competitiveness, announcing the new ACAS Code on 8 June 2000)

A comprehensive grievance procedure is the most fundamental piece of the jigsaw. The starting point for an accurate procedure is the current ACAS Code of Practice on Disciplinary and Grievance Procedures (the ACAS Code) which came into force on 4 September 2000. It gives guidance on the statutory right of workers to be accompanied at disciplinary and grievance hearings. It addresses absence and the distinction between illness absenteeism and other absenteeism, poor performance, counselling, confidentiality, data protection, what is meant by 'gross misconduct', the concept of natural justice, and what factors make up reasonableness when imposing a disciplinary sanction. All in all, it is an extremely useful reference tool when preparing or auditing a grievance procedure and should be the starting point for all charities when drafting procedures of their own. The Code can be obtained free of charge at www.acas.co.uk. It is likely to be updated in 2004.

Failing to follow the ACAS Code of Practice will not in itself cause the employer to be guilty of an offence. However, if not followed, it is useful evidence for an employee before a tribunal that the employer has failed to handle his or her complaint appropriately. Tribunals will often cross-examine employers on their familiarity with the ACAS Code and it is therefore relevant to any unfair dismissal claim. Proposed changes to the law mean that it is also relevant to any claim where the employee has raised a grievance, for example, in respect of sex, race or disability discrimination.

20.2.1 The procedure

The charity's grievance procedure should be simple. It should be set down in writing and should clearly explain the purpose of the procedure and how it is to operate. It is sensible to provide employees with examples of the types of issues that might give rise to a grievance. These might be disputes about terms and conditions of employment, health and safety, relationships at work, new working practices, organisational change and equal opportunities.

Grievance hearings should be confidential and it is important that the records of the hearing and any associated investigation remain confidential.

20.2.2 Statutory right to be accompanied at a grievance hearing

Under the Employment Relations Act 1999, a worker is entitled to be accompanied at certain grievance hearings. This right applies to all workers, including temporary and contract workers. Only the genuinely self-employed and volunteers are excluded.

The right to be accompanied applies specifically to hearings which could result in:

- the administration of a formal warning to a worker by his or her employer;
- the taking of some other action in respect of a worker by his or her employer (eg suspension without pay, demotion or dismissal); or
- the confirmation of a warning issued or some other action taken.

Whether the worker has the right to be accompanied depends on the nature of the hearing. In grievance hearings, the right will apply only if the grievance concerns the performance of 'a duty by the employer' that arises from statute or the contract of employment.

One could argue that, strictly speaking, there is no statutory right to be accompanied in the case of an informal interview or counselling session which does not result in the administration of a formal warning. However, the wording is broad and it is safest for charities to offer the option of a representative at all times. Bearing in mind that the merest squabble between employees could lead to a variety of claims, it is wise to presume that the right to be represented applies rather than not. Generally, workers are less inclined to want a representative if they are making the grievance complaint themselves. They are more likely to want representation when they are asked to attend a hearing as a witness or, more obviously, at disciplinary hearings.

The right is to be accompanied by a fellow worker or a trade union official who has been reasonably certified by the union as having experience of or training in acting as a worker's companion at such hearings. The companion should be given paid time off to attend the hearing and to have prior meetings with the worker if required.

The companion is permitted to address the hearing and to confer with the worker, in private if necessary. However, he or she is not allowed to answer questions on behalf of the worker. A worker denied this right may complain to an employment tribunal, which may award him or her up to 2 weeks' pay as compensation and, potentially, a much larger award for unfair dismissal compensation if that is claimed.

20.2.3 Ensuring managers are aware of the procedure

To operate effectively the procedure needs to be publicised and understood. In particular, the line managers responding to complaints need to be trained to respond in accordance with the procedure. The ACAS Code requires managers and work representatives to be conversant with the rules. The fact that the training of managers is now set out in this Code will increase the likelihood of a manager being cross-examined about the level of training received in these procedures in any subsequent tribunal hearing.

Whilst a lack of training on the part of the manager is unlikely to lead to a finding against the employer in itself, tribunal members often decide cases on the credence they attach to a particular witness. If the charity can prove that it has provided appropriate training, that is likely to work in its favour if it is disputed that the correct procedure was followed.

For their part, workers should either be given a copy of the procedure or have ready access to it, eg in a staff handbook or via the intranet. Special allowance should be made for workers who may suffer from a disability or have difficulty understanding the procedure.

20.2.4 Benefits to the charity

A clear grievance procedure, well known to all employees, is essential as its use alerts charity employers to problems at an early stage. This is vital because it will help to avoid the breach of certain employment duties to employees.

Charities must also remember that a failure to be proactive in these situations can, in itself, lead to tribunal claims. This is particularly the case where serious allegations are made, say of bullying and harassment.

Example

In *Wigan Borough Council v Davies* [1979] IRLR 127, the tribunal found that there is an implied term in employment contracts that the employer will take reasonable steps to support the employee in his or her duties without harassment or disruption from colleagues.

Employers are also under an implied contractual duty to provide a safe workplace. If, for example, bullying poses a threat to an employee's safety, the employer has an obligation to deal with this. In *WA Goold (Pearmak) Limited v McConnell & Another* [1995] IRLR 516, the tribunal found that an employer has an implied duty to 'reasonably and promptly afford a reasonable opportunity to their employees to obtain redress of any grievance they may have'.

20.3 EMPLOYMENT ACT 2002

New law on grievance and disciplinary hearings will come into force under the Employment Act 2002 (EA 2002) from 1 October 2004.

The Act deals expansively with dispute resolution. Whilst it is estimated that 90% of large employers have disciplinary and grievance procedures, a huge number of small employers, including charities, who face tribunal claims have no procedures in place at all. Accordingly, statutory procedures covering both disciplinary and grievance issues will put in place minimum standards which will be implied into every contract of employment. Under no circumstances will an employer be permitted to contract out of these minimum standards, and existing procedures will need to be fully audited to ensure that they comply.

The aim is to implement a fixed period prior to any tribunal claim being lodged during which parties can attempt conciliation. The standard procedure sets out the following basic requirements:

- each step must be taken without unreasonable delay;
- timings and locations of the meetings must be reasonable;
- the meetings must be conducted in a manner enabling both employer and employee adequately to explain their case;
- appeals, so far as reasonably practicable, should be heard by someone more senior than the person who took the original decision.

The procedure is initiated by the employee's grievance statement, which must be in writing and sent to the employer. The employer must then invite the employee to a grievance meeting to discuss the matter and the employee is required to take all reasonable steps to attend that meeting. After the meeting, the employer must inform the employee of the outcome and advise the employee of the right to appeal if the employee is dissatisfied with the outcome. Once the appeal has been conducted the employer must inform the employee of the outcome.

Failing to follow these statutory procedures could result in serious sanctions: they will be implied into every contract of employment, including those of employees who have insufficient service to qualify for unfair dismissal rights. Accordingly, a failure to comply with the procedures could result in a breach of contract claim from any member of staff.

In addition, if a grievance procedure has not been used or followed, the party at fault may be prohibited from proceeding with the claim. An employee will not be able even to lodge a claim for discrimination or equal pay without following an internal grievance procedure.

Where the tribunal claim goes ahead, an employer's failure to follow the procedure will automatically lead to an unfair dismissal. Equally, and crucially, employees who fail to follow the procedure before going to tribunal will be penalised. A failure by either party to follow the procedure adequately will result in a reduction or increase to the compensatory award of between 10% and 50%.

This is a new power given to tribunals, and both charity employer and employee are well advised to follow the procedure.

20.4 BULLYING AND HARASSMENT

In addition to ensuring that disciplinary and grievance procedures comply with these minimum statutory requirements, charities would be wise to review and consider the other matters closely linked to grievances.

A significant number of grievance applications emanate from bullying, harassment and discrimination. Charities should ensure that they have comprehensive policies dealing with such sensitive matters (see Chapter 7). The policies should clearly enunciate the charity's position, with guidance on what constitutes bullying, harassment and discrimination both legally, where possible, and by way of examples. The policy should explain to the employees what they should do in the event that they are subject to, or witness to, such activities, and the potential consequences of a finding that such an act has taken place. These procedures should dovetail with the grievance and disciplinary procedures, where applicable.

20.5 SHOULD A GRIEVANCE POLICY BE OPEN TO NON-EMPLOYEES AND EX-EMPLOYEES?

It is sometimes the case that people leaving the organisation for a specific reason will have a grievance about the way in which they have been treated. In that case, they may wish to pursue a grievance against the charity. Most grievance policies, however, limit the use of a grievance process to current employees. The general rule is that if someone is no longer employed then they cannot pursue the grievance, and any current grievance which has started will come to an end on the termination of employment.

It is sometimes the case that a charity may feel that the grievance process should continue because of the allegations raised. This is often the case where the grievance relates to a beneficiary of the charity. In these circumstances, it is important for the charity to ensure that it accepts that it may set a precedent in the way that it deals with grievances pursued by ex-employees. After all, a charity can continue to investigate the allegation without involving the ex-employee or pursuing the grievance policy.

The EA 2002 provides for grievances to live beyond employment by requiring employees bringing claims for discrimination and equal pay to pursue internal grievances (save in exceptional circumstances) before lodging complaints with the Employment Tribunal. It is therefore accepted that ex-employees will be able to make use of a charity's grievance procedure after their employment has terminated, from 1 October 2004.

20.6 'THE WHISTLE-BLOWERS ACT'

The Public Interest Disclosure Act 1998 (PIDA 1998), nicknamed 'The Whistle-blowers Act', provides protection from dismissal or detriment to workers who, acting in the public interest and in good faith, report actual or suspected wrongdoing by their employer. The PIDA 1998 applies to all 'workers' as opposed to the narrower category of 'employees'.

In order to be protected, the disclosure must be a qualifying disclosure. This is information which, in the reasonable belief of the worker, shows one or more of the following types of malpractice:

- that a criminal offence has been committed, is being committed or is likely to be committed;
- that a miscarriage of justice has occurred, is occurring or is likely to occur;
- that the health and safety of any individual has been, is being or is likely to be endangered;
- that the environment has been, is being or is likely to be damaged;
- that a person has failed, is failing or is likely to fail to comply with any legal obligation to which he or she is subject (a relevant failure); or
- that information tending to show any matter falling within any one of the above paragraphs has been, is being or is likely to be deliberately concealed.

To be a protected disclosure, the disclosure must be made to the appropriate party as specified in the PIDA 1998:

- to the worker's employer or, in cases where the information relates to the conduct of another person or to matters for which a person other than the employer has legal responsibility, that other person;
- to a legal adviser in the course of obtaining legal advice;
- to a Minister of the Crown where the worker's employer is:
  (a) an individual appointed under any enactment by a Minister of the Crown; or
  (b) a body whose members are appointed by a Minister of the Crown;
- to a person prescribed by an Order made by the Secretary of State for the purposes of receiving qualifying disclosure information of relevant categories;
- to other people *only* if the worker makes the disclosure in good faith, reasonably believes the information to be substantially true, does not make the disclosure for personal gain, one of a number of conditions are satisfied and in all the circumstances disclosure is reasonable.

The conditions referred to above are:

(1) that the worker reasonably believes that he or she will be subjected to a detriment by the employer if the disclosure is made to the employer or a prescribed person; or
(2) that, in cases where there is no prescribed person, the worker reasonably believes that evidence relating to the wrongdoing will be concealed or destroyed if a disclosure is made to the employer; or
(3) that the worker has previously made a disclosure of substantially the same information to the employer or a prescribed person.

In considering whether the worker has acted reasonably in making the disclosure, the tribunal will take note of the identity of the person to whom the disclosure is made, the seriousness of the relevant failure, whether such a failure is likely to occur again, whether the disclosure was made in breach of a duty of confidence owed by the employer to another person, the action which the employer or person to whom a previous disclosure was made might reasonably have been expected to take, and whether the worker complied with any procedure, the use of which was authorised by the employer.

The final category relates to disclosures of exceptionally serious failures. The worker must make the disclosure in good faith, believing it to be true, not for personal gain, when the relevant failure is of an exceptionally serious nature and where it is reasonable to make the disclosure.

Any dismissal of an employee because he or she has made or intends to make a protected disclosure will be automatically unfair and any compensation awarded will not be capped. Further, there is no qualifying period of employment or upper age limit.

Therefore, where there is a possibility of the PIDA 1998 applying, it is vital that the charity is sure that it is dismissing for a potentially fair reason and is not motivated by the fact that the employee may have 'blown the whistle'. Compensation can also be awarded if the worker is subjected to any other detriment, such as failing to give promotion or training opportunities.

If a worker raises a concern with the charity which could potentially fall under the provisions of the PIDA 1998, the charity should consider the following:

- the individual may wish to remain anonymous – this wish should be respected as far as possible;
- a thorough investigation of any protected disclosure should be carried out by an independent and responsible person;
- a report should be completed within a reasonable time period, and a copy should be supplied to the appropriate person, in order to take action in respect of any findings;
- the individual should receive feedback on any action taken, with the exception of details of any disciplinary action taken against other individuals;
- the charity should ensure that all details of the complaint are kept confidential;
- notes should be kept of all conversations with the individual and witnesses, in a safe place. It may not be appropriate to place these on the employee's file.

If the charity does not deal with a disclosure of malpractice effectively and expeditiously, the worker has far greater scope to repeat the allegations elsewhere, such as to a regulatory body or the press, which could cause the employer a great deal of damage and embarrassment, even if these are subsequently discovered to be unfounded.

Examples

Of the cases which have been brought under the PIDA 1998, one of the most notable was *Fernandes* (unreported, July 2000). The employment tribunal awarded Mr Fernandes £293,441 in the first case of its kind under the PIDA 1998. Mr Fernandes was sacked for 'gross misconduct' almost immediately after he had faxed the US management of his telecommunications company, Netcom Consultants (UK) Ltd, claiming wrongful behaviour on the part of a senior executive. The tribunal was satisfied that the disclosure was a 'qualifying disclosure' made in 'good faith' and therefore protected. It was held that the accountant had been unfairly dismissed and that there had been 'a clear attempt to intimidate and pressurise Mr Fernandes to resign'.

In another case, a worker successfully claimed that his dismissal resulted from his complaint about a lack of adequate on-site supervision. The worker claimed that the lack of supervision gave rise to a breach of contract and therefore amounted to a 'protected disclosure' within the meaning of the PIDA 1998. This means that any complaint that there has been a breach of contract of employment, which leads to victimisation or dismissal, may attract a remedy under the Act.

Other situations where 'whistle-blowing' might arise include workers publicising faulty or dangerous equipment, the cover-up of relevant evidence or a policy of discrimination in recruitment.

The importance of implementing a proper policy cannot be understated in the current climate, especially in the light of a recent case concerning Mr Holden, a train driver who acted as a health and safety representative for Connex South Eastern Limited. Mr Holden had sent two reports detailing potential dangers facing both employees and passengers to Her Majesty's Railway Inspectorate. Following a severe reprimand by Connex, Mr Holden was told that he would be dismissed if another report was sent out. He resigned and brought proceedings against Connex. He was subsequently awarded £54,320 for unfair dismissal.

20.6.1 Policies

As with grievances, charity employers need to be proactive and ensure that they have the policies and procedures in place to deal with a possible whistle-blower. However, a disclosure is not the same as a grievance and it is inadvisable simply to let workers use the grievance procedure in such situations.

The unique nature of the provisions of the PIDA 1998 means that charities need to implement comprehensive policies dealing specifically with these disclosures and ensure that they are published and understood by managers and workers alike.

20.6.2 Practical guidance

The whistle-blowing policy should:

- form part of the staff handbook and, like the grievance procedure, be readily available to staff in a handbook or on the intranet;
- explain the rationale behind the PIDA 1998, ie its purpose, and, in so doing, distinguish between this policy and those dealing with grievances, discrimination or harassment;
- clarify to whom it applies legally but also specify if the charity wishes, say, non-worker contractors to comply with it if they become aware of activity covered by the PIDA 1998;

- state to whom the worker can make a disclosure (some charities identify a trustee or board member to whom a disclosure can be made, thereby emphasising their independence);
- explain what is covered by the PIDA 1998 and what the worker must do if he or she becomes aware of a relevant act;
- list the stages of the procedure, ie investigation, hearing, appeal; and record retention should be covered;
- deal with the issues of confidentiality, anonymity, victimisation and malicious allegations;
- provide guidance notes for those who may have to respond to disclosures; and implement comprehensive training on all aspects of the PIDA 1998 and its effects.

Chapter 21

DEALING WITH ALLEGATIONS

21.1 INTRODUCTION

From time to time charities receive allegations, against employees and against board members/trustees. Allegations may be varied and of a minor character, such as an allegation that an employee is persistently late for work; sometimes they are considerably more serious and concern serious misconduct, such as allegations of discrimination or fraud.

It is essential that charities, whatever their size, respond fairly to such allegations. This is especially important where there is an allegation about the charity's activities or funds, which will impact on the beneficiaries of the charity. This chapter adopts a step-by-step approach and guides a charity through a fair process when responding to allegations.

22.2 STAGE 1A: AN ALLEGATION IS MADE BY AN EMPLOYEE

When an allegation is made the charity should respond immediately by following its grievance policy or other appropriate policy (such as a bullying and harassment policy), which should state explicitly how to follow a proper procedure in documenting and recording the complaints. As mentioned in Chapter 20, the charity should have previously identified and made available to staff details of an appropriate person to whom the allegation should be made. Usually the person to whom the complaint is made will be an HR officer, with a second optional officer to cover the situation where the HR officer is the alleged perpetrator.

The HR officer should follow a prompt procedure in recording the complaint. This means clearly writing down full details of the allegations made, including any dates, names and places where the acts are alleged to have occurred. All information of a personal nature recorded against the alleged perpetrator will be subject to the provisions of the Data Protection Act 1998 (DPA 1998), and the Code of Practice on Data Protection. In short, these give workers rights of access and confidentiality in respect of data recorded about them.

At this preliminary stage, the charity will also want to recall the main provisions on whistle-blowing, in case such an issue arises. As dealt with at **20.6**, the Public Interest Disclosure Act 1998 (PIDA 1998) protects workers against victimisation or dismissal if they report malpractice by their employers or third parties. The law gives special protection to any worker who makes a 'qualifying disclosure' in accordance with the provisions of the PIDA 1998, including protection to an employee who is dismissed because (or principally because) he or she has made a protected disclosure. The complainant should, in such circumstances, be assured of the charity's protection.

The charity will also want to bear in mind its duties in relation to the victimisation of complainants under discrimination legislation.

Once the allegations have been recorded, the charity should form a commonsense view and classify the allegations as either of a serious or minor nature in order to decide what action needs to be taken.

Prudent charities will have distinguished between serious and less serious misconduct in their disciplinary and capability policies (see Chapter 20) For very minor offences, the worker may be approached on an informal basis and a basic oral inquiry made. For more serious allegations, it will be necessary for the charity to implement its disciplinary procedure.

21.3 STAGE 1B: AN ALLEGATION IS MADE ANONYMOUSLY OR BY SOMEONE WHO IS NOT AN EMPLOYEE

It is not unusual for charities to receive anonymous allegations about senior members of staff or board members or trustees. Allegations are also sometimes made by people working with charities who are not employees, or by beneficiaries.

Ex-employees will have a right to be treated in accordance with the grievance procedure under the Employment Act 2002 (EA 2002), which is due to come into force on 1 October 2004. However, at present, ex-employees who make allegations do not have the right to be treated in accordance with the grievance procedure.

All allegations should be treated seriously. It is sensible in these circumstances to follow a process which is not dissimilar to a grievance procedure. Some charities formalise this as a 'complaints procedure', which is publicised to beneficiaries and board members, but followed in every instance where an allegation is made. A person should be given the role of investigating the allegation insofar as he or she is able and consideration should be given to appointing a third party who is external or independent to the charity to investigate serious allegations. This is especially the case where serious allegations are made against senior staff.

Charities should note that if an allegation is made, even if it is anonymous and unsubstantiated, and the charity does nothing, where the allegations are proved to be true the charity will have legal risks which it will face at a later date.

If the allegation is anonymous there will be practical difficulties in carrying out a full investigation. Attempts should be made to speak to the informant if contactable, if that is the only way of investigating the complaint.

What is more common is an informant who is content to co-operate with the charity in making the allegations, but wishes to remain anonymous (see detailed guidance in Chapter 20). The basic principles are that a charity cannot always guarantee anonymity and should not make such promises, but it is possible to take such allegations seriously and investigate them further if necessary.

21.4 STAGE 2: DISCIPLINARY ACTION AGAINST STAFF – FAIR DISCIPLINARY RULES AND PROCEDURES

Where an allegation against a member of staff could result in disciplinary action, the charity must then implement the appropriate disciplinary policy.

There should be a preliminary stage to the disciplinary policy, which provides that minor complaints be dealt with informally in the first instance. For more serious offences, and allegations of repeat offences, the disciplinary procedure must be followed.

21.5 ALLEGATION MADE AGAINST A NON-EMPLOYEE INCLUDING A BOARD MEMBER OR TRUSTEE

Where an allegation is made against someone who is not an employee, the board will be expected to have acted reasonably to ensure that it is acting in accordance with its duties to beneficiaries and the expectations of the Charities Commission. If the person concerned is likely to continue to have dealings with staff and 'reoffends', the way in which the charity dealt with the original allegation is relevant to any subsequent problems.

If the allegation is serious, the charity should give consideration to terminating the relationship with the person concerned. This is particularly important where that person has dealings with staff or beneficiaries, or where the allegation is serious enough to warrant press interest in the charity's dealings with him or her.

Where the allegation is less serious, it is probably preferable for a quiet word to be had with the person concerned, and where appropriate for a record to be kept of the discussion. Note, however, that such a note will be subject to the DPA 1998 and the Code of Practice on Data Protection and may require to be disclosed at a later date.

It is also relevant for the charity to consider offering support to the individual concerned about the allegation – for instance, offering a board member training on how to deal with certain situations.

21.6 EXPECTATIONS OF THE CHARITY COMMISSION

Complainants do, from time to time, involve the Charity Commission in complaints made against individuals concerned with charities. The Charity Commission expects complainants to contact it only where other procedures have been exhausted, and will investigate complaints and intervene only where there is a serious risk of significant harm or abuse to the charity, its assets, beneficiaries or reputation.

Charities should also consider advising the Charity Commission of events where internal investigation uncovers similar 'significant harm or abuse'.

CASE STUDY 1

A is a charity which provides home improvements to people with disabilities in the community. A police informant names a senior manager, Charlie, as linked to a tendering scam. This information is passed to the Charities Commission, which advises the charity of the allegation. Ben, the Chief Executive, reacts by undertaking a detailed analysis of the tendering and obtains company searches on all of the relevant contractors. Nothing comes to light, and this is reported to the Charities Commission.

Ben is not satisfied. Although no further action is technically necessary, the charity appoints private investigators. They begin to uncover possible links between Charlie and one of the contractors. Ben confronts Charlie, who admits the relationship with the contractor and that it has lasted for over 10 years. Charlie resigns and the charity withholds making further payments to the contractor.

The charity then commissions a detailed independent investigation of the work carried out by the contractor to assess whether the work has been properly undertaken and for a reasonable price. It also reviews its tendering procedures and makes a number of changes.

The independent investigation of the work shows that the contractor has undertaken the work to a reasonable standard and for a fair price. It is not therefore necessary or appropriate for the charity to seek recovery of the sums paid over to the contractor.

Practical Guidance

- Allegations should be taken seriously irrespective of the source.
- Allegations should not be 'investigated' by a colleague or line manager as there may be a conflict of interest or a perception that the allegation is not being taken seriously.
- Where checks on procedural compliance can shed light on an allegation, then such checks can be undertaken internally, but it may be best to deal with matters externally to ensure that the investigation is not too narrow in its scope; and external investigations are perceived to be more independent by outside parties.
- Where irregularities come to light, the charity should not assume that it has reached the root of the problem until related areas have been checked.
- Charities should undertake such checking without waiting to be told to do so by the Charities Commission.

CASE STUDY 2

An allegation of racism in relation to appointments was made against a black senior manager by an ex-employee. Continuing legal action in relation to an unfair dismissal claim complicated the position as it was not appropriate for the charity to 'second guess' what the outcome might be.

There was nothing particularly wrong with the charity's policies and procedures in relation to recruitment and equal opportunities. However, it was inconsistent in following them. In one area of the charity's work, 50% of recruitments had not been openly advertised. Although there was no evidence of discrimination, the failure to recruit openly left the senior manager vulnerable to a charge of favouritism.

Equal opportunities monitoring was not adequate but the board was aware of the way in which the recruitments had taken place. The board was ignorant of several key aspects of employment law.

The charity's failure to follow its own procedures was used as evidence in a later employment tribunal that its procedures were not sufficiently robust, and the tribunal did not give credence to the witness evidence of the HR team on the procedures used on recruitment.

Practical Guidance

- Disciplinary and grievance procedures should be sufficiently robust to cope with situations in which they arise contemporaneously. In such situations, the manager taking disciplinary action cannot also hear the grievance.
- Procedures should also be sufficiently robust to cope with situations in which a further grievance is raised before the first one has been considered or resolved.
- Where grievances concern complaints of racial or gender discrimination, the charity should normally make arrangements for these to be heard or assessed by someone who is black or female, accordingly. If necessary, the charity should seek external assistance with this.
- Charities should look for patterns of disciplinary action or grievances, which may be signs of institutionalised behaviour that could undermine their equal opportunities objectives.
- Where an allegation is made that relates to a specific area of the charity's activities, there should be a thorough check of compliance with policies and procedures.
- Compliance checks of non-financial procedures are a key safeguard against accusations that can be damaging to a charity's reputation.
- Policies are valueless if they are not followed and a tribunal will look beyond the existence of such policies, if challenged, to see that they are being used.

Chapter 22

DEALING WITH MISCONDUCT AND POOR PERFORMANCE

22.1 WHAT SHOULD CHARITY EMPLOYERS DO?

22.1.1 Act fairly

All charity employers will want to help and encourage their employees to achieve and maintain acceptable standards of performance and conduct whilst at work. This chapter looks at how to encourage improvement in individuals' conduct and how to impose sanctions for unsatisfactory performance.

The best way for a charity employer to maintain fairness when dealing with disciplinary and capability issues at work is to implement and follow a disciplinary and capability policy or policies (whether one or two policies). This ensures that staff are treated fairly and consistently.

The policy should clearly set out the procedures to be followed should a disciplinary or capability issue arise. It should be communicated to all employees and made readily available for them to read – for example, on an intranet or in a staff handbook. Employees such as managers and human resources staff will need to be particularly familiar with the provisions of the policy so that they are able to play their part in its implementation. Some charities have a separate disciplinary procedure for their senior employees. The main difference is likely to be the length of time between stages and the ability to jump stages.

Although an individual charity's disciplinary and capability policy will need to be drafted according to the charity employer's specific requirements, there are a number of basic principles which all policies should cover, and these are discussed below.

22.1.2 Take proportionate action

Disciplinary action will normally be taken following an allegation that there has been a breach of company rules. It is common for a policy to distinguish between less serious offences and more serious offences of gross misconduct. Although it is not necessary to provide a definition of every form of misconduct (some forms of misconduct will be obvious to both employer and employee) it is important to make all disciplinary rules and procedures clear and unambiguous. Employment tribunals will normally accept that a rule is reasonable provided there is a good commercial or operational reason for it, and that the penalty falls within the 'range of reasonable responses' open to the employer to choose as a sanction.

22.1.3 Involve representatives in formulating procedures

The ACAS Code of Practice on Disciplinary Practice and Procedures in employment recommends that management should secure the involvement of employees when formulating new, or advising on existing, rules and procedures. Trade unions or employee representatives, where recognised, should participate fully with management in agreeing the procedure and arrangements which will apply to their members and in seeing that these arrangements are used consistently and fairly.

22.2 TYPES OF DISCIPLINARY OFFENCES

22.2.1 Misconduct

The following is a (non-exhaustive) list of behaviour which may be regarded by a charity employer as misconduct and which may be listed in a disciplinary policy as such. Offences of a similar nature will also be dealt with under the disciplinary procedure:

- bad time-keeping;
- unreasonable or unexplained absence;
- minor breaches of confidentiality or company rules and procedures;
- damage to company property;
- poor performance due to negligence.

22.2.2 Gross misconduct

A finding of gross misconduct normally results in dismissal. A finding of gross misconduct should not be made before a full investigation has been undertaken to establish the facts of the case and the employee concerned has been given an opportunity to state his or her case. The decision to dismiss should not be taken without reference to a senior manager, and should be made only after full consideration of the range of reasonable responses open to the employer. The employee should be notified of the dismissal in writing and should be reminded of the right to appeal. The following are examples of behaviour which may be regarded as gross misconduct:

- fraud, dishonesty or falsification of documents;
- wilful or negligent damage to or misuse or unauthorised use of the employer's property or facilities;
- working whilst under the influence of alcohol or non-prescribed drugs;

- serious negligence leading to loss, damage or injury;
- gross insubordination;
- serious incidents involving discrimination, bullying and/or harassment on the grounds of sex, race, or disability;
- violent, dangerous or intimidatory conduct;
- serious breaches of confidentiality or of the employer's rules and procedures;
- serious infringements of health and safety rules;
- misuse of the employer's property or name;
- serious breach of confidence.

The list is not exhaustive and serious incidents of misconduct may also be regarded as gross misconduct.

22.3 FOLLOWING A PROPER DISCIPLINARY PROCEDURE

It is not necessary to carry out a detailed investigation if the employee either admits his or her guilt or, in the case of criminal offences, the employee has already pleaded guilty to the offence in a court of law. In all other cases, including those where an employee has been charged with an offence but has not been tried, an employer will have to be satisfied, on a 'balance of probabilities', that the employee is guilty of the offence. This means carrying out a detailed investigation before any disciplinary hearing.

22.3.1 Stages in procedure

A disciplinary procedure for dismissal normally includes the following stages.

Stage 1: The investigatory stage

The charity should:

- interview relevant witnesses, making a statement of their evidence;
- pay particular attention to the factual detail such as the date, time and place of each and every observation or incident, the opportunity to observe the incident clearly and with accuracy, any circumstantial evidence tending to support what the informant is saying, any reason why the informant might be lying or have any other reason to fabricate a statement;
- undertake further investigation to try to collaborate the informant's statement;
- interview the accused (he or she may be accompanied by a workplace colleague or a union representative and should be advised of this right); and then, having considered all the evidence
- decide whether to convene a disciplinary hearing.

Stage 2: The pre-disciplinary hearing stage

The charity should invite the accused to a disciplinary hearing. The invitation should:

- state when and where the disciplinary hearing will take place and who will chair it;
- inform the accused of his or her right to be accompanied by a workplace colleague or union representative;
- state the charges the accused has to face – for instance, detailing the charge of gross misconduct, being an allegation that, on a certain day, the employee used possessions of the charity for his own use; and
- disclose any relevant evidence to enable the accused to prepare his or her case.

Stage 3: The disciplinary hearing stage

The charity should:

- introduce those present, explaining the role of various attendees;
- inform the accused of the case against him or her;
- disclose all relevant evidence;
- allow the accused (or his or her representative) to challenge the evidence against him or her if he or she wishes; and
- allow the accused (or the representative) to make other representations he or she wishes – for example, in mitigation.

Either at the hearing or after the hearing, the person hearing the allegation should reach a decision both as to the guilt of the accused and the appropriate penalty, inform the accused of that decision (in person, preferably), but at least confirm the decision in writing and inform the accused of his or her right to appeal and the procedure for appealing.

Stage 4: The appeal hearing stage

The nature of this stage will depend on whether the appeal is by way of a review of the original decision or a rehearing.

- *Review*: The person conducting the review should invite the appellant to set out his or her grounds for appeal and give him or her (or his or her representative) an opportunity to make representation. The person should then review the decision, informing the appellant of the outcome. Any decision should be confirmed in writing.
- *Rehearing*: The person holding the appeal should follow the same procedure as set out in stage 3 above.

22.3.2 Particular aspects of procedure

The various procedural stages are now considered in more detail.

Suspension

Charity employers should not automatically respond to an allegation by suspending the employee. Instead, they should consider whether the allegations are well founded and whether it is necessary to suspend the employee while the investigation is ongoing. If it is necessary to take the employee away from his or her current duties, the charity should consider various options: the employer should, for instance, first consider whether the employee can be transferred to another post or department or could be given time off on holiday. Suspension should be for not too long a period; not more than weeks, rather than months. The employer should also be sensitive and tactful in advising the employee that an investigation is to take place.

Where informants who make the allegations wish to remain anonymous

Where allegations concerning an employee's conduct are made by an informant, a careful balance must be maintained between the right of the informant to remain anonymous (especially where the informant has a genuine concern for his or her safety) and the right of the accused to have a fair hearing.

If the informant is not prepared to attend a disciplinary hearing, or to be identified by the written statement, management must decide whether the fear is genuine and whether the hearing should go ahead. If the hearing does go ahead, the case should be outlined in as much detail as possible to the accused without identifying the informant and, if necessary, the hearing should be adjourned to enable management to ask the informant to comment on any significant factual matters that are disputed by the accused.

Anonymity should not be guaranteed. It is inadvisable for charities to guarantee anonymity to an informant as it will often be possible for the accused to identify the informant from the statement.

Where the allegation is against an anonymous employee

The courts have recognised that it is open to employers to dismiss a group of employees if it is impossible to establish or identify who is guilty of the particular offence and every employee in the relevant group has had the opportunity to commit the particular offence. However, the following criteria must be met:

- the employer must be satisfied that the act was sufficiently serious to justify the dismissal of an individual;
- there was a sufficiently thorough investigation by the employer to seek the identity of the culprit;
- as a result of that investigation, the employer reasonably believed that more than one person could have committed the act;

- the employer acted reasonably in identifying the group of employees who could have committed the act and each member of the group was individually capable of doing so; and
- as between each member of the group, the employer could not reasonably identify the individual perpetrator.

22.4 TRADE UNION OFFICIALS

Disciplinary action against a trade union official can lead to a serious dispute if it is seen as an attack on the union's function. Although normal disciplinary standards should apply, no disciplinary action beyond an oral warning should be taken until the circumstances of the case have been discussed with a senior trade union representative or full-time official.

22.5 CRIMINAL OFFENCES OUTSIDE EMPLOYMENT

Such offences should not be treated as automatic reasons for dismissal, regardless of whether the offence has any relevance to an individual's duties as an employee. The main consideration should be whether the offence is one that makes the individual unsuitable for his or her type of work or unacceptable to other employees. A employee should not be dismissed solely because a charge against him or her is pending or because he or she is absent through having been remanded in custody; the principle is that a person is innocent until proven guilty. Having said that, if an employee is on remand for a long period of time there will come a time when it is appropriate for an employer to take action to dismiss him or her. Such matters must be treated very carefully as the employee will not be in the best position to defend himself or herself.

22.6 STATUTORY RIGHT TO BE ACCOMPANIED AT A DISCIPLINARY HEARING

Under the Employment Relations Act 1999, an employee or a worker is entitled to be accompanied at disciplinary hearings. The right to be accompanied applies specifically to hearings which could result in:

- the administration of a warning to an employee by his or her employer;
- the taking of some other action in respect of an employee by his or her employer (eg suspension without pay, demotion or dismissal); or
- the confirmation of a warning issued or some other action taken.

Whether the employee has the right to be accompanied depends on the nature of the hearing. Arguably there is no right to a companion at an investigation hearing, as it is not a hearing that could result in the administration of a formal warning. However, as a formal warning can result from an investigation it is safest to interpret the law widely, and it is good practice to encourage employees to have the support of a companion for all disciplinary hearings. It is sensible to include such a right in the disciplinary procedure; it is also sensible to limit the representation allowed to specific classes of companions to ensure that it cannot be a legal representative.

The right is to be accompanied by a fellow worker or a trade union official who has been reasonably certified by the union as having experience of or training in acting as a worker's companion at such hearings. The companion should be given paid time off to attend the hearing and to have prior meetings with the employee if required.

The companion is permitted to address the hearing and to confer with the employee, in private if necessary. However, he is not allowed to answer questions on behalf of the employee. If the employee is denied this right he or she can complain to an employment tribunal, which may award up to 2 weeks' pay as stand-alone compensation and, potentially, a much larger award for unfair dismissal compensation.

CASE STUDY

The importance of following a fair procedure and not assuming guilt is illustrated by the decision of the Court of Appeal in the case of *Gogay v Herefordshire County Council* [2000] IRLR 703.

The employee in the case was a residential care worker who was placed in a difficult position by a child inmate who had been abused at the home and who had formed an attachment to the employee. This led the employee to stress-related absences. Later, during a therapy session, the child made remarks leading the employer to instigate an investigation, during which the employee was suspended. The employee was told of her suspension by a bluntly worded letter relating to an 'allegation of sexual abuse', which caused the employee extreme upset. Although the investigation eventually found no case to answer, the employee suffered clinical depression and was unable to return to work.

The employee sued the employer for breach of the employment contract, claiming lost earnings and damages for personal injury. She was awarded damages of £26,000 and the court found that the employer had been in breach of the implied term of trust and respect in the manner in which she was suspended.

The court found that it was not necessary for an employer to suspend an employee automatically, especially where there was no immediate risk to the child in question. Here the employer had overreacted, and the facts did not actually show an 'allegation' of abuse at all; there was no well-founded allegation. The employer should have given more thought to lesser measures than suspension, such as a period of transfer to other duties.

22.7 DISCIPLINARY SANCTIONS

22.7.1 Considerations

Before taking disciplinary action, an employer should consider various factors to ensure that the action taken is fair and reasonable. These factors include taking into account:

- penalties which have been imposed in previous similar cases;
- special mitigating circumstances; and
- the employee's past record and service.

22.7.2 Penalties/Sanctions

The following penalties or sanctions may be considered by an employer.

Warnings

Warnings, whether written or oral, should be recorded and kept on file. In the case of oral warnings, it is important to have evidence that they were given and to have certainty of their content. The employee should not be in any doubt that an oral warning has been given. All warnings should specify the reason for the warning, improvement expected (if relevant) and the time scale for achieving the improvement. There should also be a date after which the warning will be considered 'spent' if no further breaches of discipline occur. If further warnings are given, it is sensible to include a provision that all existing warnings will be taken into account if future disciplinary action is necessary. The following illustrates the normal ascending severity of warnings given.

(a) **Stage 1: An informal warning**
At this stage of the disciplinary procedure, it is sensible to warn an employee about what is coming next. While no formal warning is given, a note of the conversation should be kept on the file of the individual concerned.

(b) **Stage 2: A formal oral warning, and Stage 3: A formal written warning**
If, after a full investigation, an employee is found to have committed an act of misconduct, the charity can give the employee a formal warning which will be disregarded as 'spent' for further disciplinary purposes after a stipulated period of time – for example, 6 months.

(c) **Stage 4: A final written warning**
Where an incident of misconduct or gross misconduct has occurred but the charity has not felt it necessary to dismiss the employee, it

can give the individual a final written warning. The final written warning should be disregarded after a stipulated period of time, say, 12 months, and should make it clear that the individual will be dismissed for a further breach of the disciplinary policy.

(d) **Stage 5: Dismissal**
There must be a valid reason for dismissal, and the employer must act reasonably and follow procedures. It is usual for charities to dismiss only where there is an incident of gross misconduct or where less serious disciplinary sanctions have been given and accrued.

Unless a dismissal is for gross misconduct, notice of termination must be given in accordance with the terms of the contract and in line with the statutory minimum periods of notice. Failure to give proper notice may lead to a claim for wrongful dismissal.

Suspension

Unless there is an express right in the contract of employment to suspend without pay, such a suspension will be a breach of contract and may give rise to a claim for constructive dismissal.

Suspension with pay for a reasonable period will not be in breach of contract and is advisable while investigations are carried out, particularly where there is a suspicion of dishonesty. The employee should be told the length of the suspension, which can be extended if investigations are not completed. However, it is an element of fairness that these matters are dealt with speedily. Suspension should be seen by employers and employees alike as a measure taken as part of the disciplinary procedure rather than as a penalty in itself.

Fine

It is unlawful to make a deduction from an employee's wages as a disciplinary penalty unless the employee has given prior written consent to such a deduction; if this is a sanction the charity wishes to include, then it must make provision in the contract.

Demotion

A demotion will generally be a breach of contract and may give rise to a claim for constructive dismissal (which may not necessarily be unfair). However, if the employee agrees to the demotion because the alternative is dismissal, this will be acceptable. If the employee's misconduct was itself a serious breach of contract, the employer can demote.

22.8 KEEPING RECORDS

The ACAS Code of Practice recommends that records should be kept, detailing the nature of any breach of the disciplinary rules, the action taken and the reasons for it, whether an appeal was lodged, its outcome and any subsequent development. These records should be carefully safeguarded and kept confidential, in accordance with the provisions of the Data Protection Act 1998 (DPA 1998).

A record should be kept of all warnings. In the case of a written warning, an employee should be asked to acknowledge the receipt of the warning and his or her acceptance of the accuracy of the information contained in the warning. This can be very helpful if the matter subsequently goes to an employment tribunal.

Records should be kept for all disciplinary hearings and it is recommended that a member of management attends the disciplinary hearing as a 'note taker'. An employee may be invited to sign and confirm that any such note is an accurate record of what took place. This, again, is useful if the case goes to an employment tribunal. The same procedure should be followed at an appeal hearing.

It should be remembered that nearly all documents created in a disciplinary procedure will be discloseable in any future employment tribunal.

22.9 LACK OF CAPABILITY

It is common for employers to confuse when a matter becomes one of capability rather than misconduct. The following are examples of lack of capability. Similar circumstances may also be dealt with in the same way:

- poor performance;
- incompetence;
- unsuitability for the position; and
- ill health.

This procedure should normally be followed in cases of poor performance and should be set out as a policy for use across the charity. In more serious cases, one or more of the earlier stages may be omitted. The principle of the policy is that the employer should, wherever possible, provide training, support and additional supervision.

22.9.1 Stages in procedure

Stage 1: Formal oral warning

If, after a full investigation, an employee's performance is found not to meet the standards required by the employer, then the problem should be brought to the employee's attention in the form of an oral warning. The employee's superior should remind the employee of the standard of work expected and seek an explanation for the poor performance. The employee should be told of the improvement required and a time scale, if any, for achieving the improvement. He or she should also be warned that further action may be taken if there is no improvement. A brief note of the conversation should be put on the employee's personnel file, but should be disregarded for disciplinary purposes after a stipulated number of months – for example, 6 months. The employee's manager should first consider whether the lack of capability is caused by disability and, if so, there may be a duty upon the employer to make reasonable adjustments in accordance with the DDA 1995 (see Chapter 7).

Stage 2: First written warning

Where, after the period specified in stage 1 above, it is found that an employee's work has not reached the required standard (but it is felt that the employee is capable of attaining the standard), the employee should be informed by his or her supervisor of the particular respects in which performance is still inadequate and given a further reasonable period in which to attain the required standard. The employee should be warned that further action may be taken if there is no improvement; and this should be confirmed in writing. A copy of the warning should be kept on the employee's personnel file but disregarded after a set period of time, for example, 6 months, subject to satisfactory service in the meantime.

Stage 3: Final written warning

Where, after a first written warning has been issued, it is found that an employee's work has still not reached the required standard but it is still felt that the employee is capable of obtaining the standard, the employee should be informed by his or her manager of the particular respects in which their performance is inadequate and given a further reasonable period in which to attain the required standard. The employee should be informed that he or she may be dismissed with immediate effect at the end of the period if the required standard has not been attained; and this should be confirmed to the employee in writing. A copy of this warning should be kept on the employee's personnel file, eventually to be disregarded, subject to satisfactory service.

Stage 4: Dismissal

Where a final written warning has been issued, and the period in which the performance is to be improved has resulted in no such improvement, whether or not by reason of the fact that the employee is not capable of attaining the required standard, consideration should be given to offering the employee an alternative position within his or her capability. If such an alternative is not available, the charity employer is likely to be justified in dismissing the employee. The decision to dismiss should be taken only after full consultation with the employee.

During the process, if it is clear that the employee is unable to attain the standards set, the charity can make the decision to move directly to dismissal; this would be appropriate in some circumstances, such as where the job changes to the extent that the current job holder is not capable of carrying out the job as he or she lacks the relevant qualifications.

22.10 EMPLOYMENT ACT 2002

Those parts of the Employment Act 2002 (EA 2002) that relate to grievance and disciplinary hearings are due to come into force on 1 October 2004.

The EA 2002 deals expansively with dispute resolution. Whilst it is estimated that 90% of large employers have disciplinary and grievance procedures, a huge number of small employers who face tribunal claims have no procedures in place at all. Accordingly, statutory procedures covering both disciplinary and grievance issues will put in place minimum standards which will be implied into every contract of employment. Under no circumstances will an employer be permitted to contract out of these minimum standards, and existing procedures will need to be fully audited to ensure that they comply.

The aim is to implement a fixed period prior to any tribunal claim being lodged during which parties can attempt conciliation. The standard procedure sets out the following basic requirements:

- each step must be taken without unreasonable delay;
- timings and locations of the meetings must be reasonable;
- the meetings must be conducted in a manner enabling both employer and employee adequately to explain their case;
- appeals, so far as reasonably practicable, should be heard by someone more senior than the person who took the original decision.

The procedure is initiated by the employee's grievance statement, which must be in writing and sent to the employer. The employer must then invite the employee to a grievance meeting to discuss the matter, and the employee is required to take all reasonable steps to attend that meeting. After the meeting, the employer must inform the employee of the outcome and advise the employee of the right to appeal if the employee is dissatisfied with the outcome. Once the appeal has been conducted the employer must inform the employee of the outcome.

Chapter 23

RESIGNATION, DISMISSAL AND SETTLEMENTS

23.1 INTRODUCTION

There will be occasions when charities find it necessary to dismiss an employee or an employee decides to leave an organisation. This chapter looks at what happens when an employee wishes to leave an organisation, and what is expected of employers when terminating the employment of an individual.

23.2 RESIGNATION/TERMINATION OF EMPLOYMENT BY MUTUAL CONSENT

An employee can bring the employment relationship to an end by giving notice to terminate his or her contract of employment. The notice is usually set out in the contract and is what is reasonable in the circumstances. If an employee has been continuously employed for one month or more, he or she must give at least one week's notice. In practice, most charities require staff to give at least one month's notice.

If an employee resigns his or her employment it is good practice for the charity to enquire why. Larger employers institute formal 'exit interviews' giving an opportunity for an employee to explain the reasons for leaving. Most employers find these of great use.

Charities should be wary of accepting resignations that are given in haste or in a fit of pique. There is case law which suggests that an employer should in these circumstances allow for a cooling off period, and it is suggested therefore that charities ask a resigning employee to reconsider his or her resignation, if it is given in these circumstances.

Another difficult situation arises where an employee gives notice in circumstances where he or she indicates that it has been precipitated by something at work. An aggrieved employee may resign as a precursor to taking action against an employer for constructive dismissal. If the charity suspects that this is what is intended, it is worth discussing the matter with the employee and trying to ascertain what the complaint is. From October 2004 it will be necessary for employees to pursue a grievance before making out a claim.

If an employee does not resign but comes to an agreement to leave, it is often because there is a mutual termination of the contract of employment. This is advantageous to a charity, as an employee who leaves by mutual agreement cannot bring a claim in respect of dismissal against the charity. Charities should also note that a resignation or termination by mutual agreement under threat of dismissal is treated in law as a dismissal. However, such a route is not as attractive to an employee as it does not necessarily attract the same tax benefits on severance.

23.3 DISMISSAL

Employees can attain contractual rights from the outset of the employment relationship and so a dismissal will be unlawful if not conducted in compliance with the terms of the contract. In addition, all employees with more than one year's continuous service have the statutory right to claim unfair dismissal. Bringing the employment relationship to an end also sometimes precipitates other claims, such as discrimination claims. It is therefore important for a charity to adhere to a fair and thorough procedure when the dismissal of an employee is a possibility, to minimise the risk of such claims.

23.3.1 Fair dismissal

A fair dismissal is a legal term; employers can dismiss fairly for certain reasons. These are listed in the Employment Rights Act 1996 (ERA 1996) and constitute what an employer must prove as the 'substantive' fair reason for dismissal. There are five fair reasons for dismissal.

Reasons

The following are acceptable reasons for dismissal:

(1) reasons related to the capability or qualifications of the employee for performing work of the kind which he or she was employed to do;
(2) reasons related to the conduct of the employee;
(3) the employee was redundant (for the definition of 'redundancy' see Chapter 25);
(4) the employee could not continue to work in the position held without contravention (either on his or her part or on that of the employer) of a duty or restriction imposed by or under the enactment; or
(5) some other substantial reason that would justify the dismissal of an employee holding the position which that employee held.

Procedure

It is equally important that a charity follows a fair procedure in dismissing an employee. In addition to proving the substantive fair reason for dismissal, the employer must also prove that it has complied with its statutory obligation to act reasonably in the circumstances. This is something of a 'catch-all' provision and enables the employment tribunal to consider all aspects of the dismissal, including, for example, the size and administrative resources of the employer, in deciding whether dismissal was a reasonable response in the circumstances. If a fair process has not been followed, the tribunal is likely to find that a dismissal is unfair and possibly in breach of contract.

When dismissing an employee for one of a variety of different reasons, it is important to use the appropriate procedure for that reason. Thus, where a charity dismisses an employee for misconduct, it is appropriate to follow a disciplinary route (see Chapter 19). When dismissing an employee for incapability, it is appropriate to follow a capability process, ideally set out in a capability procedure (see Chapter 22). When dismissing an employee for incapability due to sickness absence, one should consider all possible consequences and consider taking the action suggested in Chapter 12. When making an employee redundant, it is appropriate to follow the correct procedure for redundancy (see Chapter 25).

The two other 'fair ' reasons for dismissal under the law are illegality and 'some other substantial reason'. These are not normal routes for a charity to use when dismissing an employee. The best example of a dismissal for illegality is where the employer becomes aware that it will be illegal to continue employing an employee – for instance, where he or she does not have the appropriate immigration status to remain employed (see **4.4.2**).

The other reason, 'some other substantial reason', could be perceived as being a catch-all provision. Perhaps because of this, the courts have interpreted the provision very restrictively. It can be relied on when enforcing a change to terms and conditions of employment by dismissing employees and then re-employing them on different terms (see Chapter 26). It is also relied on in one-off situations, say, where an employee is dismissed to make way for the employment of the owner of the business.

It is not possible, under the current law, to dismiss an employee just because the relationship has reached a natural end. This situation does occur from time to time, but it is not possible to dismiss an employee fairly, simply because this is the charity's view. In these circumstances, the best route is to reach a mutual agreement with the employee to terminate the employment relationship. The employment will then come to an end, not through dismissal, but by mutual agreement.

23.3.2 Notice

When dismissing an employee, a charity must give adequate notice to terminate the contract. The notice provisions in the contract should specify a minimum notice period. Notice given must be at least the statutory minimum notice, which is not less than one week's notice if the period of continuous employment is less than two years, and not less than one week's notice for every completed year of continuous employment up to a maximum of 12 weeks' notice.

It is common for most staff who are paid monthly to be entitled to be given one month's notice, and it is also more usual for senior staff to have longer periods of notice. A director of a charity will, normally, be entitled to 3 months' notice as a minimum.

23.4 COMPROMISE AGREEMENTS

An employee cannot waive his or her statutory employment rights except where he or she has signed a valid compromise agreement, or where ACAS completes a settlement agreement. It is therefore important, where either a charity dismisses an employee and is unsure that the reason or the process is fair, or the charity reaches a mutual agreement that the employment should terminate, that the employee enters into a compromise agreement.

In order for the compromise agreement to be valid, the following criteria must be met:

(a) the agreement must be in writing;
(b) the agreement must relate to a particular complaint;
(c) the employee must have received independent legal advice (usually from a solicitor) as to the terms and effect of the agreement;
(d) there must be in force, when the employee receives the legal advice, a policy of insurance covering the risk of a claim by the employee in respect of any loss arising in consequence of the advice;
(e) the agreement must identify the adviser; and
(f) the agreement must confirm that the conditions regulating compromise agreements under the ERA 1996 are satisfied.

Generally speaking, an employee will not sign an agreement unless the charity offers some form of financial inducement. There is also an argument that a compromise agreement is not valid unless an ex gratia payment is made to an employee in consideration of agreeing to terms. A propensity to settle any potential claim may lead to employees taking advantage of the employer and, therefore, making a deal in every case is inadvisable. However, the ability to settle a claim and provide all parties with finality can be an extremely useful tool and should always be considered as an option when the employment relationship with an employee breaks down.

23.4.1 Practical guidance

A compromise agreement should contain the following:

- a statement of why and when the employee is leaving the employment of the employer;
- terms setting out the severance payment or agreement for the employee's benefit.

There is usually some negotiation about the financial package. The age of the 'fat cat' has not as yet arrived in the charity sector, and a charity employer must consider the level of payment to be made to an outgoing employee very carefully, in light of its overarching obligations to beneficiaries.

In considering the level of severance payment, a charity should take into account:

- any outstanding sums due to an employee on the termination date;
- any sums due for his or her notice period;
- any sums that would be paid if the employee took legal action against the charity.

The charity should also consider non-financial severance terms, such as:

- the provision of training or outplacement counselling (which can be tax deductible);
- an agreed reference;
- an agreed statement of reasons for departure to be given to staff;
- an agreed press release, in the case of senior staff;
- the transfer of charity property to the employee (such as mobile phone);
- the transfer of capital payments into the employee's pension scheme rather than payment to the employee.

A charity will also want to protect its own interests and may wish to include terms:

- to protect its own confidential information;
- requiring return of charity property;
- requiring confidentiality about the terms of departure.

In all circumstances, a compromise agreement is an effective conclusion to a departure of a senior member of staff, and one that charities should consider using to avoid conflict and litigation.

Chapter 24

EMPLOYMENT TRIBUNALS

24.1 INTRODUCTION

Sometimes it is not possible to resolve disputes with employees before they leave employment and matters are left to employment tribunals, (formerly known as industrial tribunals). The employment tribunal is the forum most frequented by parties seeking redress for disputes associated with the workplace. Tribunals were originally intended to be an informal means of supplying a swift and decisive resolution to employment disputes. Although to a lay person the system can today appear just as official as the one found in courts, the tribunals have in fact retained some of their original informality, which is possibly why so many individuals still choose to represent themselves in disputes.

The workload of the tribunals has increased hugely since they were originally created in 1964. From a low of 29,304 applications registered in 1988/9, the number of applications rose to 130,408 in 2000/1. The increase in claims is driven by the introduction of new law and the extension of the tribunals' jurisdiction but it is undoubtedly enhanced by the fact that employees and workers are becoming more familiar with their rights. In recent years, the number of applications has dropped slightly, but is still high.

This chapter sets out the principal elements of the employment tribunal system to provide an insight into what to expect if faced with a tribunal application.

24.2 COMPOSITION OF THE TRIBUNAL

An employment tribunal panel is usually composed of three individuals. The chairman, who is currently appointed by the Lord Chancellor and must have a 7-year legal qualification, is appointed on either a full-time or part-time basis to chair the panel that hears the claim. The chairman is customarily drawn from either a legal professional background or a legal academic background. He will sit in the centre of the three individuals hearing the application. On either side of the chairman will sit a lay representative. One lay person is required to have an employee-biased background, ie somebody with union experience. The second lay member is required to be representative of employers, ie somebody with a business background, who may have been an employer. Thus, in theory, a balanced panel hears the claim.

A full tribunal comprising all three members is required for the hearing of the majority of claims within its jurisdiction. There are, however, exceptions where a chairman may sit alone. Examples of the most common exceptions include:

- applications regarding an unlawful deduction from wages;
- applications with regard to a failure to pay a protective award (in collective redundancy or business transfer scenarios); and
- claims for breach of contract.

Tribunals are usually public hearings, so one will often find members of the public, including the press, attending a particularly interesting hearing. There are exceptions to this rule, such as the conducting of directions hearings (concerning management and running of the case), although it would be rare to exclude members of the public if both parties were agreeable to their inclusion. The tribunal has authority to direct a private hearing where it believes that the evidence would consist of information which, if disclosed, would breach a statutory prohibition or which was disclosed to a witness in confidence, or which, if disclosed, could cause substantial damage to a witness's business for commercial reasons. However, these exceptions are rare.

Tribunal hearings are conducted in rooms. The three members of the tribunal panel sit at the head of a room, generally on a raised platform. The applicant employee and the respondent employer, or their representatives, will sit at tables facing the tribunal members. The witness giving evidence will sit at a table located either in the centre of the parties or occasionally to one side. The chairman is addressed as either 'Sir' or 'Madam'.

24.3 INITIATING PROCEEDINGS

An individual who wishes to bring a claim is called an applicant. The applicant commences proceedings by presenting form IT1, the originating application claim form, to the appropriate tribunal office. The application is deemed as presented when it is received, as opposed to when it was sent. This is extremely important for applicants because the time-limits for presenting tribunal applications are strictly enforced by the tribunals; even if a claim is presented one day over the time-limit, it can be barred from proceeding any further.

Accordingly, parties to proceedings tend to favour faxing crucial documentation to the tribunal so as to ensure that they have evidence to support their position in the event of a dispute. However, there is technically no difficulty in either the documentation being sent or presented in person.

Form IT1 will provide basic information concerning the claim. It will include the details of the employer and the employee, the dates of employment, the salary details and a space for the employee to provide the factual details of his or her complaint.

As noted, claims to employment tribunals must be presented within a specified time frame. This varies according to the nature of the claim, and any extension of time permitted to individuals who submit their claims late also varies depending upon the nature of the claim. It is beyond the scope of this chapter to set out the time frame for every claim which can be brought before an employment tribunal. However, it is useful to know the general rule and how it applies to the most common claim.

In a claim of unfair dismissal, the period of time in which an employee can present a tribunal application runs from, and includes, what is called the 'effective date of termination'. In layman's terms, this is the date upon which the dismissal is communicated to the employee and not, if it differs, either the date upon which the employer decides to dismiss or the date that the dismissal letter is sent. The communication can be verbal or in writing. The employee has 3 months from the effective date of termination to present his or her application.

24.4 THE NEXT STEP

When the employment tribunal receives the complaint, it will send this to the employer, who has 21 days from receiving the complaint to submit a response. This entails completing form IT3, which largely mirrors the details provided by the applicant on form IT1. The employer must set out its name and address, whether it has a representative, whether it agrees that the individual was dismissed and, if so, the reason for this. Dates of employment and salary details are requested and, finally, it provides space to set out the grounds of defence.

The consequences of submitting the IT3 late can potentially be very serious. It is possible for the tribunal to prohibit the respondent from taking any further part in the proceedings. However, the respondent does have the opportunity to make an application to the tribunal to enter its IT3 late. The tribunal is not obliged to grant the extension but, provided there is a good reason why the response was not provided within the 21-day period, there is a reasonable chance that the tribunal will grant the extension. However, the consequences of submitting a late IT3 can be serious and a respondent should always endeavour to comply with the 21-day limit.

Once the respondent has submitted its response, the tribunal will consider it together with the applicant's complaint and decide what, if any, preliminary and case management issues need to be addressed before the claim proceeds to a full hearing.

24.4.1 Practical guidance

On receipt of an IT1, the following steps should be undertaken:

(a) Note in a diary the date by when the charity must respond with the IT3.
(b) Complete the information on the form IT3, putting forward a clear version of the facts argued, with or without legal representation.
(c) Consider whether it is possible to argue any points of the claim. If so, the charity will need to set out its counter-arguments.
(d) Collect and collate all relevant documents, ideally in date order.
(e) Ask the relevant witnesses to put together statements of their version of events.

24.5 DIRECTIONS HEARING

The most frequent interlocutory matter a tribunal will consider is a directions hearing. This is a short hearing of 30 minutes or so when the parties are asked to appear before a tribunal chairman, sitting alone, in order to consider the management of the case. This will involve the chairman identifying the critical legal and factual issues which will be heard at the full hearing. He or she will also deal with matters such as the exchange of evidence, the provision and exchange of witness statements and obtaining agreement on how long the full hearing should be listed for. The purpose is to ensure that at the full hearing there is no, or less, confusion on what the central arguments are and to ensure that the tribunal has the best chance to consider the case properly.

Directions hearings are extremely useful where an applicant is representing himself or herself. Often, the form IT1 can be unclear and, even if it identifies the exact claim the individual is bringing (ie unfair dismissal), the facts surrounding the complaint can be missing or so ambiguous that the employer has little chance of understanding exactly what it is defending. The tribunal will often note this ambiguity and use the directions hearing as an opportunity to speak to the applicant in person, ask exactly what he or she is alleging and provide the parties with a record of what the applicant is claiming so that, in effect, an amended claim is comprehensively and succinctly set out by the tribunal.

It is not always the case, however, that the tribunal will take it upon itself to consider whether a directions hearing would be useful. There is nothing preventing either the respondent or the applicant writing to the tribunal and suggesting that such a hearing would be useful. Alternatively, and often in an effort to save on costs, the parties can write to the tribunal setting out the directions they believe would be useful and ask the tribunal simply to approve those directions. This is often the procedure followed if the respondent and the applicant are both represented.

24.6 PRE-HEARING REVIEWS

A pre-hearing review can also be ordered by the tribunal of its own volition, or can be requested by one of the parties. The purpose of a pre-hearing review is to decide whether one party's case, or a particular submission of one party, has 'no reasonable prospect of success'. If the tribunal accepts that this is so, it can either issue a costs warning against the offending party or it may order the offending party to pay a deposit as a condition for being permitted to proceed to a full hearing.

The maximum deposit that a tribunal can order in these circumstances is £500. It is usually the applicant who is asked to pay this deposit on the basis that the claim is spurious and unlikely to succeed. However, one can easily envisage a case where a respondent could be subject to such a penalty – if there was a clear case of a failure to pay wages, for example.

If the deposit is ordered it must be paid within 21 days and, if the party concerned fails to pay, the claim should be struck out. The deposit is just that and, therefore, it may be refundable to the paying party unless an order for costs is made against that party at the full hearing. Therefore, if at the full hearing the tribunal decides that the claim has real merit, then the deposit would be refundable.

24.7 PRELIMINARY POINT HEARINGS

A third type of interlocutory hearing which is often conducted by an employment tribunal is a preliminary point hearing. Such a hearing is considered appropriate where there is a particular issue, independent from the main body of the claim, which should be considered before the merits of the claim are heard.

By way of example, a preliminary point hearing often heard is where the employee has presented his claim to the employment tribunal late and, therefore, on the face of it the tribunal does not have jurisdiction to hear the claim. As there are certain provisions which allow the tribunal to extend the time-limits, it will consider this issue and decide whether to allow the claim to proceed. This issue is a discrete point, which can be heard independently of the merits of the case. If the tribunal accordingly finds that there is justification for extending the time-limit, the matter will proceed. If, however, the tribunal finds that the applicant should have presented his or her complaint within the prescribed time-limit, it will strike out the claim at this point.

Another common example where a preliminary point hearing is useful is where the status of an individual is unclear. Certain claims (for example, unfair dismissal) are available only to employees as opposed to workers or contractors. Often, it is unclear whether an individual fits into the category of employee or one of the wider categories. Without needing to consider the circumstances surrounding the 'dismissal' of the individual, the tribunal will consider, as a preliminary point, whether the individual is an employee and, accordingly, whether the claim can be presented at all. If the tribunal finds that the individual is not an employee, it can dismiss the claim immediately without spending time considering the merits of the case.

24.8 SETTLEMENT AND ACAS

Aside from these interlocutory matters, the primary consideration for an employer in this interim period is to consider whether settlement is an option. An assessment can be made from a commercial perspective as to whether the cost of management time and legal fees incurred in defending the proceedings will, regardless of the case merits, render settlement a favourable option. When considering settlement, the preferred procedure is to utilise the services of ACAS, which is a publicly appointed body whose role is to conciliate between the parties to tribunal proceedings. Although ACAS is not a source of advice, it can often prove a useful conciliator even if it is simply to pass on information. If a settlement can be reached using the services of ACAS, a settlement agreement prepared by ACAS, known as COT3, can be prepared which, if properly drafted, can act as a binding agreement between the parties providing closure on all employment claims between the parties.

The alternative way in which to settle a tribunal claim is by way of a compromise agreement, the details of which are provided at **23.3**. However, the services of ACAS are generally preferred because often the applicant is not legally represented and, by conciliating the matter via ACAS, there is no need for the applicant to obtain the independent legal advice he or she would need in order legally to complete a compromise agreement. Thus, the cost of seeking and obtaining such independent legal advice can be avoided.

24.9 THE TRIBUNAL HEARING

If matters proceed, each party will have arrived at the tribunal with an agreed indexed and paginated bundle of documentary evidence, with witness statements drafted and signed for all those witnesses it is intended to call at the hearing. It is to be hoped that each party will have exchanged these statements in advance with the other side so that each side understands what the other will be bringing to the fore at the hearing.

The hearing will commence with the tribunal chairman possibly outlining the key issues and reminding the parties of the areas for deliberation; then the party who must prove its case will commence proceedings. This will differ depending upon the type of claim which is being brought.

However, in unfair dismissal cases, for example, the burden of proof is upon the employer to prove that the reason for dismissal was fair in law and therefore the onus will be upon the employer to present its evidence first.

The tribunal procedure does vary in different tribunals but, in cases of unfair dismissal, the employer's witnesses will ordinarily read out their statements and refer to any of the relevant documentation within the bundle. After the witness has concluded reading out his or her witness statement, the opposing party will cross-examine the witness on that evidence. In this respect, the way in which the tribunal hears evidence is identical to a court. Once the cross-examination has been concluded, the representative for the witness has the opportunity to re-examine the witness on any particular issues raised during cross-examination. It is then usual for the tribunal members to ask the witness questions they believe to be pertinent and the witness will then be released. It is customary for one party's witnesses to be heard in succession before the opposing party's witnesses are called. However, this can be varied if circumstances so dictate.

Once all the witness evidence has been heard, the parties' representatives will make their submissions on the case and, finally, the tribunal will retire to consider its decision. The tribunal may reach a unanimous or a majority decision. Whether a decision is promulgated on the final day of the hearing will largely depend upon time. Often, if the matters are particularly complicated and there is a detailed set of witness statements and bundle of documentation, the tribunal members may send the parties away and choose to provide their decision in written form at a date in the near future.

24.10 ANCILLARY ISSUES

Parties are often curious as to whether they will successfully recover the costs they incur in either initiating or defending proceedings. The rules governing costs are distinct to those found in the court system, where costs are generally awarded to the successful party.

The tribunal has the power to make an order containing an award of costs against a party where it believes that either a party or a party's representative has, in conducting proceedings, acted 'vexatiously, abusively, disruptively or otherwise unreasonably, or the bringing or conducting of proceedings by a party has been misconceived'. This last part was added with the introduction of the Employment Tribunals Regulations 2001, which assist employers in particular where an employee initiates a claim which has no legal basis and is, therefore, misconceived.

In cases where costs will be sought by a party, it is helpful to his or her cause if the cost-seeker notifies the other party in advance of the hearing of this intention and the basis for it. The tribunal has the authority to award up to £10,000 on its own. If a party's costs exceed £10,000 and it wishes to recover all of its costs, it is possible to make an application to the tribunal that the costs be assessed by a taxing officer. The taxing officer can award an unlimited amount of costs.

Once the tribunal's decision has been made, there is scope for the unsuccessful party to appeal to the Employment Appeals Tribunal (EAT). However, the party is limited to appealing on a point of law as opposed to a factual finding. This is not always an easy distinction to make and professional guidance is generally taken to ascertain whether there is an identifiable point of law on which to base an appeal.

Chapter 25

REDUNDANCY AND RESTRUCTURING

25.1 INTRODUCTION

This chapter looks at the law on redundancy and restructuring and provides guidance to charities on managing a redundancy and restructuring programme.

25.2 THE DIFFERENCE BETWEEN REDUNDANCY AND RESTRUCTURE

An employee is dismissed by reason of redundancy if the dismissal is due wholly or mainly to the fact that the employer has ceased or intends to cease to carry on the business for the purposes for which the employee was employed by it, or to cease to carry on the business in the place where the employee was so employed.

Dismissal by reason of redundancy will also take place if the requirements of the business for employees to carry out work of a particular kind, or for employees to carry out work of a particular kind in the place where the employee was employed by the employer, have ceased or diminished or are expected to cease or diminish.

Once an employer has established the reason for the dismissal, it must also follow a fair procedure in making the dismissal. There are three main stages to this: consultation, fair selection for redundancy and the offer of suitable alternative employment. Failure to carry out any part of the process can render the dismissal unfair.

A restructure has no statutory definition, but generally occurs where there is no change in numbers of the workforce. Thus, a restructuring exercise does not necessarily mean a diminution or cessation of the work. Rather, the employer undertakes a reorganisation such that the work is carried out in a different way. This could involve deleting old posts, creating new posts and redistributing the work accordingly. Case law has established that an employer is allowed to reorganise its working practices, for example, to allow it to adapt to modern developments in technology, as no job is likely to remain the same forever. A charity employer can also restructure its working practices by providing that the dismissal of an employee is fair by being a dismissal for 'some other substantial reason ... such as to justify the dismissal ... where there is a necessary reorganisation of the business'. An example of such a situation would be where a charity has reorganised its existing shift patterns, or has introduced a new computer system to be used by employees. However, the charity will have to show that the reorganisation is both necessary and proper, and an employment tribunal, in scrutinising the changes, would expect to see a substantial need for differences between the old structure and the new structure.

The procedures for redundancy and restructure that employers are required to follow are slightly different and are considered separately below.

25.3 REDUNDANCY PROCEDURE

25.3.1 Consultation

The first stage that will occur in a redundancy is consultation. It is an essential element of any redundancy exercise that the charity consults with the employee. Consultation should take place both individually with the employee affected and collectively, where more than 20 redundancies take place, with the union or employee representatives.

Such consultation should include the reasons for the redundancy, any proposals put forward to avoid the redundancy, the criteria to be used for selection, the reason for which the employee was selected for dismissal under the criteria, and any representations made as to the selection.

Clear written records should be kept at all stages of the process.

Consultation is an ongoing obligation up to the date of termination of employment.

Duty to consult with representatives

There are obligations set out in the law for an employer to consult with employee representatives where 20 or more employees are proposed and contemplated to be redundant (whether or not such redundancies are connected with a transfer of an undertaking). The employee representatives must be appropriate representatives elected for consultation (see Chapter 15), who will be trade union representatives where an independent trade union is recognised and, where there is no recognised trade union, employee representatives.

Consultation should begin when a charity proposes to dismiss employees. Under UK law an employer does not 'propose' to dismiss until it has reached the stage of formulating a specific proposal. However, recent case-law has held that the word 'propose' used in the legislation, is too restrictive and fails properly to implement European law. An employer should begin consultation where redundancies are 'envisaged' or 'contemplated', ie at an early stage in the decision-making process.

The consultation should begin 'in good time' and, in any event, where 100 or more employees are likely to be made redundant at one establishment, an employer must begin consultation at least 90 days before the first of the dismissals is due to take effect. Where an employer is proposing to dismiss as redundant 20 or more but less than 100 employees at one establishment, consultation must begin at least 90 days before the first of the dismissals is due to take effect.

If redundancies are planned in connection with a transfer of an undertaking, they will also trigger the obligation to consult under TUPE because such redundancies will count as 'measures' (see Chapter 26).

If the employer fails to consult in such a situation it is possible for a separate award to be made in relation to each of the obligations to consult, without one being offset against the other.

If more than 20 employees are proposed to be made redundant, it is also necessary for the charity to notify the DTI. Forms can be obtained from the DTI direct on www.dti.gov.uk.

Duty to consult with individuals

If there is a dismissal by reason of redundancy (involving any number of employees) and subsequent claims of unfair dismissal are made, then one of the key features which an employment tribunal will consider in determining whether the redundancy dismissal was fair is whether there was meaningful consultation with the individual (in addition to any consultation with appropriate representatives). Therefore, if any redundancies are planned (whether or not they are in connection with a transfer), it is important to consult with the individuals concerned.

The individual consultation should, in particular, consider the following:

- reasons for the proposed redundancy programme;
- reasons for the proposed selection of the employee for redundancy, including the selection criteria applied. The employee should be given an opportunity to query the application of those criteria if necessary;
- the availability of alternative positions within the employer's company or group of companies (the employee should be asked whether he or she wishes to work elsewhere and whether he or she has any suggestions);
- terms and conditions relating to alternative jobs (these do not necessarily need to be the same as existing terms and conditions);
- details of the trial period applicable to any alternative position;
- time off to look for alternative employment;
- calculation of the redundancy payment; and

- details of the charity's grievance procedure, which the employee should use if not satisfied.

Individual consultation should be an ongoing process until the date of termination of the contract of employment. If a tribunal finds that there has been insufficient consultation for a particular individual, it may make a finding of unfair dismissal.

25.3.2 Fair selection for redundancy

Where it is necessary to select one or more employees to be made redundant from a group of potentially redundant employees, that selection must be carried out fairly.

The criteria to select the employees for redundancy must be fair and also be applied fairly; they should be objective – for example, the employee's attendance record, efficiency, experience or length of service. An employer should seek to ensure that the selection is made fairly in accordance with these criteria and must consider any representations made by the employee (or any union on behalf of the employee) to the contrary.

The first stage is to identify the pool from which the redundant staff will come. This might be a class of certain types of employees within a specific location – for instance, all secretaries at head office.

The practical way to consider selection is to consider all employees who are identified as being within the pool for redundancy against criteria, marking them against a grid designed for the purpose. It is sensible for more than one person to be involved in the selection process in order to ensure objectivity and to counter any accusation of bias.

25.3.3 Suitable alternative employment

A charity making a member of staff redundant must offer any existing suitable alternative employment to that employee or the dismissal may be considered unfair. A redundant employee should be offered an available vacancy even if it is at a lower salary or of a lesser status than the post from which he or she is being made redundant.

The fairness of a dismissal will be judged not simply at the date on which notice is given but also with regard to events up to the date on which it takes effect. Hence, if a suitable vacancy arises during the notice period it should be offered to the otherwise redundant employee.

The employer will have to be prepared to ring-fence posts elsewhere in the organisation as these other jobs may be objectively suitable.

A person loses the right to a redundancy payment where he or she unreasonably refuses the offer of suitable alternative employment and the employee is said to have resigned. It is therefore important to consider what is suitable alternative employment.

The question of suitability of an offer of alternative employment is an objective matter; examples of factors affecting suitability include the same terms and conditions as the old job or suitable for the employee's experience and skills. The reasonableness of the employee's refusal of the offer depends on factors personal to the employee and is a subjective matter to be considered from the employee's point of view – for example, refusal might not be considered unreasonable where the job is in a new location which makes travelling to and from work difficult, or where the new job is on a different level within the organisation and is perceived as a loss of status.

Where there is no suitable alternative employment, but other vacancies exist, an employer must offer these vacancies to those employees in a redundant situation. If more than one redundant employee is interested, an employer should follow a fair process, akin to a recruitment process, in selecting the individual for the new position.

25.4 STATUTORY REDUNDANCY ENTITLEMENT

To be eligible for statutory redundancy pay, staff must have 2 years' continuous service whilst over 18 years of age and must not have reached the normal retiring age for the organisation where that is less than 65; or, in any other case, the age of 65, and must not have been offered suitable alternative employment.

Redundancy pay is calculated as follows, subject to a maximum of 20 years' service and to a financial limit which is reviewed annually:

- for each year of employment in which the member of staff was aged 41 or over: one-and-a-half week's pay is allowed;
- for each year of employment in which the member of staff was aged 22 or over, but under 41 years: one week's pay is allowed;
- for each year of employment in which the member of staff was aged 18 or over, but under 22 years: half a week's pay is allowed.

Entitlement to pay is reduced for staff who have passed their 64th birthday and at the moment there is no entitlement to a redundancy payment for staff over the age of 65. No payment is due for part of a year.

From 1 February 2003, a week's pay is set as being the lower of the gross weekly wage or £260. This means that the maximum statutory redundancy payment that can be made is £7,800 (after 20 years of service over the age of 41). A statutory redundancy payment is treated as tax free to the employee receiving it.

As part of the consultation on new law outlawing age discrimination, there are proposals to simplify the calculation of redundancy pay, so that older employees do not receive a higher payment than those who are younger.

25.5 UNFAIR DISMISSAL EXCLUSION UNDER THREAT

The UK Government is obliged by EU law to implement by 2006 law which will outlaw any discrimination on grounds of age alone. At the same time as consultation on such new law takes place, cases are currently progressing through the employment tribunal system which are making the matter more complicated. An example of such a case on redundancy is *Rutherford and Another v Towncircle Limited* [2002] IRLR 768. Mr Rutherford was 67 years old when he was told that he was to be dismissed by reason of redundancy. He felt aggrieved with the decision to dismiss him and brought claims for a redundancy payment and unfair dismissal against his employer.

Before the tribunal, Mr Rutherford alleged that his claims were not barred by sections in the Employment Rights Act 1996 – which provide that the tribunal has no jurisdiction to hear a claim where the applicant is over the normal retirement age of 65 – on the basis that these provisions were indirectly discriminatory on the grounds of sex (because they impacted more on men than women). The tribunal decided that the provisions disproportionately affected men and that the law could not be justified objectively. The tribunal was of the view that the Government was put on notice some time ago to the possible discriminatory impact of the legislation and should have taken measure to amend it. The tribunal therefore disapplied the relevant statutory provisions and allowed the claim to proceed. In the event, the EAT overturned the tribunal's decision although the case remains a good example of how law is 'structured' by new cases being brought to tribunal.

25.6 CONTRACTUAL REDUNDANCY PAYMENTS

It is common for charities to provide for contractual redundancy payments. The statutory redundancy payment scheme is not particularly generous, so charities will often increase the payment they are obliged to make to employees on redundancy, often by retaining the same calculation, but removing the cap on weekly wage of £260 so that it reflects more clearly the earnings of staff whose salaries are more than £13,520 per annum.

A contractual redundancy payment is also tax free to the extent that an employee can receive £30,000 of a severance payment tax free on a redundancy.

25.7 REDUNDANCY POLICY

Given that the law on redundancy is onerous, it is sensible for a charity to formulate a procedure to follow in cases where redundancies are necessary. The benefit of a policy is that both employees and managers know where they stand if they follow a procedure. The disadvantage is that if a charity fails to follow its own procedure, this could be a breach of contract or evidence that the individual has not been treated fairly.

25.8 TERMINATION OF EMPLOYMENT ON REDUNDANCY

A redundant employee is entitled to notice to terminate their contract, or payment in lieu of notice.

A written statement covering the reasons for and the terms of the redundancy should accompany formal notice of redundancy. The statement should also include a calculation of the redundancy payment, showing what part of it is the statutory redundancy payment.

Employees are entitled to reasonable time off to look for work and for interviews during the notice period. Many charities go beyond the minimum requirement and assist a redundant employee in finding alternative work outside the charity. This can be done by offering help with an employee's CV or interviewing techniques, or making charity journals available to redundant staff, even if they have already left employment. Any practical assistance is generally welcome and can be of no cost to the charity.

25.9 PRACTICAL GUIDANCE – REDUNDANCY

A redundancy should incorporate the following key steps:

- Decide on the number of employees to be made redundant. (This will be because there is a reduction in the number of employees required to carry out a certain role.)
- Decide which areas of the business those redundancies are to come from. (This is to define the 'pool' from which the charity will select redundant employees.)
- Inform all the employees in the pool that there is a need for redundancies.
- Start the consultation process by advising employee representatives of the position (if more than 20 employees could be made redundant) and setting out a programme of consultation meetings (both collectively and individually with employees).

- Decide which criteria are to be used to select employees for redundancy. Possible criteria include: experience, length of service, attendance record, disciplinary record, performance record as objectively tested through appraisals, key skills.
- Inform all the employees in the pool as to the selection criteria to be used.
- Using the selected criteria, mark each of the employees against each of the criterion.
- Meet each of the employees individually and explain whether or not they have been *provisionally* selected for redundancy. Confirm this in writing.
- Offer each of the provisionally selected employees an opportunity to suggest alternatives to redundancy (eg retirement, alternative work, part-time working, job share, short working hours). It is important that any alternatives to redundancy be properly considered by the charity and the reasons why they are not viable be communicated to the employee. The provisionally selected employee should also be informed why he or she has been selected (ie that his or her score is lower than others – NB there is no need to explain other employees' scores; in fact, to do this would be inappropriate).
- Consider whether there are any alternative positions in the charity that would be suitable for the provisionally selected employee.
- When the consultation process has progressed to show the way forward and staff have been redeployed, write to the employee giving notice to terminate his or her employment for redundancy and explaining what will happen on the redundancy.
- If the employee has 2 years' service, a redundancy payment must be made in accordance with the statutory formula.
- If the employee works his or her notice, an opportunity to take time off to seek alternative employment should be given.

25.10 MANAGING RESTRUCTURES

It is an essential element of any restructuring exercise that a charity should consult with the individual employees affected by the changes. Such consultation should include:

- the reasons for the restructuring;
- any proposals put forward as alternatives to the restructuring;
- specific changes proposed to existing working practices and how these will affect individual employees; and
- the criteria to be used for selection where new posts are created in place of existing posts.

Even when carrying out a restructuring exercise (which, technically, does not involve a redundancy situation where the statutory information and consultation provisions outlined above apply), a charity must consult with each of the potentially affected employees individually. It is also good practice for a charity to consult with any trade union or employee representatives; and, of course, it should consult those which have been officially recognised by the charity for consultation in the circumstances. The charity should also keep clear written records at all stages of the process.

As in redundancy, the dismissal of an employee during restructuring may be considered unfair if the employee concerned is not consulted according to a fair and proper procedure. Furthermore, best practice dictates that consideration be given by a charity to finding employees other suitable jobs within the organisation.

Part and parcel of the consultation process will be discussion of any alternative employment offered to employees. This may occur where an employee refuses to work according to the changes proposed but the charity is able to offer him or her some other position instead. In this type of situation, consultation may be necessary at a number of separate stages, including to establish why the employee cannot work according to the changes (for instance, due to child care arrangements) and to decide if the employee can be employed in another post.

25.11 PRACTICAL GUIDANCE – RESTRUCTURING

In order to carry out a fair restructuring exercise, a charity should follow this checklist.

- Consult affected employees individually.
- Consult at the collective level with recognised trade unions and employee representatives and attempt to gain their agreement to the changes. (Note that employee representatives can often help to 'sell' the changes to disgruntled employees.)
- Consider possible alternatives to the restructuring arrangements initially outlined.
- Consider representations made by the employee on how his or her job will be affected.
- If an employee rejects the changes to his or her current working practices, investigate the possibility of offering alternative employment with the charity employer.
- Give employees time off to seek other employment should they wish to do so.
- Pay all monies due.
- Conduct an appeal if the employee's contract of employment requires it.

Chapter 26

TRANSFER OF UNDERTAKINGS (PROTECTION OF EMPLOYMENT) REGULATIONS 1981: STAFF TRANSFERS (INCLUDING PUBLIC SECTOR)

26.1 INTRODUCTION

Charities must consider the services they provide and whether they are provided properly, cost effectively and in the interests of the charity's beneficiaries. This often results in charities contracting out various services to contractors (for instance, cleaning services) and also providing services to other organisations under contract. In each case it is possible that the staff providing their services will transfer their employment from or to the charity. This generally involves the application of the Transfer of Undertakings (Protection of Employment) Regulations 1981 (TUPE).

TUPE was enacted in the UK in order to implement the EC Acquired Rights Directive (1977). The principal aim of the Directive and TUPE is to protect employees' rights when their employer changes involuntarily. Until the early 1990s, TUPE applied only to undertakings that were in the nature of a commercial venture. It was therefore assumed that, as charities were non-profit-making, they were not affected by TUPE.

Since 1993, TUPE has applied to a broader range of transfers: this has led to a certain amount of confusion about when TUPE will apply to the transfer of staff. The effect of TUPE's application to a transfer is onerous on the new employer, and the effect is therefore considered regularly by the courts. It is not unusual to describe the law around TUPE as a 'minefield' which is difficult to negotiate. Some help is hopefully at hand: changes to TUPE have been proposed by the Government and are likely to come into force during 2004.

Charities involved in the provision of public services will also need to consider the additional Government guidance that applies on transfers of public services.

All charities, whether transferor or transferee, involved in reorganisation should therefore be alert to TUPE's implications, and should initially consider whether TUPE applies in the circumstances of individual transfers.

26.2 WHEN DOES TUPE APPLY?

The legal test of whether TUPE will apply is, at present:

(a) whether a recognisable economic unit is transferred;
(b) which retains its identity as a separate economic entity after transfer, with regard to all the facts of the transfer.

As recently as January 2002, the European Court of Justice considered how best to decide whether an economic entity has transferred, in particular when assets do not transfer, such as on a change of contractors. Where there are no assets to transfer, the decision about whether TUPE will transfer is always a difficult one, and requires much consideration of the composition of the recognisable economic entity before and after transfer. This is a charity's starting point in deciding whether TUPE will apply to the transfer of services.

How does a charity decide on the composition of a recognisable economic entity? The courts have always taken a practical approach to the problem (which leads to differing and somewhat confusing decisions). The courts' approach is to list the various constituents of the economic entity and then decide whether the entity is 'sufficiently autonomous in its management and structure to constitute a recognisably distinct entity'. The charity, therefore, needs to start the exercise by making what is known in legal parlance as a 'shopping list'. For example, if a charity is contracting out its cleaning services, those services are likely to comprise: the service of cleaning; the essential utensils; the relationship of the provision of the services to the charity; and the staff who carry out the cleaning. The charity must then consider whether, before the transfer, the services are provided in a recognisably distinct unit. This is unlikely to be the case if, for example, the employees carrying out the services also carry out other services (for instance, security).

If the services are then contracted out, TUPE may well apply if the services retain their identity after transfer. It is possible for a charity to ensure that TUPE will apply when contracting out services by obliging the incoming contractor to retain the identity of the economic entity or take on the staff under TUPE. However, it is not uncommon for contractors to be resistant to taking on staff and to resist such contractual provisions, or to increase the price of the service accordingly to take into account additional costs.

It should be remembered that if TUPE does not apply in a contracting-out situation, the charity may find itself overstaffed by a group or number of staff, and may be obliged to make redundancies.

It is also the case that it is very difficult for employers to take TUPE avoidance measures effectively, without legal challenge. For instance, if an employer refuses to take on the staff (and therefore tries to ensure that it will not take on the entire economic entity), the court can look at the reason for not doing so to see if the purpose of not taking on staff was to avoid TUPE's application.

The current position is that TUPE may apply in a wide variety of situations, including the following:

- the transfer of a charity or part of a charity in a merger or take-over situation;
- outsourcing and insourcing, including competitive tendering situations;
- transfers from one contractor to another;
- transfers from one organisation to another within the same group;
- all transfers to and from public sector bodies.

Detailed consideration of each situation is necessary before any decision is taken on whether TUPE will apply.

The proposed changes to the law anticipated in 2004 seek to regularise the position and ensure that TUPE will apply where there is doubt. The first proposed change is a provision that TUPE will apply on public sector transfers, whether or not TUPE applies as a matter of law (ie confirming the existing position set out in Government guidance).

The second proposed change is that TUPE will apply on any service provision change in the public or private sector.

26.3 WHO WILL TRANSFER WITH THE UNDERTAKING?

It is necessary to assess the work that each individual employee carries out before deciding whether any particular post will transfer as part of the undertaking. There are no hard and fast legal rules that can be applied to decide whether any employee transfers; it is a subjective test.

The starting point for a charity is to consider what proportion of work is carried out for the undertaking. There are various ways of assessing this – for instance, by assessing what percentage of working day the employee spends on work for the undertaking.

Where an employee is engaged primarily within that part of the business which is to be transferred or spends more than 50% of his or her time on work related to the undertaking, the employer should consider whether that employee will be protected by TUPE. Where an employee spent 70% of his time on the work of an undertaking, the court found that he was protected by TUPE. There is also an argument that if staff are not 'assigned' to the part of the business that transfers, even if they work within it, they do not transfer. However, it should also be remembered that the courts usually try to protect employees and so, if an employee would otherwise lose his or her job, the court is likely to find that he or she is protected by TUPE instead.

26.4 OBJECTION TO TRANSFER

An employee has the right to object to the transfer. If he or she lodges an objection, the employee will be taken to have resigned, without remedy, from employment with the transferor, without protecting his or her rights to claim constructive dismissal against the transferor.

26.5 THE EFFECT OF TUPE

Onerous obligations are imposed on an employer by TUPE – this can lead to both short-term and long-term issues, which need to be resolved.

The principle is simple. As a result of TUPE, employees who are deemed to work in the undertaking to be transferred are automatically transferred from the transferor employer to the transferee on the same terms and conditions of employment, currently with the exception of pensions. All obligations in relation to employees that were previously the responsibility of the transferor become the responsibility of the transferee, who is said to step into the shoes of the transferor.

This includes hidden liabilities such as liability for personal injury claims brought by employees with a right to transfer under TUPE. A new employer also inherits the right to rely on the old employer's existing insurance provision to cover the relevant injury.

Both employers must provide information and consult recognised unions or other employee representatives.

Any dismissals of transferring staff which are deemed to be related to the transfer are deemed unfair unless the employer can show that the dismissal was for an economic, technical or organisational reason entailing a change in the workforce ('an ETO reason'). An employee who is dismissed as a result of the transfer, and not for an ETO reason, can sue his or her employer for unfair dismissal and damages in respect of the breach if he or she has more than one year's service.

The Acquired Rights Directive allows European Union Member States to provide in their own regulations that the transferor and the transferee shall be jointly and severally liable in respect of obligations to transferring employees which arose before the date of transfer. The proposed change to TUPE is that there be joint and several liability for personal injury claims arising before transfer in the public sector.

In the meantime, charities should negotiate appropriate contractual protection to deal with such liabilities after transfer. It is reasonable for an employer to request that the transferor employer retain liability for events that occurred before the transfer.

26.6 CHANGES TO STAFFING

If, before the transfer, and unconnected to it, the transferor moves employees with their consent to alternative positions or dismisses them, these employees will be unaffected by TUPE.

A transferring employee may object to the transfer and will be deemed to have resigned. TUPE precludes the employee from claiming unfair dismissal or redundancy in this situation, unless the employee resigns due to the belief that a substantial change has been made to his or her working conditions to his or her detriment, in which case he or she will have a claim for constructive dismissal.

If either employer wishes to change the staffing as a result of the transfer, or connected with it, that employer should be mindful of the fact that any dismissal will be unfair unless it is for an ETO reason. The changes must be to either the number or functions of the workforce and must be necessary. A genuine redundancy situation may be an ETO reason and, in a recent Court of Appeal decision, a transferor's requirement for the transferee to dismiss an employee for economic reasons was an ETO reason. Changes in terms and conditions of employment or significant changes in the functions of employees will not usually amount to an ETO reason.

26.7 TERMS AND CONDITIONS

There will probably be disparity between the terms and conditions of transferring staff and those of existing staff (if any) employed by the transferee. This is a common problem, especially where staff transfer from the public to private sector, and it can cause industrial relations problems. This is what is referred to as the 'two-tier workforce', which has been addressed by guidance on local authority transfers (see **26.13**). Specific legal problems also arise for the two-tier workforce.

- Transferring employees may be employed on terms which are the subject of negotiation under a collective bargaining agreement such as pay negotiations in local government. The transferee employer may be unable to take part in future negotiation resulting in amendments to the collective bargaining terms, although it will be bound to abide by these new terms.
- Some terms to which transferring employees are entitled may be inappropriate when the transferee employer takes on the transferring employees, such as bonus arrangements, share option schemes and in-house procedures, such as disciplinary procedures.
- If the terms and conditions of transferring employees are substantially better than the terms under which existing staff are employed, difficulties may arise under the Equal Pay Act 1970 if

employees of a different sex are doing like work employed on different pay and benefits.

26.7.1 Changes to terms and conditions

Any negotiations to change terms and conditions should be carried out with circumspection. Changes to terms and conditions as a result of the transfer may be ineffective unless for an ETO reason. This matter has been debated endlessly in the courts. As a result of these cases, an employer can make changes to terms and conditions on a transfer by dismissing an employee and re-employing him or her on different terms in particular situations where the variation is economically necessary for the continuance of the recognisable economic entity.

If an employer changes terms, the employee will have a claim for automatic unfair dismissal unless the employer can show that the change was for an ETO reason.

If an employer makes changes to terms and conditions on a transfer and related to it, by trying to negotiate changes with the employee or by imposing charges, it is not clear from the judgments whether this would result in an effective change, or be susceptible to challenge by the employee in the years after the change that his or her previous contract should be upheld. Charities are advised to proceed with caution.

A charity can, of course, negotiate changes to terms and conditions if those changes are not related to the transfer.

The proposed amendment to TUPE is that employers should be able to make changes to terms and conditions for ETO reasons, thus giving more flexibility to employers.

26.8 TRADE UNIONS

A duty is imposed by TUPE on the transferee employer to recognise those trade unions that are already recognised in relation to transferring staff. Transferee employers should be alert to any recognition arrangements, whether or not in writing. If, once the transfer is completed, the transferee chooses to ignore the arrangements or terminate them, it may do so, cognisant of any rights of action that trade unions will have and the adverse effect on industrial relations.

The transferee employer also takes on obligations under any collective bargaining agreements. As stated above, if collective bargaining terms form part of employees' terms and conditions, those terms (and subsequent amendments to them) will be enforceable against a transferee employer, although that employer has no rights of negotiation in respect of those terms.

The proposed change to TUPE is that recognition ordered by the Central Arbitration Committee (CAC) should transfer.

26.9 CONSULTATION

Even if employers have no existing trade union arrangements, they should be aware of their obligations to inform and consult affected employees on a transfer to which TUPE applies. 'Affected employees' are not just those staff that transfer; they are staff that are actually affected by the transfer, and so will include those staff that do not transfer but whose jobs will be affected by the transfer.

There are also onerous obligations for employers to inform and consult with affected employees through trade unions, employee representatives or staff directly. If a recognised trade union does not exist, the employer is obliged to appoint employee representatives by election. A recent case indicated that it is not enough to have an informal appointment process for employee representatives; it is more appropriate (but not clearly regulated) to have a secret ballot process electing the representatives.

If apathy prevails and employees fail to elect employee representatives, it is necessary to consult with affected employees directly.

Consideration should also be given to consulting with staff directly, in addition to the required collective consultation. The consultation exercise on the transfer will also have to be widened if redundancies take place on that transfer.

26.10 PENSIONS

The transfer of occupational pension schemes is, currently, specifically excluded under TUPE. Case law confirms that TUPE does not apply to pensions and the transferee has no strict legal obligation under TUPE to provide the same occupational pension scheme to transferring employees.

There is a proposal, in a consultation paper issued in 2003, to provide for the transfer of pensions. If, under the terms of the existing scheme, the employer is required to make contributions, the proposal will oblige an employer to match employee contributions of up to 6% into a stakeholder scheme or equivalent alternative.

In the public sector, this is an area which has already been addressed by Government guidance through the Statement of Practice on Public Sector Transfers. On public sector transfers, a new employer must protect transferring employees either by providing a broadly comparable pension scheme or by becoming admitted to the appropriate public sector pension scheme. The Government accordingly widened the admission criteria to the Local Government Superannuation Scheme in 2000 to encourage private sector bodies to become admitted to it.

26.11 INSOLVENCY

The Acquired Rights Directive sets out useful provisions on the insolvency of an employer. It gives Member States the option to provide that, in order to save jobs when the undertaking of an insolvent employer is transferred to a buyer, the transferor's outstanding debts to the transferring employees will not transfer to the buyer. It also permits Member States to allow employee representatives to negotiate changes to terms and conditions in order to save jobs when the undertaking of an insolvent employer is transferred.

The proposed changes to TUPE echo the new Directive. Until that time, TUPE applies on the transfer or sale of an insolvent business.

26.12 PUBLIC SECTOR TRANSFERS

Employers involved in transfers involving the public sector are advised to take specialist advice on the morass of applicable guidelines.

The Statement Of Practice on Public Sector Transfers issued in January 2000 applies in principle to all public sector transfers, and sets out stringent obligations on a transfer, including an obligation that the new employer should provide a comparable pension scheme, taking into account accrued pension rights.

The DETR has also issued guidance (in 2001) which regulates the handling of workforce issues on best value.

There is also guidance on transfers from particular parts of the public sector, such as local authorities (see **26.13**) and the NHS (see **26.14**)

26.13 LOCAL AUTHORITY TRANSFERS

Charities taking a transfer from local government must also consider the 'Code of Practice on Two-Tier Transfers', published in February 2003. For contracts advertised after 13 March 2003, staff in the private sector providing public services to local authorities will benefit from increased employment protection. The review follows trade union criticism of the growth of a two-tier workforce in local authority services, with significant differences in pay and conditions between staff transferred from local authorities to private contractors, and those employees recruited after a contract has been awarded.

Local authorities are under a duty to deliver services according to clear standards relating to cost, quality and cost-effectiveness. The Best Value performance framework requires local authorities to publish annual performance plans and review all their services every 5 years. Authorities must show that they have applied Best Value to every review.

26.13.1 Proposals for change to contracting process

Local authorities must now select private or voluntary sector partners on the basis of their ability to deliver high quality services, not by cutting costs and downgrading staff terms and conditions. The Code will also prevent good contractors with high employment standards from being undercut. The Government states that the changes will help prevent abuse of the local authority contracting process. The Code is non-statutory, which means that it is not law, although it will be enforced as part of any contract with the relevant local authority.

The Code sets out various obligations:

- contractors must offer new staff 'fair and reasonable terms and conditions, which are, overall, no less favourable to those of transferred employees'. The comparison will be made by looking at the overall package rather than considering salary and benefits separately;
- consultation involving a genuine dialogue for agreement on the terms and conditions of new recruits between recognised trade unions and the contractor;
- membership of the local authority pension scheme, or membership of a good quality employer's pension scheme. This will require employers to match employee contributions up to a maximum of 6% for an employer's own defined contribution scheme (although either could pay more if wished), or membership of a contracted out, final salary defined benefit pension scheme; or employer contributions to stakeholder pensions matching those of the employee up to a maximum of 6% (although either could pay more if wished);
- the Code will form part of the service specification and conditions for all contracts between local authorities and contractors involving a transfer of staff;
- the contractor is to provide the necessary information to the local authority to enable it to monitor compliance with the Code;
- enforcement of the Code's obligations is the responsibility of the local authority, unless staff have been transferred to a sub-contractor, when the primary contractor is responsible;
- local authorities must certify that all contracts comply with the Code, as with all Best Value requirements; and
- the operation of the package will be kept under review to ensure that it delivers fair terms and conditions for new recruits.

26.13.2 Issues

A number of difficult issues result as a consequence of the Code.

- How will the transfer guarantees work in practice in situations involving complex group structures and transfers to existing charity employers? For instance, how does an existing employer deal with equal pay issues when it takes on a public sector workforce and recruits new staff on matched terms and conditions?
- What exactly will constitute 'no less favourable [terms and conditions]'?
- A charity may have difficulty in providing terms and conditions no less favourable than the public sector terms.
- There may be an impact on existing staff representation at the charity.
- The Code addresses one of the main reasons why private sector contractors tender for local authority contracts and will undoubtedly have an effect on the viability and future of such transfers.

26.14 NHS TRANSFERS

Charities also need to take account of guidance and new developments in the NHS concerning how transfers should be dealt with. Charities should take advice if involved in public finance initiative (PFI) transactions.

26.15 NEW TUPE

The Government is committed to updating TUPE. In 1997, proposals were published for consultation on amendments to the Acquired Rights Directive, and following this a further consultation document was published in December 2001 setting out proposed amendments to TUPE. The changes are likely to come into force in 2004.

26.15.1 Age-related payments

At present there is some confusion over whether a contractual right to payments usually made to employees on redundancy which are related to age (and therefore pension rights) transfers, although recent case law has found that it does (*Beckmann v Dynamco Whicheloe Macfarlane Ltd* (C-164/00) [2002] IRLR 578, ECJ). The Government proposes to ensure that this type of payment would transfer under TUPE. The practical effect of this is most likely to be felt in the public sector, where payments into pension schemes are common on redundancy. The proposal obviously brings certainty to an issue, at the expense of added costs to the transferee employer.

26.15.2 Transfer of information

This proposal is both long awaited and sensible, addressing one of the main oversights in the original drafting of TUPE. At present there is no obligation upon a transferor employer to give any information to the new employer about the staff it will inherit. Where there is no contractual provision providing for this, it can lead to 'poison pill' transfers where transferor employers organise their workforce before transfer to ensure that specific staff transfer, or that staff transfer on enhanced terms and conditions to increase the burden on the next contractor.

The proposal is that the transfer will give 'written notification of rights and obligations [of transferring employees]' to the new employer. The notification must be updated to include changes to original information provided and given in good time and before the transfer.

The incentive to employers to ensure compliance will be that they could face claims for compensation if the new employer fails in its obligations. This therefore increases the burden on transferor employers and proposes that they may have residual liability for staff after transfer.

26.15.3 Changes to terms and conditions

The only proposal that employers are likely to embrace is a limited suggestion to make it easier for employers to make changes to terms and conditions of employees.

At present it is not possible to make transfer-related changes to terms and conditions of transferring employees unless the changes are as a result of a dismissal of staff for 'economic, technical or organisational reasons entailing changes in the workforce' ('ETO reasons') and their re-engagement on different terms. In effect, this means that the changes can be implemented only if there is a change in the numbers and functions of the workforce.

The proposal is that employers should be able to make changes to terms and conditions for ETO reasons, without a related dismissal. However, the proposal does not address the definition of ETO reasons. This means that employers will still be required to make changes to the numbers and functions of the workforce if making changes to terms and conditions. It will not, however, be necessary to dismiss and re-engage staff in order to make the changes.

The proposal, therefore, has a limited effect unless it is possible for employers to dismiss members of the workforce. This is not always possible, especially where staff numbers are regulated (for instance, by care standards). However, it is an acceptance of the difficult position experienced by employers when inheriting an expensive workforce. It also makes it easier for the courts to interpret 'ETO reasons' in a broader fashion, perhaps accepting that a restructure and related change to terms and conditions falls within the current narrow definition.

26.15.4 Joint liability for pre-transfer personal injuries

The law on TUPE has developed to ensure that, while employers must accept liability for injuries to staff that occur pre-transfer, they can also rely on the existing insurance provision to cover that injury. In the public sector, there is no strict legal obligation on public sector bodies to carry that insurance, so employers taking staff from the public sector cannot always rely on it.

The proposal is that public sector bodies must now accept, for such pre-transfer personal injuries, joint liability after the transfer.

26.15.5 Insolvency

Perhaps importantly in times of recession, the Government has suggested major reforms to TUPE where the outgoing employer is insolvent.

The Government has taken up both options offered under the Acquired Rights Directive in proposing that changes to terms and conditions by reason of the transfer will be permitted if they are not contrary to UK law and are either agreed between the employer and employee representatives or designed to safeguard employment opportunities by ensuring the survival of the business.

26.16 CONCLUSION

Charities which believe they may be affected by TUPE must consider matters carefully. Wherever possible, a charity affected by TUPE should negotiate warranties and indemnities to cover itself in a contract providing for the transfer.

26.17 PRACTICAL GUIDANCE – FREQUENTLY ASKED QUESTIONS CONCERNING TUPE

What is 'TUPE'?

TUPE is the Transfer of Undertakings (Protection of Employment) Regulations 1981. It was introduced in order to comply with European law, which protects the position of employees when their employment transfers to a different employer.

When does TUPE apply?

TUPE applies when there is a transfer of an 'undertaking' or part of an undertaking from one employer to another employer. An undertaking is defined as any 'trade or business', whether or not it is of a commercial nature. In practice, this means TUPE will apply where staff are organised in a discrete autonomous unit of management. The Government's Statement of Practice for Staff Transfers in the Public Sector also recommends that all public sector bodies apply the principles of TUPE, even where TUPE does not technically apply.

Which employees will TUPE apply to?

TUPE applies to and protects all employees who are 'wholly or substantially' employed in the undertaking which is transferring. Accordingly, employees of an employer who are wholly or substantially employed in providing services immediately before transfer will transfer to the contractor.

Other employees, to whom TUPE does not apply, may transfer to the new employer by agreement between the old employer, the new employer and the relevant employee. This sometimes happens in order to avoid any redundancies.

Can my new employer change my terms and conditions after the transfer?

If your employment transfers to the new employer under TUPE, you will be entitled to the same terms and conditions of employment that you currently enjoy with your old employer. The new employer cannot make changes to your terms and conditions if the reason for the changes is related to the transfer or otherwise without your agreement. Any changes to terms and conditions of employment on or after transfer, which are related to the transfer, will be ineffective.

Furthermore, the transfer will not affect your continuity of employment, and your length of service will be carried over. Any collective agreements with trade unions will also continue to be in force after the transfer. The practical effect of TUPE (if the transfer goes ahead) will be to substitute the name of your new employer for that of your old employer in your contract of employment.

Can I object to being transferred?

Yes. If you are an employee who would transfer across under TUPE, but you do not wish to do so, you are entitled to object to your employment transferring. Any such objection will terminate your contract of employment with your old employer, and your objection is treated as a resignation. Your old employer is not obliged to redeploy you but may wish to offer to redeploy you at its discretion.

What if my new employer has a different structure?

If the new employer has a different operational staffing structure, there will be a simultaneous restructure on transfer and those employees who do not transfer directly into a new post will be considered for suitable alternative employment. It is unlikely that there will be any redundancies. However, you are still entitled to be employed on the same terms and conditions as previously unless you expressly agree otherwise.

Is my employer required to carry out any consultation prior to the transfer?

Yes. It is required to provide employee representatives of the recognised unions with information concerning:

- when the transfer is to take place;
- the reasons for it;
- the legal economic and social implications of the transfer for affected employees; and
- the measures which either it or your new employer envisage taking in relation to those employees and, if no measures are envisaged, that fact.

Your old employer will also be required to consult, through the same employee representatives, in respect of measures that will be taken by either it or the new employer.

What will be the process for determining who transfers?

The employees who will transfer will need to be identified. This is usually done by the old employer in the first instance. The transferring employees identified are listed on the 'TUPE/transfer list', which continues to evolve until just before the transfer takes place.

Chapter 27

CARE WORKERS

27.1 INTRODUCTION

The charity sector is involved in a wide variety of activities which include care; approximately 63% of the voluntary sector is involved in the provision of care services (*UK Voluntary Sector Almanac 2002*), and charity employers need to be aware of their obligations in relation to employing care workers .

The Government introduced the Care Standards Act 2000 (CSA 2000) to regulate the care sector and provide a better standard of care for both child and adult service users. The CSA 2000 established the National Care Standards Commission (NCSC) and made provision for various regulations to be issued in relation to staffing, the environment of the home, the health and welfare of service users, management and training, and the financial position of care establishments and agencies. The CSA 2000 has also led to national minimum standards being published, which will be applicable to care establishments and agencies.

Numerous regulations and national minimum standards have been issued in relation to various care services. The General Social Care Council (GSCC) has also issued Codes of Practice for both social care workers and their employers.

A detailed consideration of individual legislation is beyond the scope of this work, and this chapter will briefly consider some of the general issues that will affect charity employers of care workers.

27.2 DEFINING CARE SERVICES

Set out below are details of the various care services that are regulated under the CSA 2000:

- care homes;
- children's homes;
- domiciliary care agencies;
- fostering service;
- nurses agencies;
- independent hospitals and clinics;
- residential family centres;

- voluntary adoption agencies;
- boarding schools;
- residential special schools;
- accommodation of students under 18.

In addition to the CSA 2000 and the Children Act 1989, the key legislation, regulations and standards that may be applicable for each service are:

- Regulations:
  - Care Homes Regulations 2001;
  - Children's Homes Regulations 2001;
  - Private and Voluntary Health Care Regulations 2001;
  - Domiciliary Care Regulations;
  - Nurses Agencies Regulations;
  - Residential Family Centres Regulations;
  - Fostering Services Regulations;
- National Minimum Standards:
  - Care Homes for Older People;
  - Care Homes Younger Adults and Adult Placements;
  - Care Homes for Adults 18–65;
  - Domiciliary Care;
  - Nurses Agencies;
  - Children's Homes;
  - Adoption;
  - Residential Family Centres;
  - Fostering Services;
  - Independent Health Care;
  - Boarding Schools;
  - Residential Special Schools;
  - Accommodation of Students under 18

Charity employers should ensure that they are familiar with the specific legislation that may affect their care service.

Charity employers should be aware that if their care service falls within any of the services listed above, it is likely that the service should be registered under the CSA 2000.

The NCSC is currently responsible for inspecting registered care services. However, from April 2004, two new independent inspectorates, the Commission for Healthcare Audit and Inspection (CHAI) and the Commission for Social Care Inspection (CSCI) will be established. The CSCI will take over the NCSC's social care functions, while the CHAI will take on the NCSC's independent healthcare functions.

The NCSC will take into account the appropriate national minimum standards to identify whether the care service is being run properly. If the service does not meet the standards in only a few respects it is likely that only a written warning would be issued. If, however, a regulation is breached, then the NCSC will serve a notice specifying the action which must be taken to avoid a prosecution. The regulations and national minimum standards cover a variety of aspects of the organisation of care services, and in the employment context, there are a number of onerous provisions which charity employers should understand.

27.3 RECRUITMENT

Charity employers need to be aware of key provisions in relation to the recruitment of staff to work in a registered care service. Although the regulations will vary depending on the nature of the service provided, no person should be employed in a registered care service unless he or she is fit to work in the service. This means that the charity will need to be able to show that workers:

(a) are of integrity and good character;
(b) have the necessary skills, qualifications and experience; and
(c) are physically and mentally fit to perform their duties.

The various regulations specify that an employer must have seen the following documents relevant to the employee:

(a) photographic ID;
(b) birth certificate;
(c) current passport (if any);
(d) documentary evidence of any relevant qualifications;
(e) two written references (see below); and
(f) criminal records check (see below).

Charity employers should ensure that there is a recruitment checklist on each personnel file to record when the documents have been seen, and by whom. Charity employers will not be able to retain the originals of many of these documents on the personnel file and therefore should ensure that they take copies, which are marked with the date on which they were compared against the original, together with the signature of the person who has seen the original document.

The following wording can be used:

> *'Confirmed as a true copy of the original this*
> *[ ] day of [ ] 2003 by*
> *[insert full name and job title]*
>
> ....
> *Signature'*

As a general rule, charities should also ensure that similar safeguards are in place for people who are not employees, but who come into contact with service users. This will include volunteers.

27.4 STAFFING LEVELS

If a charity employer is providing care services which are registered under the CSA 2000 it needs to ensure that there are sufficient qualified and competent staff working in the services. In deciding what staffing levels are appropriate, charity employers should take into account the size of the service, the number of service users and their needs.

Although the specific minimum standards vary according to the nature of the service provided, as a general rule the standards indicate that staff should be appropriately matched to the service users regarding gender, age, cultural background and personal interests. This raises very specific recruitment issues, especially when taking into account the existing obligation to recruit in compliance with equal opportunities legislation. (See Chapters 4 and 7.)

Charity employers should therefore exercise great care in specifically recruiting from one gender or racial group. If there is a genuine occupational qualification for the job which can only be performed by someone of a particular racial group or gender, charity employers may be able to take advantage of this exception to the rules on race and sex discrimination. (See Chapter 7.)

27.5 CRIMINAL RECORDS CHECK

This is covered in more detail in Chapter 4.

Charity employers must also ensure that they have been provided with the relevant certificate from the Criminal Records Bureau (CRB) in relation to all new employees employed since 1 April 2002.

Following the creation of the CRB, employers now have wider access to criminal record information to help them identify candidates who may be unsuitable to enter the social care workforce.

Employers wishing to take advantage of the CRB's disclosure service must be registered in advance of a check being carried out. In addition, employers must comply with the Code of Practice drawn up by the CRB, which is designed to ensure that all disclosed information provided about candidates is handled confidentially and fairly. The Code specifically advises that if a CRB certificate is not clean, the employer should not automatically refuse employment. The type of offence, sentence passed and the subsequent behaviour of the individual should all be taken into account.(See Chapter 4.)

Charity employers should be aware that new care staff may not be confirmed in post until a satisfactory police check has been completed. In the meantime, charities should follow good recruitment practice and ensure that any new recruit is assigned to an established member of staff as a mentor. New staff who have not received CRB clearance should not have unsupervised access to children or vulnerable people. CRB clearance will also be required for existing members of staff by 31 October 2004. Consultation regarding how this will be undertaken closed on 31 July 2003, and one proposal is for employers to apply by the end of November 2003 so that applications can be processed over 12 months, as and when the CRB has capacity.

Set out below is a summary of the CRB requirements for each service as at the time of writing.

Service	*New Staff Employed (since 1 April 2002)*	*Existing Staff (excluding managers and providers)*	*Managers and Providers*
Care home	✓	Check by 31 October 2004	✓
Children's home	✓	✓	✓
Domiciliary care agency	✗	✗	✓
Fostering agency	✓	✓	✓
Nurses agency	✗	✗	✗
Independent hospitals and clinics	✓	✓	✓
Residential family centres	✓	✓	✓
Voluntary adoption agencies	✓	✓	✓
Boarding schools	✓	✓	✓

Service	*New Staff Employed (since 1 April 2002)*	*Existing Staff (excluding managers and providers)*	*Managers and Providers*
Residential special schools	✓	✓	✓
Accommodation of students under 18 by further education colleges	✓	✓	✓

✓ = check required

✗ = no check required

Care providers must also consider the difficulty in ensuring that staff inherited under the Transfer of Undertakings (Protection of Employment) Regulations 1981 (TUPE) are of a satisfactory standard and that appropriate checks have been carried out. Charities who inherit staff under TUPE should seek appropriate contractual protection, in case satisfactory criminal records checks have not been received.

There will be three levels of disclosure available, depending on the work involved.

(a) **Basic disclosure**
Although it is not yet available, this will be the lowest level of check and will be issued to individuals (rather than employers) on request. The Criminal Conviction Certificate will contain only details of convictions which are unspent under the Rehabilitation of Offenders Act 1974.

(b) **Standard disclosure**
A Criminal Record Certificate has been available since April 2002 for staff who have regular contact with children or vulnerable adults. A joint application by the employer and the individual must be made for a Criminal Record Certificate. It will contain details of both spent and unspent convictions as well as any cautions, reprimands or warnings held on the national police computer. The standard disclosure will also reveal whether a person is banned from working with vulnerable adults.

(c) **Enhanced disclosure**
An Enhanced Criminal Record Certificate is the highest level of check available for those staff who have unsupervised contact with children or vulnerable adults. Enhanced disclosure will contain the fullest information available from the CRB such as details of arrest, suspected offences and names of suspected associates.

27.6 REFERENCES

The majority of regulations and minimum standards explicitly set out that two written references must be obtained before any member of staff is appointed. In the interim, before CRB clearance is obtained, at least one of these references should be followed up verbally. In the case of children's homes, one of these must be from the person's most recent employer. Given that care service managers will continually request and provide references for staff, it is important that they are familiar with the legal obligations in relation to references.

There is no legal obligation on an employer to provide a reference. However, the code of practice for care employers that was issued by the GSCC in September 2002 specifies that employers must both seek and *provide* reliable references. (See Chapter 5 for detailed discussion on references.)

27.7 TRAINING

Charities should ensure that all staff receive appropriate training for their roles. In fact, the majority of minimum standards specify that all new staff should receive induction training (to the equivalent of national training organisation standards) in the principles of care, safe working practices, the organisation and the worker's role, the needs of user groups and the particular requirements of the service setting. Staff should then receive follow-up foundation training within the first 6 months of employment.

In addition to standard induction and foundation training, charity employers should be aware that the majority of standards require that all staff have an individual training and development programme in order to assist each of them in meeting the requirements of his or her role. A number of standards specifically set out that employees should receive a certain number of paid days training per year. Charity employers need to check the appropriate national minimum standards to ensure that they are complying with the various training requirements. Charity employers must put in place procedures to enable them to comply with the obligations imposed.

27.8 LIST OF UNSUITABLE PERSONS

The CSA 2000 introduces a 'list of unsuitable persons' who cannot be employed as care workers with vulnerable adults.

Adults are considered vulnerable if they receive nursing or personal care in a care home, at home, in any type of health care establishment, or if they have a substantial learning or physical disability, or any physical or mental illness.

If a charity wants to employ an individual in a position where he or she will be working with vulnerable adults, the charity must check the list to see if the individual is included. Any person on the list cannot be offered such employment.

A charity can also check with the CRB (see **27.5**), and the disclosed information will include a statement as to whether the individual is on the list.

In addition, any person who provides care to vulnerable adults is obliged under the CSA 2000 to refer any person to the Secretary of State for inclusion on the list if that person has:

- been dismissed; or
- been made redundant; or
- transferred to another position; or
- resigned; or
- been suspended,

in circumstances where that person has allegedly failed in his or her responsibilities and a vulnerable adult was harmed or placed at risk of harm.

The Secretary of State will then consider evidence from the charity employer and the worker. If the Secretary of State considers that he or she is unsuitable to work with vulnerable adults, the worker shall be placed on the list. The procedures for reporting a person to the Secretary of State have not yet been announced.

Whenever charities consider suspending an employee, they need to carry out a preliminary investigation before suspending, to establish whether there is a well-founded allegation against the employee (see Chapter 21). As mentioned above, it is also necessary to consider whether suspension is the only option and to consider alternatives, such as moving the employee to another position. Charities should also ensure that suspension takes place only for a period of days or weeks rather than months. Employers should only suspend reasonably or the employer will be deemed to have breached the employment contract, which could lead to legal claims. Specific regulations for each sector deal specifically with this issue and may vary between sectors. A detailed analysis is beyond the scope of this work.

27.9 DOCUMENTATION

In addition to the requirements set out in the GSCC's Code of Practice for employers, the majority of minimum standards set out specific obligations in relation to the documentation that must be supplied to and made available to employees.

As a general rule, charity employers of care workers should ensure that the following documentation is in place and/or supplied to employees:

- GSCC Codes of Practice (supplied to employees);
- a written statement of terms and conditions (supplied to employees);
- disciplinary and grievance procedures;
- written policies on confidentiality, equal opportunities, risk assessments, substance abuse, record keeping, acceptance of money or gifts from service users;
- individual training and development programmes;
- a written recruitment process. (See Chapter 5.)

This list is not exhaustive and charity employers should ensure that they check the specific regulations and standards for their care service to identify what documentation will be required.

27.10 QUALIFICATIONS OF SOCIAL CARE WORKERS

The CSA 2000 introduces a requirement that care workers should have an appropriate qualification in social care. The requirement is a long-term goal, although the national minimum standards set short-term targets that vary depending on the specific sector. With a short-term target of 50% of staff attaining NVQ level 2 by 2005 for the majority of sectors, this rises to 80% of staff attaining NVQ level 3 by 2005 for children's homes. Charity employers should ensure that they are taking steps now to reach these targets by 2005.

27.11 REGISTRATION OF SOCIAL CARE WORKERS

In April 2003, the GSCC launched the Social Care Register, which will ultimately ensure that all social care workers have met the GSCC standards for qualifications, health and good character and have agreed to abide by the Code of Practice for Social Care Workers. The long-term aim is that only those social care workers registered with the GSCC will be permitted to work in care services. However, with a social care workforce of over 1 million, this is likely to take several years to complete. In England, the GSCC will start by registering social workers at certain organisations that have been agreed already. Other groups that will be registered early on will be residential child care workers and care home managers. Once this process is under way, charity employers will need to ensure that their social care workforce is appropriately registered.

INDEX

References are to paragraph numbers.